D0216362

CLIMATIC RACES AND DESCENT GROUPS

CLIMATIC RACES AND DESCENT GROUPS

By

GROVER S. KRANTZ

THE CHRISTOPHER PUBLISHING HOUSE
NORTH QUINCY, MASSACHUSETTS 02171

Library of Congress Catalog Card Number 79-90767
ISBN: 0—8158—0390—7

PRINTED IN
THE UNITED STATES OF AMERICA

Dedicated to the four "whipping boys"
whose theories of racial classification
are used to contrast with my own:
Alfred L. Kroeber
William C. Boyd
Stanley M. Garn
Carleton S. Coon

PREFACE

This book was developed largely from class lectures which began in 1966 at the University of Minnesota and which continued through five more semesters on the subject of human races taught at Washington State University from 1970 to 1977. This work is not based on extensive world travel as I have done little of that. Rather it is a compilation of data from many more accessible sources of reading and observation. More than that it is the first presentation, in print, of a novel arrangement of this data—an arrangement that unfolded only gradually over the years as I taught the course on human races.

It will be assumed that the reader is reasonably familiar with world geography, Mendelian genetics, some human anatomy, and with the process of evolution by natural selection. The book is liberally provided with maps of human trait distributions but it is assumed that the reader will know (or can look up in an atlas) the locations of various countries, major rivers, mountain ranges, deserts, and the like, that are mentioned in the text. Genetic inheritance of various traits will be mentioned, where known, and it will be assumed that the reader knows a "dominant" trait does not tend to become more common over time, nor a "recessive" trait progressively rarer. A thorough knowledge of human anatomy is not required here and most detailed structures are illustrated and described as far as is pertinent, but a sense of how the body parts are integrated would be helpful. The process of natural selection from the raw material of genetic variation is simple enough to understand but some of the detailed ramifications are discussed, particularly the influence of genetic drift and other random factors in evolution. Accordingly, this book is intended mainly for the educated layman and not for the novice. Its use as a text for a course in human races is entirely feasible, but the students should have some grounding in basic biology or physical anthropology, otherwise the instructor will have to fill in a great deal of basic material.

The first section of each chapter is a summary of the major points contained therein. These summaries alone might be read consecutively by those who wish to get just a general picture of the entire book without reading the mass of detail on which the various conclusions are based. Some readers will be largely familiar with that detail. Other readers may choose not to become familiar with it, so this layout gives them a short-hand means to speak with a semblance of knowledge on the subject. Still others may wish to read the summaries again after reading each chapter, as well as before, especially if the material is largely new and possibly confusing. The summaries could have been placed as easily at the end of each chapter, but I chose to put them at the beginning where they are easier to find.

References to other works are kept to a minimum and a selected reading list is provided at the end for those who wish further information on the subject. This is done partly to provide an easy flow to the text without the usual interruptions for citations as are found in most scientific works. Also, much of the unreferenced material is already in print in so many other works as to make a citation of one, to the exclusion of others, seem almost picky. It is also true that much of the material and interpretations are original here, and if these were stimulated by other sources, they are long since forgotten.

A few words should be said here about the use of the word "man." Of its many definitions, two stand out; both are spelled and pronounced the same, but are quite different words. The general term, man, includes all people, male and female, young and adult. The special term, man, includes male adults only, and omits the other three categories of young males, young females, and adult females. The general word is linguistically different in that it does not have a plural form and does not take a definite article. Which of these two meanings of "man" is intended can be gathered from the context—I never have any difficulty deciding which is meant when I encounter the word. There are also other more ambiguous uses of the word man and they are avoided here.

There is also a certain amount of ill-feeling in some quarters about the use of the word Negro and there is a movement to replace it with "Black." In Latin and many of its derived languages Negro means black, or one who is black. With the great variety of words meaning black in various languages, the choice of the Latin word seemed the most reasonable procedure long ago. If English is to become the world language, then the substitution of Black for Negro would obviously be correct.

As noted above, this work derives from many sources over many years, and none particularly stands out for special mention. All credit for its value, as well as any blame for its shortcomings, rests solely on the shoulders of the author.

CONTENTS

ILLUSTRATIONS

CLIMATIC RACES AND DESCENT GROUPS

1.
INTRODUCTION

SUMMARY.

Human races are very much like animal subspecies. They are geographical concentrations, with ill-defined borders, of certain variations in physical appearance. Subspecies (or races) are adaptations to local circumstances, they freely interbreed with each other, and are not incipient species. Human races are usually described as being breeding populations with similar characteristics and which are descended from a common ancestor. In man, the breeding population is true only in a very broad sense and it relates somewhat to common ancestry. Possession of similar characteristics is an independent variable. Classical traits, such as skin color, commonly used in the past to delineate races, are climatic adaptations and are distributed as a result of natural selection. Categories of similarly adapted people should be called "climatic races" with no implication of breeding pool or common ancestry. Genetic traits, like blood types, are distributed largely by factors of chance and breeding limitations. Categories of people with similar gene frequencies should be called "descent groups."

There is no inherent connection between race and group as used here. Recent movements of agricultural populations have tended to bring their boundaries into geographical coincidence in many areas. This has supported the concept of basic races whereas in the natural condition of mankind the two categories were fully independent and cross-cutting. Past attempts to classify human races have met with difficulties because of a failure to recognize the original independence of the two sets of racial traits. A dual system of classification is proposed here.

SUBSPECIES.

All individuals of a species of animal or plant are not identical with one another. Variations in size, color, food preferences, temperature tolerances, and the like have long been observed within each kind of living thing. Less obvious differences in biochemistry have received more recent emphasis. Many such differences are randomly distributed over the entire range of the species, but many are not. Whenever observable variations tend to have geographical concentrations these have come to be regarded as markers of the next lower level of classification, the subspecies. To most biologists the terms "subspecies" and "race" are synonomous. In terms of normal biological practices man can be divided into several subspecies or races. But because we are classifying ourselves, and not some other animal, our concern is greater, opinions differ, and emotional implications abound.

An animal species is defined as a collection of freely interbreeding individuals that will tend to evolve as a unit. The boundaries of a species are determined by total reproductive barriers. If a species is in contact with a similar life form, but there is no significant exchange of genetic material across that line, then that is the dividing line between species. Interspecies hybrids can occur in nature, even fertile ones, but only so rarely as not to pass most evolutionary changes from one species to the other. Within a species reproductive barriers can also occur, to a degree, but these are not strong enough to prevent useful evolutionary adaptations in one population from passing to the other. Of course, many species boundaries may be difficult to define when the barrier is less than absolute—are they two species or just two well-marked subspecies? A division of one species into two over a long period of time presupposes they began as two subspecies whose distinctions gradually became greater until reproductive isolation was achieved. At the present slice in time it is expectable that some pairs of populations will be at just that point of transition.

At the other extreme it is equally difficult to say whether the differences between two populations are worthy of subspecies rank or if they are too insignificant to be so labeled. There is an old zoological procedure for this called the Rule of 75%. From each side of a proposed subspecies line a sample of specimens is collected, tagged as to origin, and mixed together. If 75% or more of the individuals can be correctly identified as to which side of the line they originally came from then this is a valid subspecies division. Of course, this is as much a measure of the biologists' skills as it is of the reality of the line.

In man these definitions are easy to apply. All humanity is a single species as they are all mutually interfertile and do regularly interbreed to some degree with their neighbors. Human subspecies are also well marked and in many cases would fulfill even a 99% rule of reallocating mixed collections to the original sources. From a biologist's point of view the description of human races is just a matter of applying a different name to a normal phenomenon in the natural world.

A potential misconception must be dealt with here. Subspecies (races) are not all incipient species. Even though all species splits must begin as subspecific distinctions, the vast majority of subspecies do not actually go on to become divisions at the higher taxonomic level. Races are geographic variations which are adapted to local conditions and which can maintain their distinctions while the entire species is making evolutionary changes in other characteristics. In the case of man the racial differences do not in any way appear to be trending toward becoming separate species. In fact, to some degree our racial distinctions have been preserved through the all-over evolutionary advance from *Homo erectus* to *Homo sapiens.*

HUMAN RACES.

In recent years most anthropologists seem to have settled on a three-part definition of human races. These are large aggregates of people (1) who form a breeding population or gene pool, (2) with similar inherited biological characteristics, and (3) that share these traits because of their descent from a common ancestral type. It is usually assumed that these three aspects of race coincide and can all be used to delineate or describe a given population from three points of view. In fact they do not coincide at all on a theoretical level, and on a practical level they agree only sometimes.

(1) A Breeding Population is one in which a majority of interbreeding (commonly over 90% of matings) takes place between members of the group. Such breeding is also essentially at random in the sense that each individual has about equal chances of mating with any other individual of the opposite sex. All individuals in such a gene pool will have face-to-face awareness of one another, or at most will be acquainted through no more than one intermediary. Thus they all know, or know of, one another. The breeding population has been called, by some, the most biologically meaningful unit between the species and the individual. To the animals this may be true, but to the overview of human observers their attention often focuses on a larger unit, race.

Human breeding populations normally consist of a few hundred individuals (men, women, and children) in a hunting community, or a few thousand such individuals in agriculturally based societies. Variations on this include ethnic neighborhoods in large cities, castes in India, and the royal family system of Europe.

Obviously a breeding population of this size cannot profitably be called a race as it would take at least a million of them to encompass all of humanity. For special studies, as in comparing one gene pool with another in a limited area, such microgeographical populations may be a useful concept. They may be called micro-races.

Breeding populations have been defined here in terms of their interbreeding potential during a given generation. This concept can be extended to a larger scale with a longer time span of many generations. Only by such an extension in time can one refer to breeding populations on a continental scale. This now becomes part of item (3) below.

(2) The similar inherited biological characteristics which are most used for racial classifications are mainly adaptations to climatic conditions. Over many generations the processes of mutation and natural selection have worked to accentuate variations in each area that are the most suitable to the environment. There is no necessary reason for continental gene pools to correlate with climatic adaptations, and they generally do not. Within a large many-generation breeding population there may be several markedly different climatic zones. The people of each zone will be under selective pressure for the best adaptations and may appear quite different from those in other climatic zones on the same continent. Likewise, the same kinds of climates can occur in separate continental breeding populations. This would lead to selection for similar biological adaptations in two peoples without there being any close relationship between them in the other sense.

What people are perhaps most conscious of when they think of race are these inherited biological traits. As one friend rather indelicately put it, "When you go to a race riot how are you going to know who to throw rocks at?" One of the major purposes of this book is to deal with just these traits—what they mean, why they exist, how they came to be where they are. Yet there is a great deal more to race, both in the minds of scientists and of the general public alike.

(3) The idea of common descent for each supposed race seems basic in most people's concept of race. We show the traits we do because we inherited them from our parents. They have these traits through inheritance from their parents. And so on, back to the original population that was the source of our race. But then where? Common ancestry by itself explains nothing about the origin of racial traits. But then, common origin in itself is the essence of race in many people's minds.

Descent can be measured in some societies who keep long records for a few thousand years at best. Even in such cases, descent is calculated along male lines or along female lines only. Whichever system is used, the genetic contributions from the other sex in each generation are quickly lost track of. For instance, my father is only half of my ancestry even though I carry his name; his father is one-fourth of my ancestry; and seven generations back, through the male line, is a man who is less than one percent of my ancestry—who were all the rest of them?

Common descent can be measured by native language except where civilization may intervene to change languages. As a general rule people are very conservative about speech and learn it from their parents. While language affiliations can change, they, in fact, rarely do. Linguistic classifications often come close to grouping people into units of common descent and may trace back to origins of 5,000 years ago or more. Blood type frequencies, with some reservations, can also classify people into descent groups that go back five or ten thousand years and maybe more.

The trouble with common descent as a means of classifying people is that it frequently disagrees with categories based on inherited physical similarities. Yet to most people, shared physical traits and common descent are one and the same thing. The major purpose of this book is to separate the two concepts and to show how they differ, and in fact that they have no automatic relation at all.

Many of the problems in understanding human races stem from this simple procedure of equating shared physical traits with common ancestry. In the short run the equation is correct; people resemble their parents. We know that over the centuries various groups of people have perpetuated their kind for many generations. However when the time scale is in tens of thousands of years or more, and we consider all the people in the world instead of just local populations, then the equation begins to break down. Since we are here considering racial origins, this larger scale is where much attention must be paid.

The first step in understanding the difference between shared traits and common descent is in examining all of the racial distinctions that have been used in the past. These fall mostly into two very different categories which I call "classical" and "genetic." The significance of this division lies in the fact that variations in the two categories of traits arose for different reasons. The two kinds of traits behave differently in populations and have different kinds of distributions around the world. The fact that classical traits tend to be geographically distributed on one pattern and genetic traits distribute themselves on quite another pattern is the crux of the problem.

CLASSICAL TRAITS.

The first group of human variations is called classical because their contrasts have been noted since man first began exploring great distances during the early civilizations and noting what they encountered.

These traits are easily seen with the naked eye. They include color of skin, eyes, and hair; hair form along with its quantity and distribution; body fat; body size and build; nose form; epicanthic eye-folds; and other traits. Variations in these traits can be measured or located on a scale from low to high expression; they are quantitative in that each shows varying quantity of more or less the same thing. Scientists for many years have measured them with a fair degree of precision using simple tools. Averages have been calculated for each trait in many populations and maps have been drawn showing their world-wide distributions.

For the most part we do not know the detailed rules of genetic inheritance of classical traits. Clearly many different genes are involved in each because there is a virtually continuous gradation in degree of expression. (By contrast, a given blood type is an all or nothing expression—either you are blood type B or you are not, and there is no itermediate condition.) Such classical traits are, nevertheless, inherited by some kind of genetic mechanisms as can easily be ascertained by anyone who looks at large numbers of parents and their offspring.

Most classical traits are in the skin and other soft tissues and thus leave no permanent record from thousands of years ago. Some, however, do involve skeletal structures. Body build and nose form can often be traced into the past as far back as we have fossils.

Variations in most classical traits can be shown to be adaptations to climatic conditions, mainly sunlight, temperature, and humidity. Mapped distributions of these traits also correspond well with variations in these climatic factors. The origin of these variations, like any others, is from genetic mutation and recombination. The development of their geographic distributions is simply by natural selection. Within each climatic environment certain variations are better suited to leading a comfortable and productive life. Since this tends also to mean a more reproductive life as well, those more favorable variations will be replicated more often in the next generation, and those less favorable will tend to be phased out.

Average degree of expression of a trait, whether it be skin color or stature or whatever, is not what is being selected for or against. Selection works mainly on the extremes, too light and too dark, too tall and too short. When selection pressure against tall individuals increases slightly and a greater proportion of them fail to reproduce their kind, then this is reflected in a slight lowering of average stature in following generations. Similarly, a slight change in average skin color means one of the extremes is under increased selective pressure.

Given enough time, natural selection will adapt each population to the environment in which it lives, as far as possible within the limits of human anatomy. By following normal zoological procedures the human species can then be divided up into zones of climatic adaptations, or climatic races. Gene flow by random mating between populations will always tend to diffuse the traits and even out their distributions. Natural selection will constantly work to maintain the uneven distribution of traits. Of course the boundaries of these climatic races will be vague in most places, just as the boundaries of climatic zones are gradual. A zone of intermediacy of varying width will occur between all such races. Greater and lesser degrees of racial distinction also naturally occur just as with climates. Greater and lesser degrees of separateness between the races would also follow.

Much emphasis has recently been put by anthropologists on genetic inheritance, diseases, and population breeding patterns. Sometines they seem to lose sight of that which is most easily seen. All people are aware of differences in classical traits and many want to know why. It serves little purpose to answer them in terms of genes and populations. They still want to know why Africans are black, why Orientals have different-looking eyes, and why Europeans have beaky noses.

GENETIC TRAITS.

Some human variations have predictable inheritance patterns so we say their genetics are known. Other traits are included here, because they behave in a similar manner in their expressions and in their distributions, even though their exact genetics are not known. For convenience, I have lumped them all under the term genetic traits even though it is not in all cases technically correct. Genetic traits are mostly all or nothing expressions, either you have it or you don't, and are thus qualitative. One does not figure averages for them, only percentages. Although a man can be of average height or average color he cannot be of average blood type. Genetic traits mostly require some kind of apparatus and/or chemicals to detect them; they are not normally visible to the unaided eye. Accordingly, the discovery and mapping of genetic traits is a rather recent phenomenon, mostly dating since World War II.

Some of the better known genetic traits are the blood types: the ABO series, the MN series, and the Rh factors. Others are the two types of ear wax and the ability, or lack of it, to taste the chemical PTC. Genetically unknown traits such as fingerprint patterns, cephalic index, and certain dental anomalies also behave in a manner rather like the genetic traits and will be included with them.

It is presumed that these genetic traits appeared through mutations just like classical traits, but that there have generally been no long-term selective forces acting upon them. Some have apparently been selected for or against, mainly blood types in relation to various diseases, but not in any consistant manner. In any given environment there rarely has been the kind of selection pressure to eliminate any of the alleles or possible variations. The geographical concentrations of genetic traits bear no relation to those of classical traits—they do not distribute by climate. The only tendency that can be observed for most of them is that they tend toward continental distributions with peculiar high points of maximum occurrence. The distributions of the various genetic traits often roughly coincide, and sometimes don't, but they do show the influences of geographic barriers to gene flow. The barriers may be mountains, seas, or sheer distance.

The primary mechanism that has caused these distributions is evidently genetic drift. This comes in two forms. Drift proper is the purely random change in gene frequency from one generation to the next. Given enough time the frequency of one allele (or variation) of a gene in particular geographic gene pool may reach unusually high or low numbers and distinguish it from other areas. The second aspect is when a population expands tremendously into a new area; this is called founders effect. The first immigrants, or founders, would likely be a small group of people whose genetic composition, by chance alone, would likely be somewhat different from the average of their region of origin. Their peculiar gene frequencies would then most likely be preserved in the resultant expanded population of their descendants in the new region. In short, genetic trait distributions are mainly the result of chance events and are maintained by barriers to gene flow. This is very different from the factors that affect the distribution of classical traits. The distributions of genetic traits and of classical traits generally do not correspond well, often not at all. The world can be divided into a few major areas where the populations tend to share genetic traits. For the populations of such areas I propose we call them "descent groups," or just "groups" for short. This is to distinguish them from "climatic races," or "races" for short. Descent groups do represent a certain degree of common ancestry, hence "descent," and they are not united by observable traits, hence the word "group" is used in order to avoid the term "race."

MEDICAL TRAITS.

There are many more traits, mostly genetic, of unequal geographic distribution which are fascinating to some people for good reasons. These are the inherited characteristics which relate to diseases, either through providing resistance or susceptibility. The genetic mechanism of sickle-cell anemia and its resistance to malaria is the best known of these. For the most part these are omitted from this work for the simple reason that they are not properly racial traits. Their distributions tend to follow the distributions of the diseases in question and bear no particular relationship to either classical traits or the regular genetic traits. The various disease-related traits also cannot be set up as a third category of human trait distributions because they have no tendency to agree with each other. Sometimes there may be a fortuitous correlation, as between sickle-cell anemia and sub-Saharan Africans. But there is nothing about having dark skin, wide noses, or spiral hair that predisposes Negroes to sickle-cell anemia. It's just that the environment leading to selection for those traits just happens to overlap broadly with the area of Africa with a high incidence of malaria. This coincidence has led to significant ramifications in the social implications of race but that is not properly the purview of this book.

Another field of medical application of racial traits, again the genetic ones, is in the field of immunology. Blood types can be very significant in terms of blood transfusions and organ transplants, but since ancient man probably did not practice such things this has no direct bearing on the origin and distribution of the blood types. Accordingly, the subject of antigens and antibodies will receive no further attention here.

CLASSICAL vs. GENETIC.

Racial classifications in the past have had to deal with the contrast between classical and genetic traits. The problem has been how to reconcile the two very different kinds of data and their different patterns of distribution over the world. The problem might not have been so bad if it had been earlier realized that the two kinds of traits have evolved and distributed themselves according to two quite different sets of rules. One reason why this problem has persisted is because almost everybody thinks in terms of race as being a kind of major division of the human species that is somehow natural and proper. Just as a genus is divided into species, a species is divided into subspecies. Races must be there—it is our task to discover and delineate them. Race is thought of as a major division of mankind, a total entity, something of great antiquity and unity. Consciousness of belonging to a particular race carries a heavy emotional load in people's minds.

There are four clearly different ways in which this contrast between classical and genetic distributions has been dealt with in the past, and a new one is offered here. At this point they will be briefly identified.

(1) Divide humanity into basic races using only classical traits and

ignoring the genetic ones. Fifty years ago this was about all that could be done as too little was yet known about the genetic traits. Still, this kind of division, and there are many variations of it, is what prevails in most people's concept of race.

(2) Divide humanity into basic groups using only genetic traits and ignoring the classical ones. In the last twenty-five years some attempts in this direction have been made which stress common descent and geographical inbreeding. They have been poorly received in most quarters simply because such groupings do not entirely agree with classical trait distributions.

(3) Use both kinds of traits at different levels of classification. This was only approached by one author who tended to use genetic traits at the broader level of continental races, then subdivided these largely by classical traits into local races. The idea that the two kinds of traits behave differently was at least touched upon.

(4) Use both classical and genetic traits together to make a single classification. This is the most emotionally satisfying solution as it accepts race as a total entity and at the same time tries to use all scientific data in formulating the classification. This approach must strain at the seams in many places, and much data has to be ignored or down-played in order to make a single set of races.

(5) Both classical and genetic data can be used, but separately, to set up two parallel systems of classifying humanity. As introduced here, this would divide the world into a set of climatic races, and at the same time, a crosscutting set of descent groups. This system recognizes the independent factors that have governed the evolution and distribution of the two kinds of traits. It has the disadvantage of splitting the concept of race into two parts which must be handled separately. Thus a population may be classed in a particular climatic race with certain other peoples, and at the same time it may be classed in a descent group with somewhat different partners. The dual classification system may be confusing, especially to the individual who seeks identification with some larger entity.

This new dual system also raises serious problems with regard to race studies in the past. Much work has been done to show correlations, or lack of them, between racial affiliation and various other attributes such as health problems, social behavior, historical accomplishments and the like. All such studies involve pooling the data from a sample of one race and comparing it with a pooled sample of data from one or more other races. The question then arises, what kind of population has been pooled? Was it a sample drawn broadly from a climatic race, or was it from a descent group? Just which theory of race was used can make a great difference. For example, when comparing the historical accomplishments of Europe vs. China, with which sample do you include India? In terms of classical traits the people of India lean strongly toward Europe; in terms of genetic traits they lean strongly toward China. This kind of problem, that of pooling data, will be dealt with in more depth later.

CLINES.

Much ink has been spilled over the clinist approach to human variation which stands in contrast to what might be called the basic race concept. Many people see themselves divided into two hostile camps on this subject, the "clinists" vs. the "racers." (I hesitate to say "racists" because that implies more than is usually the case.)

The basic race idea, as discussed above, is that races are natural units that tend to maintain their identity. When physically intermediate populations are noted, the racer will say they are mixtures or hybrids of the more "real" races. This has sometimes been called anti-evolutionary because of the implied permanence of each race. Those who adhere to the basic race concept usually do not make it clear just why the races should be considered to be so distinct. This is often treated as simply self-evident.

In contrast to this is the clinist approach which, in its extreme form, appears to deny the existence of race. A cline is a slope, incline or decline. In this case it refers to the slope on a graph which illustrates how the degree of expression of a physical trait changes over space. A simple example of this would be a graph of the average amount of melanin (dark coloring) found in human skins along a north-south line from Poland to Nigeria. (See Fig. 1.) There is little melanin in skins at the north end of this line and it gradually increases to a maximum amount at the south end. The line of melanin quantity thus slopes; it is a cline. A clinist then says that's all there is to race, just populations located at different positions along a continuum, or cline, of a particular trait. No position along this cline is any more real, basic, or original than any other position.

This skin color graph also shows a very steep section, corresponding to a region in the Sahara, where skin color changes more per km than anywhere to the north or south. This steep part of the cline is called a racial boundary by the racers, and the populations there must be some kind of mixtures of the basic races. To the clinist this is just a steep place on the cline, and nothing more. The clinist would presume that the forces operating to affect skin color change more rapidly along this one section of the cline and thus the colors reflect this. This is then a zone of intermediacy, not of intermixture. The

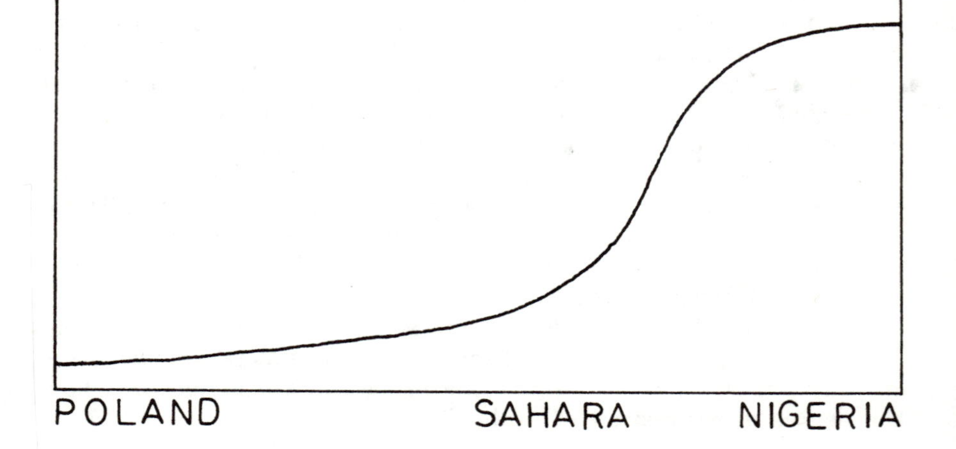

FIGURE 1. Skin color cline from Poland to Nigeria. This graph illustrates the increasing level of melanin in the skin as one approaches the equator, moving from low sunlight to high sunlight zones. The steep part of the cline in the Sahara is commonly taken to represent a racial boundary. In terms of actual solar radiation this steep part ought to be farther to the north, thus a recent population movement is suggested.

distinction may sound trivial but it is very fundamental to some people's thinking.

The clinist approach is then applied to a multitude of traits, more or less simultaneously, and the world is covered with a mass of trait clines going in all directions with every degree of slope. Classical and genetic traits are all included. Given this morass of data the extreme clinist attitude is to deny the existence of race itself. On the surface this position is absurd. Black people have black children, white people have white children—anybody can see that. Both types of people have well-known geographical centers of origin. These are facts, not opinions, and they constitute race in the minds of most people. Any attempt to deny this makes one look rather foolish.

A well-reasoned clinist approach must concentrate on the divisions between races, not their existence. How fundamental are these dividing lines, how sharp are they, how long have they lasted, how did they come into being? A clinist may also challenge the idea of a fundamental unity throughout the area of each major race. Instead, he sees a mass of clines within it, very much like the trait clines that supposedly mark its boundaries. Still, the clinist must somehow come to grips with the fact that large areas of the world are actually inhabited by masses of people who change very little over their vast territories. Whatever the clinist may say about them, these are what most people now mean by race and their existence cannot be denied. Something has caused some very steep places along trait clines, and those of many different traits often coincide far more than chance would account for.

Both the clinists and the racers are right, but in different places and at different times in the racial history of man. I will take a firm stand on both sides of this issue, and hope to show that it is not a simple one at all. The concepts will be developed at great length later in this book, but they can be stated briefly at this point.

In terms of classical traits, man's original condition was one of clinal distribution. The expression of each trait was in response to climatic factors and these are and were clinal. There are steep places on the climate clines and one can draw lines along them dividing mankind into climatic races. Such races are descriptively useful, but they do not imply any fundamental unity within each beyond the approximate sharing of a few conspicuous characteristics. People on the dividing lines are just as real as those in the middle of one of the climatic races.

In more recent times, with the advent of agriculture and large populations, the classical trait picture has shifted at least somewhat toward the basic race position. When large population expansions extend over great territories they bring their classical traits with them. Such movements will overrun and absorb lesser numbers of nonagricultural peoples and bring a frontier of their original classical traits into new areas. In this manner a clinal distribution is lost in the shuffle and a very real racial boundary builds up. When two such population expansions arise in different places and move towards one another a classic racial clash can result (pun intended). The white-black meeting in southern Africa is one of the best known of these where both groups had moved far from their homelands and met on neutral ground with a maximum of classical trait contrast between them. The black-white meeting in America is likewise an encounter of contrasting ends of a continuum, both transported to new locations without the intervening part of the trait cline. In summary, classical traits were originally distributed by clines with some steep places, but have recently shown basic-race type contrasts in some parts of the world.

In terms of genetic traits the reverse seems to be the case. The original distribution of descent groups, while clinal to some degree, probably came close to the concept of basic races. There would have been an approach to genetic uniformity within the continental breeding pools with marked distinctions between each of them. The zones between them would be mixed, and their mixture would have been maintained by gene flow (hybridization) from each of the major groups.

With the advent of massive agriculturally-based populations moving and mixing around the world, the genetic trait picture changes to one of largely clinal distributions. High and low spots remain of many genetic trait expressions but they fade out gradually from these centers now, rather than abruptly dropping off at the boundaries of the old descent groups. These groups can still be delineated but not with great precision. In summary, genetic traits were originally distributed like basic races with zones of intermixture, but have recently been diluted into a more clinal picture of distribution. Thus the present writer's position on the clinist issue is a firm stand on both sides of several aspects of the argument.

Most people, however, have grown up with the basic race concept. An individual showing traits somewhere between those of Europeans and of central Africans is immediately labeled a hybrid, or as someone ultimately descended from hybrid ancestors. Yet such an intermediate set of characteristics may be just as old and stable and as well adapted to the environment as the two extremes. One reason for the basic race-hybrid attitude is sheer weight of numbers. Many intermediate populations are small or have long ago disappeared. The agriculturally augmented peoples, often in contact and conflict with one another, now constitute most of the people in the world. Expectably, many of the people with intermediate traits are in fact hybrids. But that should not cause us to lose sight of the original conditions that gave rise to the diversity of mankind and its distribution. We should also not ignore the great numbers of truly intermediate peoples still little altered by the agricultural revolution. Much emphasis will be placed on them in the remainder of this book. Whether they are politically or economically significant is not the measure of their importance in this context. Their importance, in addition to being human beings, lies in the light they can shed on the problem of race.

SKELETAL RACES.

A final subject for this introductory chapter is that of tracing human races back into the distant past through the examination of fossil skeletal material. Much work has been devoted to this subject but its utility is highly dubious because of a basic assumption that is almost always made, that basic races are real.

The most emphasized of the classical traits relate to variations in the skin and hair and some other soft parts. These epidermal parts are not preserved in old skeletons. Most genetic traits are likewise not determinable from bones. Yet these are the very traits on which the human species is mainly classified today. Any attempt to trace the development and distribution of these soft parts by means of studying skeletons presupposes that a strong correlation not only does exist between soft and hard parts but always has existed in the past. This assumption is rarely examined and is probably only partly true.

Some classical traits, such as nose form and body build, can be read directly from bones. Some traits which behave like genetic ones are also evident in bones, such as extra sutures in the skull and certain dental peculiarities. These can then be followed back as far as the fossil record exists. If each division of humanity is freely interbreeding and owes its common traits to descent from an ancestor with these traits, then a correlation can be made.

Today, in most populations where epicanthic eye-folds are the rule, there is also a high frequency of an extra suture across the back of the skull separating part of the occipital bone as the "Inca bone." If the basic race concept were true in its entirety we need only find a few skulls to determine whether the owners had eye-folds when they were alive. Some of the half-million year old Peking skulls have Inca bones and many presume that their eyes must therefore have looked Chinese. This may have been the case, but the Inca bone does not demonstrate it. It should already be evident that these two traits have no inherent connection between them today and their near coincidence of distribution is fortuitous. Eye-folds are classical traits developed for certain arctic and mountain environments and later spread for other reasons. Inca bones have long been a genetic trait of the East Asian area regardless of the climatic environment.

Another example would be the close correlation today between dark skins and broad noses. It would seem to follow that the owner of a broad-nosed skull was also black skinned in life. These are both classical traits related to climate, but again the association is largely fortuitous. As will be shown later, broad noses are adapted to high humidity while dark skins are adapted to intense sunlight. Often these two factors correspond and a large segment of humanity today shows this. However in some parts of the world the best adaptation to the local climate is dark skin with a narrow nose, and in other places it is a lighter skin with a very broad nose. Reconstructing past skin colors from preserved facial bones is a very dubious procedure. Such reconstructions are valid only for very recent times when peoples have changed their locations and have not had enough time to adapt to the local climates.

Some of these difficulties could be avoided by constructing "skeletal races" among recent populations and then tracing them back into the past. This procedure would not be of much interest to many people as most of the usual racial traits, both classical and genetic, would have to be ignored. Not only would the modern races be confusing, but little could be said about the visual appearance of past populations.

Reconstructions of past conditions here will follow several different approaches depending on the reasons for each trait in question. All skeletal traits will be read directly wherever the evidence is available. If it is adapted to a particular aspect of climate the best guess is that the trait's distribution paralleled that of the climate in question. If the trait is of a genetic type the best guess is that it was distributed throughout the continental breeding population in which it is found. Nonskeletal climatic traits can be postulated by analogy with modern correlations, but only with great care. Nonskeletal genetic traits of the past will be estimated from relict populations and inferences about population movements and mixtures. It is all a tricky business and cannot be carried too far, as will be seen in later chapters.

2.
BACKGROUND OF THE RACE CONCEPT

SUMMARY.

Racial variations in man would not have been seen by early hunters. Their range of travel and experience would not have gone far enough to see the gradual changes which occur over geographical space. The development of early civilizations in Egypt and China first enabled certain people to travel great distances for commerce and conquest and to return with descriptions of the peoples they encountered. Since about the year 1500 A.D. Europeans have made the first full survey of the people of the world and proved they were all interfertile.

Early uses of the word race included all physical and cultural aspects of a people: appearance, size, numbers, weapons, organization, language, dress, crafts, skills, manners, etc. These were all bits of knowledge which were useful in taking advantage of such contacts. Recent biological thinking has tended to restrict race to those physical variations which are biologically inherited and which have some degree of geographical concentration.

A more recent emphasis in race studies, mainly since World War II, has been to investigate blood types and other traits not easily observable. This was partly in reaction to the apparent failure to explain race in terms of classical trait distributions. With much work and expense the new investigations have done little better.

The popular view is that mankind is divided into three basic races and these are subdivided and mixed into still more lesser races. This stems from the classical studies and has not been supplanted by anything more useful or understandable from recent research.

BEFORE CIVILIZATIONS.

Racial differences among people were largely unknown prior to about 5,000 years ago. Physical distinctions, in terms of skin color, stature, hair form, and the like, were variable from place to place but the change was gradual as was the climate change. In the space of 100 km, more than most people ever traveled as hunters and gatherers, there would have been few places where even a perceptable difference could be seen. Biochemical distinctions between peoples would be even less known, for obvious reasons.

Agriculturalists were already on the move at that time and may have brought themselves into contact with somewhat different looking people. But just a few millenia earlier even this source of contrast did not occur. Perhaps the only places where differences might have been seen would be on the slopes of mountains where high and low altitude climates come close together. Across narrow seas there would be occasional contacts of people who might have different genetic traits, but their climatic adaptations, the visible traits, should have provided no contrast.

Early man, practicing a hunting and gathering way of life, lived then as do their recent representatives in tribal territories, usually subdivided into band areas where the individual spent most of his life. Knowledge of other people was limited to the members of the tribe and to a limited awareness, often hostile, of a few individuals in the nearest adjacent tribe. Except in the relatively unproductive arctic and desert regions, hunting tribe territories rarely had diameters of over 50 km. While hunters are remarkably thorough in their knowledge of their own territories and everything in them, they are almost totally ignorant of anything far beyond those boundaries.

NONMIGRATION.

It is often asserted that various hunting peoples have made major migrations or territorial expansions in past times. Such movements of perhaps thousands of kilometers in a few generations should certainly have placed some of the migrants in contact with other people with very different anatomical features. While this would still be of no lasting consequence even if it did happen upon occasion, the fact of the matter is that most such postulated migrations could not have occurred.

Hunting peoples will fill their territories to what is for them its carrying capacity. Normally this is at or just under half the population that its resources could theoretically support; the discrepancy allows for occasional poor years in terms of food supply. All adjacent hunting territories will thus have about the same density of population. Changes from lean deserts to rich parklands are gradual and will usually involve several tribal units to show a significant difference in productivity. Hunting tribes each tend to have a rather constant total population of some 400 or 500 individuals, usually divided into a number of separate bands with subterritories of their own. Hunters forage for their food daily. They depend on each day's take of vegetables and small animals for their normal diet. Frequent, but usually not daily, hunts for larger game add to the food supply but leave almost nothing to be stored for future consumption. There is generally little along the line of real or potential military organization.

With this sketch of the hunter's way of life one might try to imagine one tribe conquering another and taking over its territory. How can this be done? Each side in the dispute will have similar numbers (few) of similarly armed fighting men. Neither side can give up the food quest for more than a few days at a time for military campaigns. Organization would be negligible, and "leaders" were rarely followed. In short, the invader would have no advantage at all over the defender. The defender, on the other hand, has a very great advantage in that he knows his territory. He knows where weapons may be stashed, where food and water can be found, good hiding places and lookout spots, good places to converge for an attack or ambush, and good escape routes. The defenders can easily plan activities over the area they know and which the invader does not know. It would be a rare event indeed when one hunting tribe could bring enough force to bear on another as to conquer it and absorb its survivors and territory into itself. The waves of population expansion that are sometimes proposed for hunting groups involve not just one action of this improbable kind, but a series of hundreds of them, all in the same direction. It is thus not likely that tribes of hunters ever moved great distances over inhabited territory and encountered new peoples of significantly different physical appearance.

There are other kinds of movements of hunting peoples over great geographical distances that have been proposed. These are equally unlikely and will be dealt with in later chapters.

EARLY CIVILIZATIONS.

Civilized societies include craft specializations which require raw materials for the manufacture of products. Often these materials must be obtained away from the place of manufacture and consumption. Civilized societies often try to conquer one another, and to defend their frontiers in an attempt to prevent such conquests. While these functions can at times be accomplished by trade and by negotiation, military domination has been the more usual method employed. Civilized societies have the means for engaging in military activities which hunting societies do not have. These include the following:

(1) Large numbers of able-bodied men to draw upon.
(2) Seasonal availability of many of these men during particular parts of the agricultural cycle when labor is less needed.
(3) Political organization with which to recruit, organize, train, and equip such men and to lead them into foreign conquests.
(4) Transportable food supplies in abundance, primarily cereal grains, to sustain the armies and relieve them of the need for regular food quests.
(5) Means of transport for this food and other equipment, and draft animals to power it and which can also become food.
(6) Often their weapons are of superior effectiveness, from design or material, though generally not from skill of use.

Different civilizations used or emphasized different parts of this list, and many other tricks as well. Some impressive conquests were made without certain items but with greater emphasis on others. Hunting societies lack these advantages. Whenever conflict erupts between them the agriculturally based civilizations will predominate over the hunters in all but the most extremes of climate or terrain difficulties.

Representatives of early civilizations traveled considerable distances investigating the world around them. They were motivated by curiosity, to establish commerce, to begin colonization where the climate was suitable, and for conquest should there be any resistance on the part of the natives to any of these goals.

The early Sumerians traveled only modest distances, probably not more than 500 km in any direction. They would have encountered little in the way of physical distinctions among the peoples within their sphere of knowledge.

At almost the same time the Egyptians were exploring greater distances, especially south into Africa along the Nile. Here they encountered people with black skins and spiral hair. That these people were seen as different from themselves is evident from their art work as well as written descriptions of some 5,000 years ago. The Egyptians indicated their own skin color as a light brown. Less than 2,000 years later people with still lighter skins are described and illustrated as a third clear-cut physical type. These were evidently invaders from civilizations to the north and were well known to the Sumerians even earlier. Egyptian expeditions even penetrated far enough into central Africa to bring back Pygmies. Educated Egyptians of the time were thus aware of a considerable range of human diversity, but they left little record of what they thought it meant or how such diversity came to be. (See Fig. 2.)

The earliest Chinese civilization in the northern part of that country dominated a considerable area, but evidently their explorations encountered only people very much like themselves in appearance. But by 3,000 years ago (approximately) Chinese influence had spread west to encounter "white" men, and far enough to the south for them to find people of distinctly darker shades of skin color and otherwise very different from themselves. Contact with early civilizations of India had begun before 3,000 years ago if we can trust the racial diagnosis of some skulls found in cities on the Indus River. It is not presently clear to Western scholars exactly how far Chinese influence penetrated in early times. Possibly they were aware of as much human diversity as were the early Egyptians.

Somewhat later, mostly within the last two millenia, several civilizations in southeastern Asia, and what is today Indonesia, explored large parts of the world. Commonly called Malays today, these were the first to emphasize sailing ships and to cross large bodies of water in their travels. Depending on the time and particular nation chosen, one can find these Malays in contact with Chinese, Melanesians, maybe Australians, peoples of India, the eastern Mediterraneans, and even with the Negroes and Bushmen of Africa. Probably no one nation contacted all these various peoples but at least a great potential was there for them to compare notes about the racial diversity of mankind.

Arab seafarers of about the same time centered their activities somewhat to the west. They may have had little knowledge of the peoples to the east of India, but they had contacts and information westward as far as the Atlantic Ocean, and to a considerable distance north into Europe. Arabs in educated circles over a thousand years ago commented on the human diversity their explorers had uncovered.

American Indian civilizations explored and conquered over great distances too, but we have little record of what they found or what they thought about it. Aztecs, Incas, and their predecessors certainly encountered great diversity in the cultures of their subjects. It is doubtful, however, that much was found in the way of human physical differences. Whatever may be said about distinctions among various Amerindians, compared to the range of physical variation in the Old World, the New World natives are remarkably uniform.

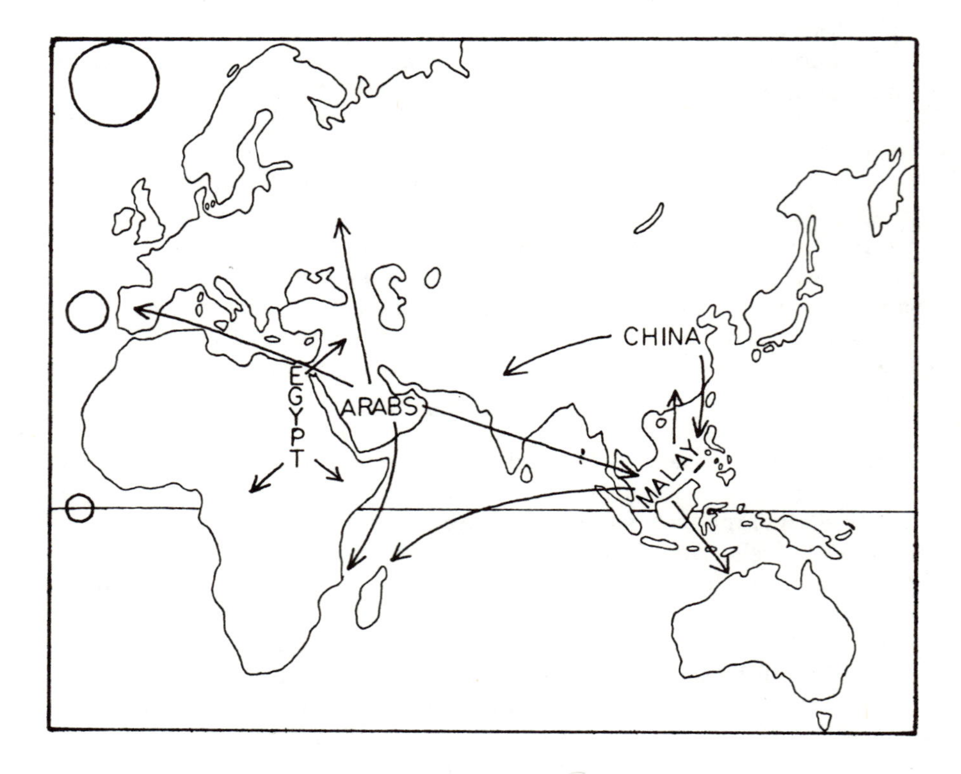

FIGURE 2. World awareness of some early civilizations. Egyptians were familiar with a wide range of physical types as early as 5,000 years ago through military, trading, and exploratory missions as indicated by the arrows. Chinese, Malay, Arab, and other contacts were later and more extensive. (This and all other maps are drawn with the Mercator Projection which exaggerates areas away from the equator in order to retain real shapes. The circles on the left edge of the map illustrate this by showing equal areas at various latitudes.)

WESTERN EUROPEANS.

The first reasonably full survey of the world's human diversity was accomplished by the maritime powers of western Europe after the year 1500 A.D. Their motives for investigating the world were the same as those before—curiosity, commerce, colonization, and conquest. To these they added another—conversion to Christianity. Improvements in shipbuilding and in navigation devices were major factors permitting Europeans to explore new routes around the world, and military equipment was paramount in their take-over of previously established commercial contacts. The vast inland areas of Asia were not immediately accessible to the maritime powers, but contact with Russian overland explorers enabled them to round-out the picture.

In addition to "discovering" the whole world from a single source, these Europeans soon settled another problem, whether or not all of humanity was interfertile, or as we say now, a single species. This was decided in the affirmative by the simple expedient of western European sailers successfully interbreeding with the women of every possible major population on earth. Fertile offspring resulted from all these crosses and proved to be quite successful. It has not yet been demonstrated whether every population is interfertile with every other, but that is not necessary for humanity to be proven a single species. It may be that Eskimos and Australian Aboriginies have never seen, let alone exchanged genes, with each other. But since English sailors have interbred with both, the genetic continuity is established.

The beginning of the European discovery of the world's peoples is usually given as the time of the first Spanish expedition to the New World in 1492. For convenience this is rounded off to the year 1500 A.D. Much exploration had been underway just prior to that time by the English crossing the North Atlantic and the Portuguese circumnavigating Africa, and much remained to be discovered well after that date. A specific year had to be chosen as part of the concept of the "ethnographic present." The ethnographic present is roughly defined as the time when a particular people was first discovered by Europeans. The concept gets rather vague in cases where some note of existence was made at one time, but fuller awareness did not commence until a century or two later. If we are to draw maps of ethnic distributions just prior to the time of European-caused disruptions, the ethnographic present is an essential base line.

In many areas, obviously including Europe itself, there is no ethnographic present because there was no particular time of discovery. The people were known all along. Any map of native distributions in the world, if it is to be complete, must set some base line for the continuously known areas as well, and 1500 A.D. is as good a date as any. Great movements of people occurred before that time, to be sure, but our historical records of them are rather incomplete, if they exist at all. Movements since 1500 are generally better known and recorded.

The year 1500 is the base line for most published race maps and will be so used here, except where otherwise specified. In effect, the goal of such a map date is to put all peoples back into what might be thought of as their more "normal" places. Many assumptions and operating procedures involved in this are less than perfect. It is assumed that all people discovered at a later date were in their discovered positions in the year 1500 as well. In mapping racial traits, people are measured wherever they are found today, but are entered on the maps where their ancestors presumably lived in the year 1500. In all cases it is assumed that inherited biological traits have not changed in any significant way in the last 500 years.

EARLY MEANING OF RACE.

The age of discovery merged into the age of exploitation. When Europeans, just like other civilizations, engaged in commerce, colonization, and conquest, it was necessary for them to have accurate descriptions of the peoples and the lands involved. The beginnings of anthropology might be traced to those descriptions of the people just as geography began with descriptions of their lands.

The explorers gathered all manner of data about the native inhabitants of each area. They described their physical appearance in terms of stature, skin color, hair form, nose shape, and the like. They learned about numbers, weapons, political organization, tactics, and anything else related to military capacity. They found out what language was spoken, and often by extension how their social organization and kinship systems worked. They learned various manners and customs that were important to each people, especially as they differed from those of the Europeans themselves. They described the skills and industries of the people in terms of what products they produced and what products they might want. All this information went into a package description of what a people was like from the point of view of a potential trader and/or conqueror. All these characteristics were seen as unchanging constants—inherited, but without any distinction being made between cultural and biological modes. This information was treated as a unit and called race.

The early concept of race was like nationality, biology, and culture all combined into the characteristics of a people. This concept of race still seems to be with us to a degree. Those who speak of the Jewish race have in mind just such a combination of biological and social traits. The late Winston Churchill used to speak eloquently about the British race, and he was a master of knowing what his listeners wanted to hear.

MODERN CONCEPT OF RACE.

With the development of the science of biology over the last century we have come to distinguish between biological inheritance and social tradition. The tendency has since been to limit the concept of race to the biologically inherited traits and to treat separately those which are passed on by cultural tradition. For the most part this can be equated with a division between anatomical traits and behavioral ones, but the basis of this distinction is not always clear.

Another major distinction between the biological and the cultural modes of transmission is the rapidity with which changes can be introduced in each. Biological evolution is based on new genetic mutations, if they are not already in the gene pool, and it requires natural selection over many generations to accomplish any kind of change. While cultural traditions are often just as conservative as is biology, changes can occur much more rapidly on occasion. Some new behavior can be learned by most adults and it is at least possible to teach totally new things to each generation. This flexibility in cultural behavior has made it a highly adaptive mechanism for survival. Individual learning by experience is the fastest kind of adaptation, but if it ends with the death of the individual it has little survival value for the species. The remarkable thing about human culture is that it incorporates learned experience, and in addition, passes this new information to succeeding generations by a mechanism just as dependable as the biological one. It is the ideal compromise between the speed of individual learning and the dependability of inherited behavior patterns. What Lamark thought he saw in biological evolution is very similar to what does in fact happen in culture.

In terms of biology, the origin of man is the evolution of our culture-bearing capacity. This must not be confused with the evolution of specific culture content. Throughout most of the Pleistocene Epoch there was an increase in man's culture-bearing capacity as well as a corresponding increase in the complexity of that culture itself. In the last 40,000 years, since the appearance of *Homo sapiens,* our individual capacity has probably not increased, but through organization and specialization some cultures have continued to grow. While various cultures differ widely in their content and even in the total quantity of their information, the individual human participants apparently do not differ in the amount that each can learn. The more complex a culture, the smaller the fraction that is known by the average person in it. It is universally accepted in anthropology that all human populations have approximately the same culture-bearing capacity. If any such differences could be found this would constitute a most significant racial trait. It would appear, however, that geniuses and fools are about equally distributed over the world.

Our modern concept of race is usually limited to inherited biological traits which have some degree of geographical concentration. Since the concept of common descent and breeding pool often enter into the definition we can get involved with cultural traits whether we like it or not. Most people, in fact nearly all, have children by mates who speak the same language. Since language is the primary criterion of nationality, it has been argued that each nation state is a breeding population, hence a race in one sense of the word. Sir Arthur Keith said as much in his book, *A New Theory of Human Evolution*. Fortunately for the sake of national prejudices this is based on a naive concept of language. Rural people, the bulk of any nation, speak dialects that differ from place to place and often grade across national boundaries with little change. There may well be a slight tendency to form national gene pools over many generations, but most nation states are neither so well bounded nor so long lasting as to make this a significant factor in long-term racial development.

The task of modern biology has consisted of three parts: (1) to determine which traits are inherited, (2) to collect enough data to give the world-wide distributions (in the ethnographic present) of the variations in these, and (3) to explain why the differences exist and why they are found where they are. Roughly speaking, the second World War marked a boundary in terms of progress along these lines. Up to that war there was almost total success in determining which traits were biologically inherited, to a fair degree these variations were mapped around the world, and virtually no progress had been made in explaining any of it.

POPULAR RACES.

Before the war the anthropologists' picture of the world's races had settled into a fairly solid mold and it is with us today in the minds of the general public who learned it from school text books. There are supposedly three major races, Caucasoid, Mongoloid, and Negroid. There are many more minor races which are subdivisions of these three and/or mixtures between them. Probably the neatest exposition of that kind of picture was by A. L. Kroeber in his *Anthropology*, published in 1948. Interestingly the 1923 edition of the book gives almost the same story.

Kroeber first gives a map of the world showing the areas of occupation by what he called the primary racial stocks (Fig. 3). The characteristics ascribed to these groups should be familiar to all readers. Then in a chart of carefully placed circles labeled as the minor races he shows a consensus as to how closely related each is to the others and to the, unlabeled but obvious, major races (Fig. 4). Kroeber's classification is one of the several basic types which we will return to later.

Climatic adaptations were only dimly known in Kroeber's time. Because of this little could be said about the reasons why the major races should originally have become separated and distinguished from each other. That there should be major races was simply accepted as self-evident and normal. How that came to be was something of a problem. Even the developing science of population genetics had little to offer in the way of explaining origins, especially the geographical distribution of classical traits on which this picture is based.

Other classifications made at this time and earlier ran into the problem of which trait to use for the first cut, which for the second, and so on. Some first divided the world into light and dark skinned people, then subdivided these according to other traits. Some made the primary division according to hair form, whether it was straight or spiral, and then subdivided by skin color and other traits. In the absence of reason one could as well make the first cut on the basis of stature or nose breadth or whatever else struck one's fancy. Kroeber's scheme, like some others, attempted to use all traits simultaneously, but obviously skin, hair, and noses were weighted heaviest. How many traits to use and how relatively to weigh them were a continuing problem for classifications of this kind. Had the anthropologists known the adaptive significance of these traits some of these problems would have been avoided.

Sharp boundaries are absent. Zones of intermediacy are almost as large as some of the racial areas themselves. To many anthropologists this was normal and expectable as a product of the presumed hybridizing along racial boundaries. Some went so far as to claim that such hybrids were not only quite normal, but even more vigorous, on the average, than individuals of either parent stock. A moment of reflection would show that if that were the case all basic races should long ago have disappeared and been replaced by the expanded hybrid populations. Since this is apparently not the case one must argue for a long separation of races and their recent recontact with each other. Such a picture should have become evident in the form of vast gaps in the

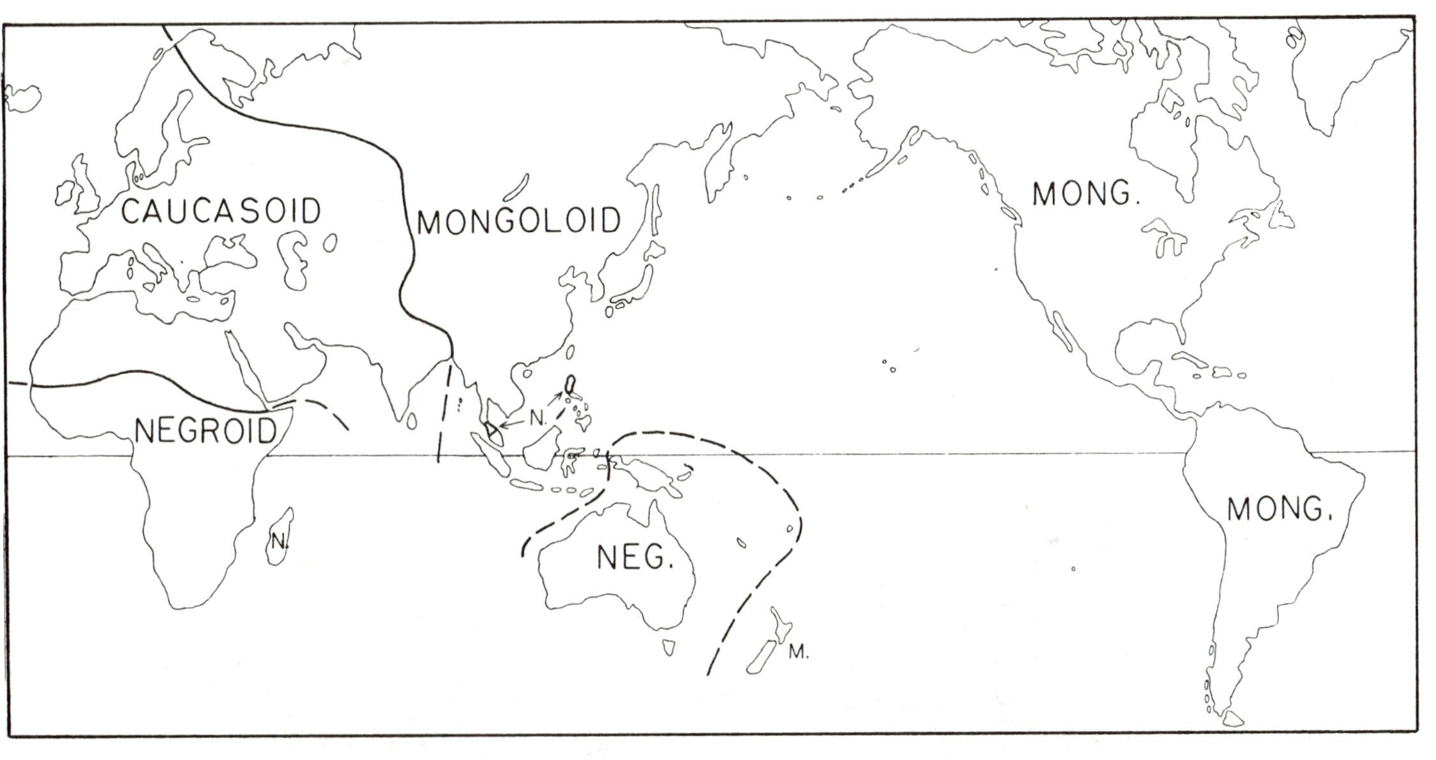

FIGURE 3. Major races of the world. This map (redrawn from Kroeber 1948) shows the distribution, in the ethnographic present, of the three races as based on classical morphology. Other authorities of the time would separate the native Australians as a fourth major race. Rather than being continental, the racial distributions tend to be circumoceanic; Negroids are on both sides of the Indian Ocean, Mongoloids almost surround the Pacific; and Caucasoids live all around the Mediterranean.

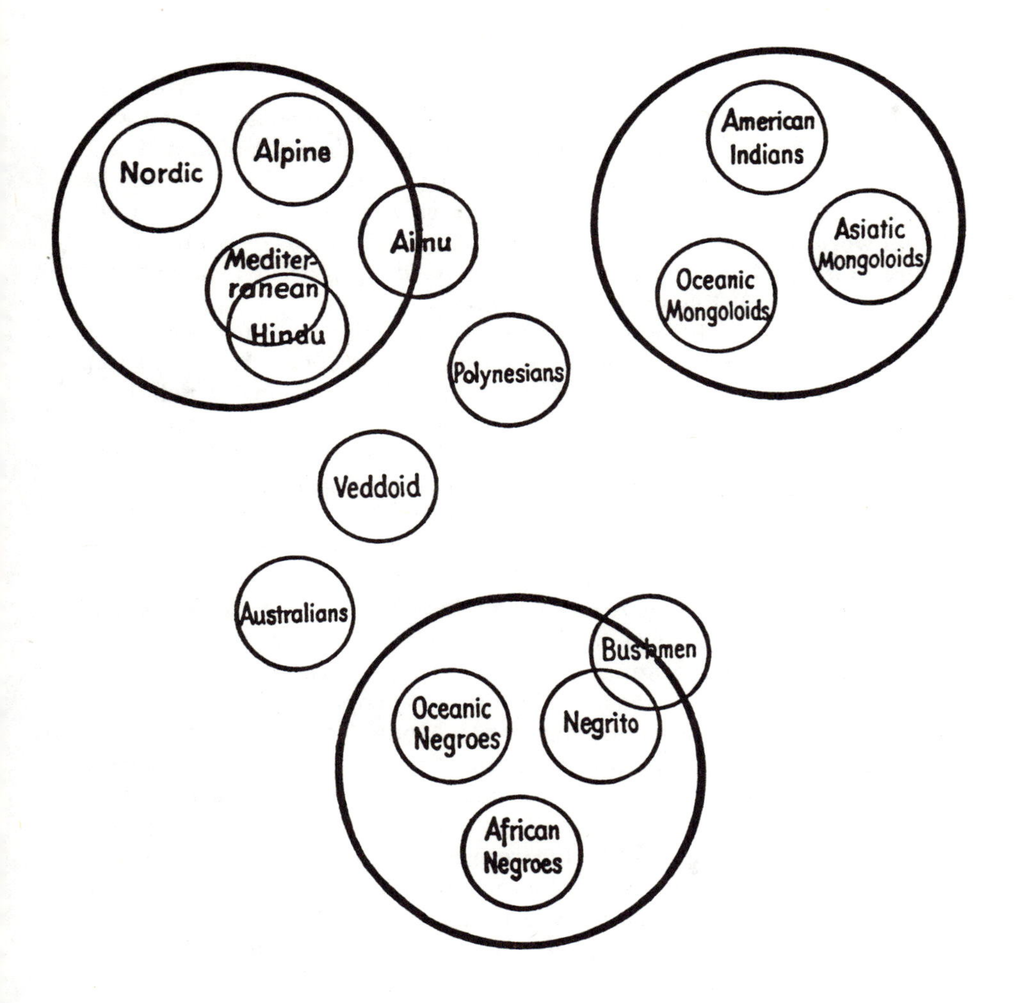

FIGURE 4. Racial distances according to classical morphology. The various races are shown here as circles, the major three being unnamed but obvious. The degree of "relationship" between these races is indicated by the distance between their centers. (Reproduced with permission from *Anthropology* by A. L. Kroeber, Harcourt Brace Jovanovich, Inc., Publisher.)

archeological record of human occupation, and they are not there. Again, the problem of the zones of intermediacy goes back to the question of how the major races came to be in the first place. The concept of basic races leaves us with a paradox.

Human beings are today distributed rather unevenly over the world. There are a few areas of very dense population and vast tracts with very sparse habitation. Some readers may be curious about this so I prepared a map (Fig. 5) which roughly outlines seventeen areas with populations ranging from twenty million up to almost a billion. These are based on population figures from 1973 and would of course be somewhat greater today. These seventeen areas contain 90% of the total world's population, yet together they encompass only about one-third of its land area. Another interesting sidelight is the fact that only 10% of the people live south of the equator.

If one combines this map of population with the map of conventional race distributions some more interesting results appear. The race map must of course be adjusted for modern distributions which have shifted somewhat. The three major races turn out not to be anywhere near equal in numbers in the world today. Comparative figures calculated by Vincent Kotshar (in Coon's *The Living Races of Man)* give Caucasoids the majority, 55.7% of the world's population, Mongoloids 37.1%, Negroids 6.8%, and as a fourth race, Australoids at 0.4%. With 1973 census data and some careful estimating I arrived at the similar figures of Caucasoids 56.8%, Mongoloids 35.1%, Negroids 7.8%, and Australoids 0.3%. These figures involved allocating mixed populations back to their original types according to ratios that are only estimates. It also means classifying the people of India with the Caucasoids and Native Americans with Mongoloids, which not everyone will readily accept. Census figures of many countries are suspect, especially where they involve noncivilized peoples. Still it takes a misallocation of over 30 million people to make even a one percent error in these figures. They cannot be far from correct. I put these percentages here as a pointed reminder to the Caucasoid peoples of the world that they are not being overrun by a rising tide of "color." It is also a reminder to the "black" peoples that in terms of the usual racial classification they are running a poor third in numbers. The "yellow peril" so often feared by Europeans is not very real.

While these population figures are rather interesting in themselves, their real significance lies in their influence on racial origins and on their classifications. I will simply note at this point that races are called major when they contain vast numbers of people with military and economic power. They are called minor when they lack these attributes. The physical distinctiveness of populations or their actual

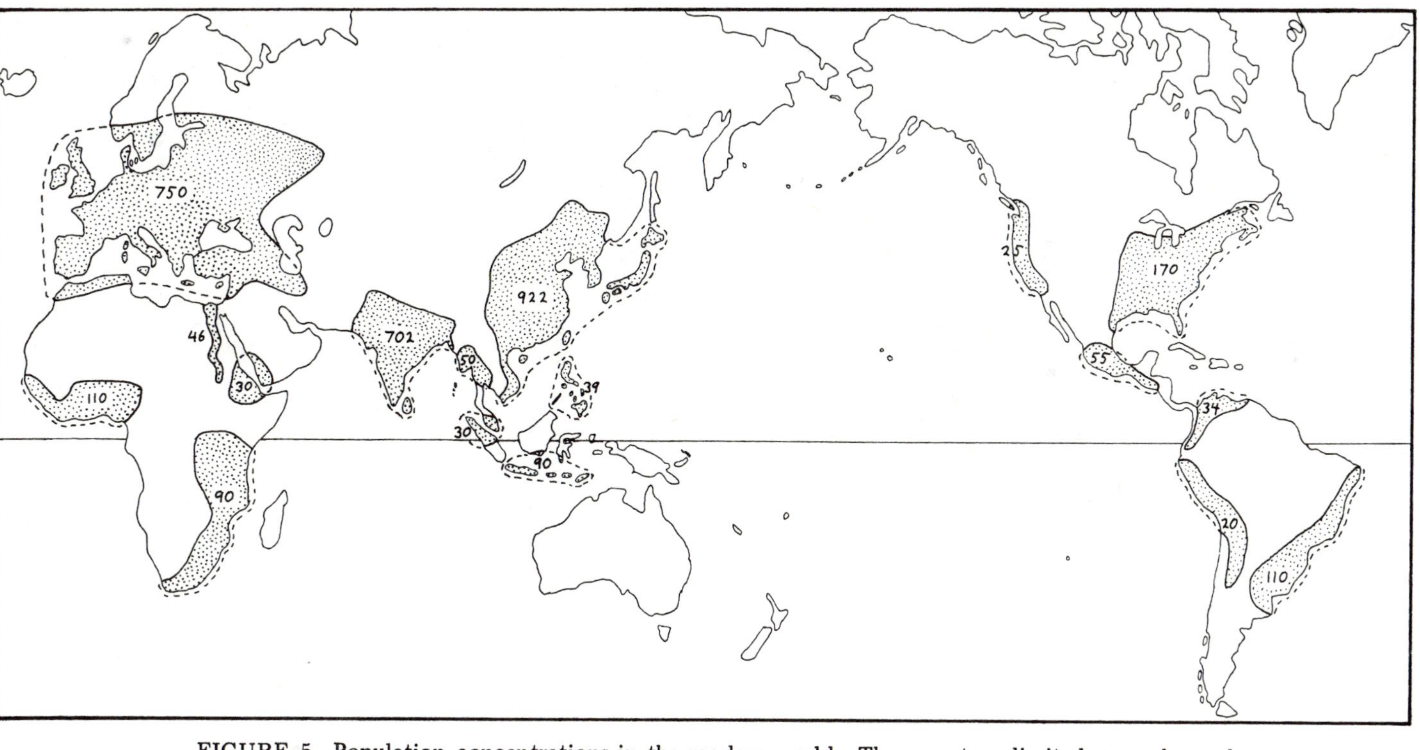

FIGURE 5. Population concentrations in the modern world. The seventeen limited areas shown here contain 90% of the world's inhabitants on about one-third of its land surface. Population figures for each area are given in millions of people and are based on 1973 estimates.

antiquity are largely irrelevant to most classifications. It is sheer power that is the basis for calling one race major and another race minor. This is unfortunate, but it is an outstanding example of how social factors get into the subject of race.

CHANGE IN EMPHASIS.

Since World War II most scientific investigations of race have shifted from studying classical traits to what I call genetic traits. This change in emphasis has occurred for various reasons, one being a feeling of futility in the older approach—it didn't seem to be getting anywhere.

Anthropometry, the measurement of man, was a relatively simple and inexpensive business when dealing with classical traits. The anthropologist brought a few measuring tools and comparison samples along with him when visiting some little known people. Often the anthropologist was mainly gathering ethnographic or linguistic data and did the anthropometry on the side. It was sufficient to have a suitcase full of measuring tools and notebooks, and sometimes an assistant to record measurements and observations while the work was being done. Exact measurements could be obtained on some samples of peoples and approximate comparisons could be noted about those who could not be treated directly. No extensive training was necessary to do a passable job and expenses were not very high. Anthropometry was certainly not what would be called a glamorous occupation. It lacked the prestige of handling large amounts of money, directing many assistants, running expensive electronic gadgets, and writing impressive reports with a team of prestigious colleagues. Still, the plodding anthropologists and educated laymen succeeded fairly well in mapping the world's distribution of classical traits. Efforts along these lines have largely ceased, not so much because the job was done, but because the emphasis shifted to what was hoped would be a more productive avenue of approach. There was a growing feeling (I think quite incorrect) that the traditional method was a dead end.

Since the war the emphasis has been on studying human variations that are not immediately observable to the naked eye. Biochemical differences have been a major focus of activity and we now have fairly complete world maps of a number of blood-type frequencies. Special adaptations to heat, cold, and high altitude are also being studied intensively. While these are variations relating to climate they are generally not the classical traits that have been noted and measured in the past.

A common thread runs through almost all recent work—it is expensive. Most anthropologists cannot afford to finance even the most modest kind of racial investigations out of their own pockets. Government and private granting agencies are the source of their funds. Given the volume of equipment, the usual team approach, and the current desire to obtain a large statistical sample of everything, this has meant that costs of such investigations are very high. Granting agencies do not want to risk funds on ideas that may not lead to something conclusive. The result of this is that only a limited number of projects are supported and these are led by established authorities in the field. Little can be done along these lines by unorthodox thinkers or by most people outside the scientific establishment.

Investigations are usually far more intensive and detailed than ever before and this has yielded much good information. But where resources are concentrated they are not dispersed. World mapping of new traits is not keeping up with their discovery. If anything, we are gradually falling behind in our knowledge of distributions, and this is what race is all about.

Another aspect of recent work has been to point out more clearly how the environment affects expression of racial traits on three different levels.

(1) There are changes which the adult organism can make in response to the environment, notably in adapting to high altitudes, as well as the mundane effect of sun tanning.

(2) The environment can affect the growing individual, again in altitude adaptations, but also in the permanent effects of diet.

(3) The environment is the major source of selection pressure favoring certain traits, whether they be climate adaptive or disease resistant.

On these three levels the environment is not just that of nature but also that of culture as well. Human cultural variations put different pressures on people in terms of how good their diet is, how hard they work, what places they choose to live in, what diseases go untreated, and how densely they are packed, just to name a few. While it is still true, as noted above, that the inherited variations are the substance of race, if these variations can be approximated by other means this may reduce certain effects of natural selection. For instance, there will be no selective pressure for light skin color in order to produce vitamin D if this substance is included in the diet. Other examples will be brought up later as appropriate. So again human cultural behavior becomes a major factor in race. It begins to look as though human races are maybe not quite the same thing as subspecies in the world of nature after all.

Modern biology still has failed to answer the questions about race that are asked by the man on the street. The ordinary man does not see the physiological details nor understand the statistical treatment of breeding patterns that he gets in books and lectures on race today. He sees different people who come from different places and simply wants to know why.

3.
SMALL POPULATIONS

SUMMARY.

In addition to the so-called major races of Caucasoid, Mongoloid and Negroid, whose descriptions are well known, there are many smaller populations that must be dealt with. These are usually treated as subdivisions of the major races, as mixtures between them, or even elevated to the rank of major races themselves in some instances.

Most of these small populations practiced a hunting and gathering economy until recently, and some still do. Some are primarily pastoralists (Lapps), a few are farmers of a primitive sort (Ainus, Polynesians, Micronesians, and Melanesians) and at least one may be classed among the civilized peoples (Basques).

These are referred to as small populations because none of them number in the tens of millions or more, like the major races. If they did they would certainly be called major races and given primary rank and a presumed great antiquity. One group, the Tasmanians, is extinct and a few others like the Ainu, Vedda, and Alakaluf are nearly gone. Melanesians, including Papuans, are in the best condition and number a few million. Others not mentioned above include the Pygmies, Bushmen, Eskimos, Negritos, and Australians.

MAJOR RACES.

Typical representatives of the popular three major racial types are probably well-known to virtually everybody and call for little description here. In brief, Caucasoids differ from the average human condition in having light skin color, prominent and narrow noses, and straight to curly cranial hair with ample beards and body hair in the males. In addition, this group includes virtually all the people with light eyes and blond hair, they usually have thin lips, and are rather large in body size with about average limb proportions.

The Negroids have dark skin color, wider and flatter noses than most of the world, and a spiral mat of cranial hair with less than average body and facial hair. They often have notable lip eversion, and while they are about as tall as Caucasoids they tend to have more slender bodies.

Mongoloids are generally light skinned, have about average shaped noses, and their hair is straight and coarse, again with a minimum of facial and body hair. Epicanthic folds cover the inner corner of the eye, cheek bones are set forward, and body build tends toward the short and heavy-set.

Further description of these supposed major types can be gleaned from the trait descriptions in the following chapters by comparing these distributions with the race locations according to Kroeber's race map. As long as one does not choose to get picky and detailed, these three major races today can encompass over 99% of the world's population.

Since it is evident that at least some of the numerical preponderance of the big three may be a recent phenomenon, a racial picture of the world must include some accounting of the numerically smaller populations. These lesser peoples, to be described below, are sometimes included as subdivisions of the major races, and sometimes they are treated as stable mixtures between them. Kroeber uses both methods of accounting for them in his scheme which thus preserves the original trinity of race. Other workers will raise one or more of these small populations to the rank of major races simply because some of them show extreme characteristics which could not have arisen from mixtures of the traits found in the big three. Australian natives and the Bushmen of southern Africa are often so elevated. Their numerical insignificance today results from the cultural fact that they were among the last to develop agriculture and thus did not participate in the population explosion this phenomenon induced elsewhere. Such circumstances of geographical location in relation to cultural events determine which races are called major and which are called minor. To so label them may be initially acceptable, but to go from there to postulate greater antiquity because of greater numbers requires further demonstration.

SMALL POPULATIONS.

The locations of the "lesser races" are mapped in Fig. 6. These are sometimes simplified in outline and exaggerated in area so they may be seen more clearly. This liberty may not be entirely misleading as some of these various peoples once did in fact cover much larger areas,

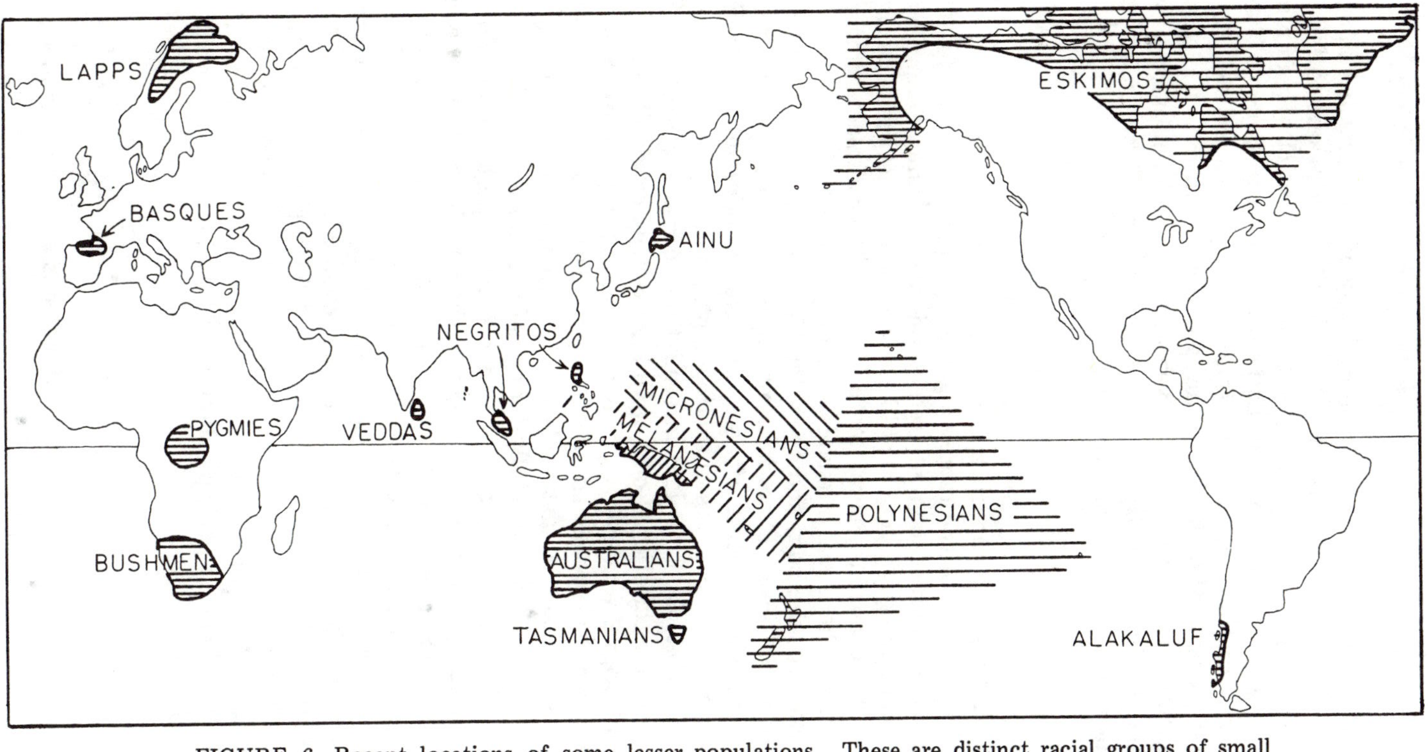

FIGURE 6. Recent locations of some lesser populations. These are distinct racial groups of small numbers which are not ordinarily classed as major human races. Their areas are shown approximately as of the ethnographic present, or 1500 A.D.

even larger than is shown on this map. Many of their detailed characteristics will be discussed in the trait-by-trait descriptions to follow, but the reader should have their geographic locations clearly in mind in order to compare with the trait distribution maps. In general, I have located them on this map as of the ethnographic present, or 1500 A.D., and my discussion of their way of life refers pretty much to that time. Original population estimates are given where possible, but sometimes we have only figures for the middle of this century. Some comments about their present circumstances may also be of interest.

LAPPS.

In the mountains and tundra of northern Scandinavia and northwestern Russia live one of the more enigmatic peoples of the world. The Lapps subsist on an economy based on reindeer herding, fishing, and some hunting and gathering of wild foodstuffs. In most respects they resemble Europeans in general, but differ from their immediate neighbors in being rather smaller in body size (but not stocky in build), and a trace darker in skin, hair, and eye color. They are also noted for their especially small teeth. There is what might be called a slight Mongoloid appearance in some of them, but this is minimal. A parallel selection for the same traits of arctic adaptation is a possibility, with or without a bit of Mongoloid intermixture to provide some of the actual genes for selection. Some would have them originally of truly Mongoloid origin, whatever that may mean, but so long exposed to gene flow from Europeans as to almost completely override their original makeup. Their linguistic relatives, the Samoyeds far to the east in northwestern Siberia, are fully Mongoloid in appearance. The same speculation has been applied to them, but reversed; perhaps they are of European ancestry now swamped by gene flow from Mongoloid neighbors. Blood types frequencies will be shown to lean strongly toward the theory of an ultimate Asiatic origin for both. Other linguistic relatives like Finns and Hungarians only complicate an already peculiar situation, and they show essentially no evidence of non-European connections.

At the turn of the century there were 31,000 Lapps, fully two-thirds of them in Norway. Since then their numbers have grown somewhat, but also some have become incorporated into the national cultures where they reside and perhaps should not any longer be counted as ethnically Lapps.

BASQUES.

In the area of the western Pyrenees Mountains and adjacent lowland parts of both Spain and France lives another anachronistic group of people. The Basque language seems to have no relationship to any other, though a resemblance to Berber of northern Africa has been suggested. Physically they do not stand out from their neighbors in any clear way. Their predominant economic pursuits of farming and sheep herding also do not serve as distinguishing marks, as compared to the Lapp reindeer herding for instance. What makes the Basques unique is their high frequency of Rh negative blood. While negative blood is a European trait in general it here reaches its highest frequency of over 50%. This and some other peculiarities of blood types have suggested to some scientists that the Basques represent an earlier substratum (whatever that means) of the European racial type. Since the Lapps also take a European gene frequency, blood type A, to its maximum expression, they too are candidates for this role. The trouble is they cannot both be proto-Europeans as the blood factors are not the same.

Basques today number about one million, and there are perhaps another 200,000 more of Basque origin in the United States and Argentina. Many of these don't speak Basque, and many more are of Basque ancestry but aren't counted here. Thus their number is somewhat arbitrary.

PYGMIES.

Certain areas of the Congo River basin in central Africa contain many small bands of Pygmies. For simplicity these are drawn as a single circular area on the map. True Pygmies of the Ituri Forest are hunters and gatherers who also trade some of their forest produce for the agricultural products of their neighbors. Ituri Pygmy males stand about 144 cm (just under 4 ft. 9 in.) and the women about 3 cm less. Other Pygmy groups are slightly larger. Pygmies are also noted for their skin color which is considerably lighter than their Negro neighbors. Blood types provide some additional distinctions.

Ituri Pygmies today number around 30,000 and are about one-fifth of the total Pygmy population of Africa. They may be expected to maintain their numbers as long as their forest environment continues to exist. But this frontier has been pushed back by farmers in many areas leaving some of the Pygmies trying to adapt to other ways of life.

BUSHMEN.

The term "Bushmen" has been used for native hunters in many regions, but for the sake of simplicity it has come to be used now only for the pre-agricultural people of southern Africa. These are again small people, but here males are mostly in the range of 150 to 155 cm, or barely over 5 ft. tall. They are distinguished by their peppercorn hair, so-called because it curls so tightly it forms little clumps over the scalp. They also have much lighter skin color than might be expected in an area of intense sunlight. Their blood types take African trends to the extreme.

There are about 50,000 Bushmen living today in various stages of acculturation. Until some economic value is found in their desert environment they should continue to exist. Their close relatives, the cattle-herding Hottentots, were in competition for arable lands with their larger black and white neighbors. The Hottentots are now gone except for mixed descendants in other populations of South Africa. They were a little larger and darker than the Bushmen, presumably from intermixture with other cattle-keeping peoples at some early date.

Bushmen and Hottentot languages are very different from those of most other Africans. A few similar languages to the north suggest remnants of the Bushman type where the language has held out but where the physical distinction was largely lost through gene exchange with their more numerous neighbors. Despite some enthusiastic claims to the contrary, no anthropologist has been able to discover an equivalent native language among the Pygmies. They speak Bantu like the local large people.

NEGRITOS.

Within the tropical rain forests of Malaya and the nearby Philippine and Andaman Islands live some small, dark people who have often been compared with Pygmies. In fact, the Spanish name Negrito simply means small Negro. It has become customary to restrict the name Pygmy to Africa and Negrito to Asia, though they both mean essentially the same thing. Like their African counterparts they hunt with poisoned arrows and gather wild vegetables. They are about as small as the Pygmies but not quite so flat nosed. They are dark, but not black, and have tightly spiraled hair. There the resemblance ends and the Negrito facial features are, if anything, more Australian than African. Their blood types are also more like their larger neighbors than like Africans.

Only those on the Andaman Islands have a language unrelated to that of their larger neighbors. Perhaps the others once did too. No relationship can seriously be proposed between these dwarfed people of Africa and Asia, but within each area they were probably once continuously distributed instead of their presently scattered enclaves. It is uncertain how many Negritos there are today, but probably they are far fewer than the Pygmies if one is to judge from the size of the areas they occupy.

VEDDAS.

Off the tip of India on the Island of Ceylon (now Sri Lanka) there are native hunting peoples who are not related to either the Indo-Europeans or the Dravidians. These Vedda tribesmen are thought to represent the aboriginal population and are sometimes combined with the so-called tribal peoples of India proper as a pre-agricultural substratum. Veddas are almost as small as Bushmen (males average 157 cm) about medium brown in color, but have the wavy hair of Caucasoids. They may be thought of as tiny versions of a southern Caucasoid group, or as dwarfed Australoids. In no sense are they a connecting link between Pygmies and Negritos. There are only a few hundred Veddas left today. The tribal people of India who are physically larger and are mostly farmers number in the millions. Just how many of these, if any, should be equated with the Veddas is unclear.

MELANESIANS.

These are the full-sized Negroid-looking people mainly in New Guinea and the Solomon Islands to the east of there, then to the south as far as New Caledonia. The name Melanesia means black islands and was based on the color of the inhabitants. The people also have spiral hair and broad noses. Melanesians are horticulturalists and fishermen, and are noted for their sea-going outrigger sailing canoes. Like the Negritos they have been compared with their African counterparts but the similarities are equally superficial. Melanesians have prominent brow ridges with a deep nasion notch at the root of the nose. They show only modest lip eversion. In blood types they are almost as un-African as it is possible to be.

There were aboriginally just over two million Melanesians. Today there are closer to three million. These fall into two linguistic groups which represent a distinction in origins. Papuan languages of most of New Guinea and parts of some of the other large islands include the majority of Melanesians. The others, never located far from the sea shores, speak Austronesian languages related to Polynesian and Indonesian. These coastal Melanesians may be relatively recent intruders who established themselves in modest numbers along the coasts and who acquired their classical traits by gene flow and selection from the more numerous previous inhabitants. In some blood type frequencies there is a notable contrast between the Papuans and the Austronesian Melanesians.

TASMANIANS.

This large island off the southeastern tip of Australia was once inhabited by natives, now extinct, who were very similar to the Melanesians. They had spiral hair, dark skins, and broad noses on an otherwise Australoid anatomy. Their location so far to the south and their simple material culture lacking water craft make it impossible to consider them just an extension of the Melanesians. Skeletons and photographs remain, but we can never get any data on their blood types. The genealogies of some supposedly mixed Australian-Tasmanian individuals are too uncertain to be of any value.

A possible connecting link, without boats, to the Melanesian homeland is a population reported from the Cairn Forest near the northeastern tip of Australia where it almost touches New Guinea. This group supposedly has spiral hair and, like most Papuans, they are somewhat smaller than most Australian natives.

AUSTRALIANS.

Already alluded to above, the native inhabitants of this island-continent have often been elevated to the rank of a fourth major race, with or without the Melanesians being included. Their's was entirely a hunting, gathering, and sometimes fishing economy at the time of discovery by European explorers. Even the bow and arrow had not reached, nor been developed by, these people. On the other hand, they had developed the throwing stick, in the form of the boomerang, to a greater degree than anywhere else. The name Aborigine, or Abo for short, has come to be used exclusively for the Australians even though it is technically correct for the natives of any region.

Aborigines have dark skins which approximate those of most Africans. Their wavy cranial hair as well as beards and body hair are like those found among Europeans. Their teeth are the largest in the world, their brow ridges are usually notable, and the root of the otherwise large nose is deeply indented. No mixing of Caucasoid and Negroid heredity would produce this kind of combination of traits. Except for their spiral hair, the Tasmanians come close to fitting into the Australian physical type.

Before contact the Abos numbered about 300,000 and are now reduced to about one-fourth of that number. In much of the Australian desert they have a good chance of surviving as the Bushmen are doing in South Africa. But the destructive impact of European technological civilization in America may yet turn out to be the model which Australia will eventually follow.

AINUS.

On Japan's northernmost main island of Hokkaido live the remnants of a people who occupied half of that country within historical times, and more even earlier. Ainus have long been noted for having European resemblances in their abundance of facial and body hair and the wavy form of that on the head. In many other features they are rather un-Mongoloid, but are just as Australian as they are European in most of these. Ainu blood types differ only slightly from their Mongoloid neighbors but some other genetic traits show more contrast.

The Ainus are essentially extinct today in the sense that too few survive to form a viable breeding population. They seem to be related to other peoples of Sakhalin Island to the north and on the mainland of adjacent Siberia. Some of these, including Gilyaks and Yukaghirs, have also been noted for their beards and not quite Mongoloid appearance. Many explanations have been offered to account for these peoples—a primitive substratum, Australoids extending up the eastern Asian offshore islands, or a Caucasoid interjection somehow.

ESKIMOS.

These sea hunters of the American Arctic are so well-known that little need be said about them. Like most Siberians they are what might be called the extreme Mongoloid type. In this they differ from most of their North American Indian neighbors who show the cold-weather adaptations to a lesser degree. Eskimo blood types also align them more with Asia than with North America and indicate a Siberian origin in the last few thousand years.

Today there are about 40,000 Eskimo and half of these are of partly European ancestry. In many areas they are becoming incorporated into the national cultures and economies.

ALAKALUF.

The southern tip of South America was inhabited by a number of tribes, many now extinct, of which the Alakaluf is the best known today. This area is the farthest south of any regularly inhabited place on the globe and the climate is rather cold. Like the Eskimo, these foraging people are cold adapted at the cost of a high intake of calories. Unlike the Eskimo, they do not have well tailored clothing—the cold is not that severe. The surviving Alakaluf are rather short (159 cm), but other southern Amerindians were as tall as northern Europeans and correspondingly massive. They now number only a few hundred at best.

POLYNESIANS.

A comparably large-bodied group of people inhabit many of the Islands of the central Pacific Ocean. Like the Melanesians mentioned before, they practice simple horticulture and much fishing from their excellent boats. Polynesians have often been considered a mixture of the three major races from their appearance, but just how this could have been accomplished has never been satisfactorily explained. Their blood types are East Asian, Amerindian, or unique, depending on which is studied. They are somehow related to the dark, spiral-haired Melanesians and speak similar languages. About half a million is a good estimate of the Polynesian population.

MICRONESIANS.

This last group is named from the small islands it inhabits located in the western Pacific. Culturally these people are much like Melanesians, with whom they have had some contact and gene flow, and the Polynesians, whose culture and language they most closely approximate. The aboriginal population was about 80,000 and has grown considerably in recent years.

OTHERS.

Many other small populations have been reported around the world which supposedly display interesting physical characteristics. Often these descriptions are too vague or too outlandish to be taken seriously. Sometimes the reputation of the observer is suspect, especially if he is trying to prove a particular theory with evidence that other observers do not see. In spite of such cautions it is good to keep an open mind to the possibility that new variations of the human anatomy may yet turn up, or old variations may turn up in unexpected places.

Veddoid peoples have been reported in Malaya, in Sumatra, and in the Celebes. These are probably not accurate descriptions, but it would at least be theoretically possible for wavy haired Veddoids to have lived there long before the southern Mongols and even prior to the spiral-haired Negritos. Negrito farmers have been reported in western New Guinea, an unexpected combination. But here it is difficult to know where to draw the line between small Papuans and large Negritos. Bushman-like desert hunters have been rumored to exist in northern Africa, and what might be mixed remnants have been observed in some recent populations there. Pygmies no doubt used to live in the tropical forests of western Africa and it has at least been wondered whether some are still there.

In the Americas there are travelers' reports of Pygmies, but these are probably just some of the smaller tribes who may average as short as 150 cm. At the other end of the size range are sailors' accounts of Patagonians well over 2 m tall. Are these just unusually tall individuals of the Alakaluf group or is somebody else involved?

There are some rather different accounts from several parts of the world of bipedal primates that have raised much interest. Such creatures as the Yeti and Sasquatch, for example, are too large, too hairy, and evidently devoid of cultural behavior. Thus they are not human, if they exist at all, and are beyond the purview of this book.

4.
CLASSICAL TRAITS

SUMMARY.

The major classical traits that are described here have been observed since civilization began. Each trait is first described in terms of its pertinent anatomy and the variations on that which lead to the differences that have been noticed. The functions of these differences are then described as far as they are known. It is found that most of these classical traits are adaptations to some aspect of the climate in which the people live in the ethnographic present, or presumably lived in not long before that.

Skin color regulates the amount of ultraviolet light from the sun that can penetrate into the deeper layers of the skin. Eye and hair color variations tend to follow skin color because they have the same cause. Sometimes they vary in an advantageous way and sometimes not. Hair form and distribution largely follow temperature zones but have been displaced a few times. Body fat tends to follow temperature, but poorly. Size and body build are clearly related to temperature, but in two different ways, which makes stature a meaningless measurement by itself. Nose forms are related mainly to absolute winter humidity, but are also influenced by such things as tooth size, cheek position, and lip thickness.

Additional variations in internal anatomy and physiology for adaptations to cold, heat, and high altitude have been studied, but world distributions of such adaptations are not known, and thus they are of little value here.

CLASSICAL TRAITS.

When man first began to explore great distances and to encounter people very different from himself, the kinds of differences he perceived were those we now call classical traits. The explorer may have been a tall, light-brown Egyptian who was looking at a darker, very tiny man with spiral hair, and almost no nose. That same Egyptian's descendants would have seen taller, lighter, blond invaders with blue eyes. A Chinese explorer would have encountered dark skins, curly hair, and very peculiar-looking eyes if he traveled far enough to the southwest. Malay sailors saw small, yellow-brown people with tiny balls of hair on their scalps off in one direction, whereas they found large and bearded ones in the other direction. Western European sailors saw them all. These are still the kinds of differences we see around us today. We still ask the same questions those early explorers asked: Why do these differences exist? Why are they found only, or mainly, in certain places?

In general terms the classical traits are those that can easily be seen with the naked eye. Thus they are epidermal (skin and hair) or they describe conspicuous variations in size and shape (nose, lips, and whole body). All of these traits show variations that can be measured on a continuous scale, whether it be in milimeters, kilograms, degree of curvature, or shade of color. The amount of expression of each trait can be noted for every individual. Range of variation and the mean (average) for each trait can be calculated for every measured population. We can also find standard deviations and do many other statistical operations with these data. These are quantitative traits because they are all measured in terms of quantity, or how much there is.

We are sure these classical traits are genetically inherited but generally we do not know the exact mechanism. Evidently each of them is determined by a large number of genes so it is difficult or impossible to trace the inheritance of just one of them. Each gene contributes such a small amount to the final expression of the trait its effect cannot be separated from that of other similar genes. Also environmental effects, especially on growing children, introduce additional slight variations that also cannot often be distinguished from what a single gene might accomplish. Still there is one classical trait, eye color, that has a known genetic mechanism for its major variation. It will be dealt with in this chapter because it is a classic, but it will be equally pertinent in the later chapter on genetic variations.

Some other traits will be discussed which are not evident upon visual inspection. Physiological adaptations to climatic extremes are pertinent here simply because the rest of the classical traits are also climatic adaptations. These physiological adaptations are also quantitatively measurable and are polygenic in their inheritance.

The general plan of this chapter will be to deal with these traits one at a time. First the pertinent anatomical structures will be described along with those variations which produce the different observable results. The known or possible functions of these variations will next be discussed. And finally, the geographic distributions of the variations will be given. It must be remembered in each case that the year 1500 A.D., or the ethnographic present, is the base line for all these distributions unless otherwise noted. For this reason one may refer to the natives of the New World simply as Americans instead of the more cumbersome American Indians or Amerindians. Likewise the Australians are the Aborigines who long preceded the present Anglo majority. South Africans are neither white nor black, but are the yellow-brown Bushmen who were there before either of them.

In many cases I will discuss the known or presumed effects of human movements prior to the year 1500. Sometimes this is obvious as in the southward expansion, with rice agriculture, of the southern Mongoloids to the equator and even beyond. In other cases it is not nearly so clear as in the case of the Tasmanian movement, with the beginning of *Homo sapiens,* down the eastern forest belt of Australia. These displacements will be shown as accomplished facts on the basic trait maps because of their time of occurrence, but in deducing the causative effects of climate on racial traits they will have to be considered in their original locations.

SKIN COLOR.

It has been claimed that skin color is one of the two most noticed of human variations, the other being stature. The range of expression from very light through the shades of brown to virtually black is almost as extreme as is possible. Practically all of this variation results from different amounts of the chemical melanin that is present in the uppermost part of the skin.

The human skin (or integument) is divided by the anatomists into an outer layer of epidermis (or cuticle) and an inner layer called the dermis (or corium). The epidermis consists largely of dead and dying cells and contains no blood vessels or nerves. This outer envelope serves to prevent unlimited seepage of body fluids and is also the body's first line of defense against foreign invasions of all kinds. The dermis contains such things as capillaries, lymph ducts, nerves, hair follicles, sweat glands, sebaceous (oil) glands, some fat, and various layers of connective tissue. Together these two layers of the skin have a thickness varying from about one to six mm. Except where calluses are well developed, the epidermis is only a small fraction of this total thickness.

Below the skin is the subcutaneous layer which contains most of the body's fat supply, more connective tissue, and through which pass significant nerves and blood vessels.

The epidermis itself is the focus of our attention here. It has been described as a series of layers (see Fig. 7) with the stratum germinativum at the base and the thicker stratum corneum on the surface. Germinativum (or Malpighian layer) is the living source for all the outer layers. Cells at this level continually divide leaving one member of the resultant pair in place while the other is displaced outward. The displaced cell eventually migrates to the surface, pushed along by other such cells behind it. In so moving, these migrating cells each temporarily occupy named positions, or layers, in their life and death cycle. Stratum granulosum is the last layer where these cells are still alive. Stratum corneum is a relatively thick layer of flat dead cells which is also referred to as epithelium.

Germinativum also contains a number of specialized cells called melanocytes, so named because they produce granules of the chemical substance melanin. Melanocytes are densely distributed throughout germinativum, in the same numbers per unit area in all peoples regardless of their skin color. It is simply the output of the melanocytes that varies tremendously. Greater numbers and larger size of melanin granules give a black color to the skin, while lesser amounts and smaller sizes of granules decline through the various shades of brown. The chemical composition of the melanin is the same in all cases, regardless of the quantity present.

Melanin granules reside only temporarily in the melanocytes, hence in the stratum germinativum. They pass out into the rest of the epidermis and slowly migrate surfaceward with the dying and dead cells around them. The melanin is also beginning to disintegrate or chemically decompose as it moves outward, eventually to be shed along with other parts of the epidermis. Ordinarily the melanin is found only in the epidermis though in very heavily pigmented people a small amount might also occur in the uppermost part of the dermis.

People of all races have the same melanin in their skins, only the amount varies, which results in their different colors. In this sense almost all of us may be referred to as "colored." A very few individuals inherit a genetic variation which inhibits the production of all melanin, whether in skin, hair, or eyes. Only these albinos can truly be called "white."

Melanin production and location is above the dermis where the last capillaries are found. To get a sense of how thin the epidermis is just think of the last time you were scratched just barely deep enough to show a trace of blood. That scratch went entirely through the melanin region and into the dermis. If beauty is only skin deep, color is even

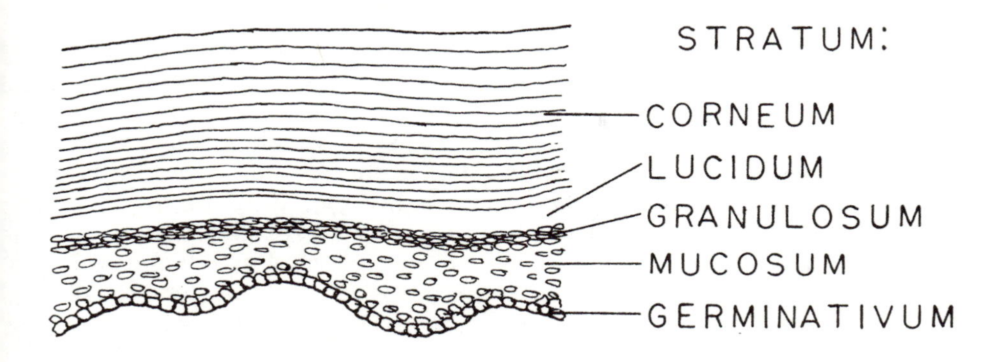

FIGURE 7. Layers of the skin in cross section. This shows the epidermis only, from the growing stratum germinativum through the outer layers of dying and dead cells. Color-producing melanin occurs only to this depth which is usually less than a millimeter.

less than that as it only involves the outer one-fourth or less of that skin.

Visible skin color consists of the light waves that are reflected from its surface. All other wave lengths are absorbed at some level and transformed into heat energy. Light-colored skin is reflecting a large part of the light that falls on it, some from the surface and some is passed through the epidermis only to be reflected back from still deeper layers. Other skins absorb most radiation, mainly in the melanin, and because so little is reflected back to be seen it appears dark in color. The more melanin there is, the more light is absorbed, and the darker the color.

On the surface (pun intended) dark skin would seem to be maladaptive in hot sunny climates where it only increases the body's heat load. This is true, but it is far outweighed by other consequences of skin color which give the opposite result. Ultraviolet radiation, wave lengths too short to be visible, are not reflected by any natural surfaces. They are either transmitted or absorbed, and they tend to do a good deal of damage wherever they reach. Depigmented skin transmits ultraviolet radiation rather well, melanin absorbs it.

When too much ultraviolet radiation reaches the dermis it quickly causes capillary congestion which makes a sunburn severe and it also slowly tends to stimulate the growth of skin cancers. Too much sunlight can cause severe damage without a layer of malanin protection.

Ultraviolet light also acts on a common chemical, dehydrocholesterol, and changes it into vitamin D. Just where this synthesis takes place has been debated, and it probably occurs in all layers of dermis and epidermis wherever dehydrocholesterol is found. What is more to the point is from what region the newly produced vitamin D can reenter the blood stream. Probably because of this, only the synthesis occurring in the dermis is functionally meaningful. This means that the amount of vitamin D production is largely controlled by the amount of melanin in the overlying epidermis which regulates passage vs. absorption of ultraviolet radiation. Too much vitamin D can cause some problems and thus adds to the reasons why melanin should exist. Too little vitamin D leads to failure of the body to utilize calcium from the food. Lack of calcium has many bad effects, best known being rickets, or soft bones. Without enough calcium laid down in them, bones can become soft enough to bend and deform under the weight and other strains of the body. People commonly survive this, but when the leg bones press together a soft pelvis of a growing female child, she and her first offspring are ultimately doomed. Lack of sufficient vitamin D can be a severe selective factor.

The atmosphere absorbs much of the ultraviolet radiation except when the sun is more nearly overhead. The amount of ultraviolet in the sunlight decreases gradually as the sun approaches the horizon and ends entirely at 20° elevation when there is still plenty of visible light. Far north (and south) of the equator this means the amount of ultraviolet light is drastically reduced. At these same latitudes, obviously the dangers from too much of this radiation are less and the need for a modest amount of vitamin D production continues. The obvious mechanism to filter through the correct amount of ultraviolet and absorb the surplus is to vary the amount of melanin in the skin. That this is indeed the case can readily be seen in the map of skin colors (Fig. 8). There are a few notable exceptions to the rule which will be discussed shortly.

In high latitudes there is not only less sunlight but it also varies by season to a tremendous degree. At noon in mid-winter there is no ultraviolet above about 45° north latitude, while in summer it should be available all the way to the pole. Progressively lighter skin colors in winter would be the most adaptive at least as far north as about the middle of France. In summer a much higher level of melanin in the skin would be desirable, and this is exactly what happens. Tanning is an increased level of production from the melanocytes which is triggered by the same ultraviolet which is the very reason why it is needed. For every latitude there are two extreme levels of available ultraviolet light, winter and summer, and likewise two levels of ideal melanin content in the skin. The lower level is the basic melanin content determined by heredity, and between it and the upper level is the seasonal gap that should be made up by tanning, another inherited capacity.

Above 45° north there is no vitamin D production for a few days in mid-winter. As one goes farther north the time of nonproduction gradually lengthens to almost the full year at the pole. It is unsure just how long people can live well without this vitamin, particularly those "at risk", such as pregnant women and young children. It is a curious fact that early human habitation sites in Europe older than 35,000 years ago come to a halt at 53° north latitude straight across the continent. This is not a winter temperature line because that runs more diagonally from the northwest to the southeast. It is also not the margin of the glacier at that time, nor is it an old sea level line. If it was, as I suspect, a limit imposed by natural production of vitamin D, then apparently a few months leeway without replenishment can be tolerated without undue ill effect. (Curiously, this same line marks the northern limits of the cave bear, *Ursus spelaeus,* though I fail to see any obvious connection with the human phenomenon.)

In order for people to live north of this line some other source of vitamin D must be found. In natural foods vitamin D is not common,

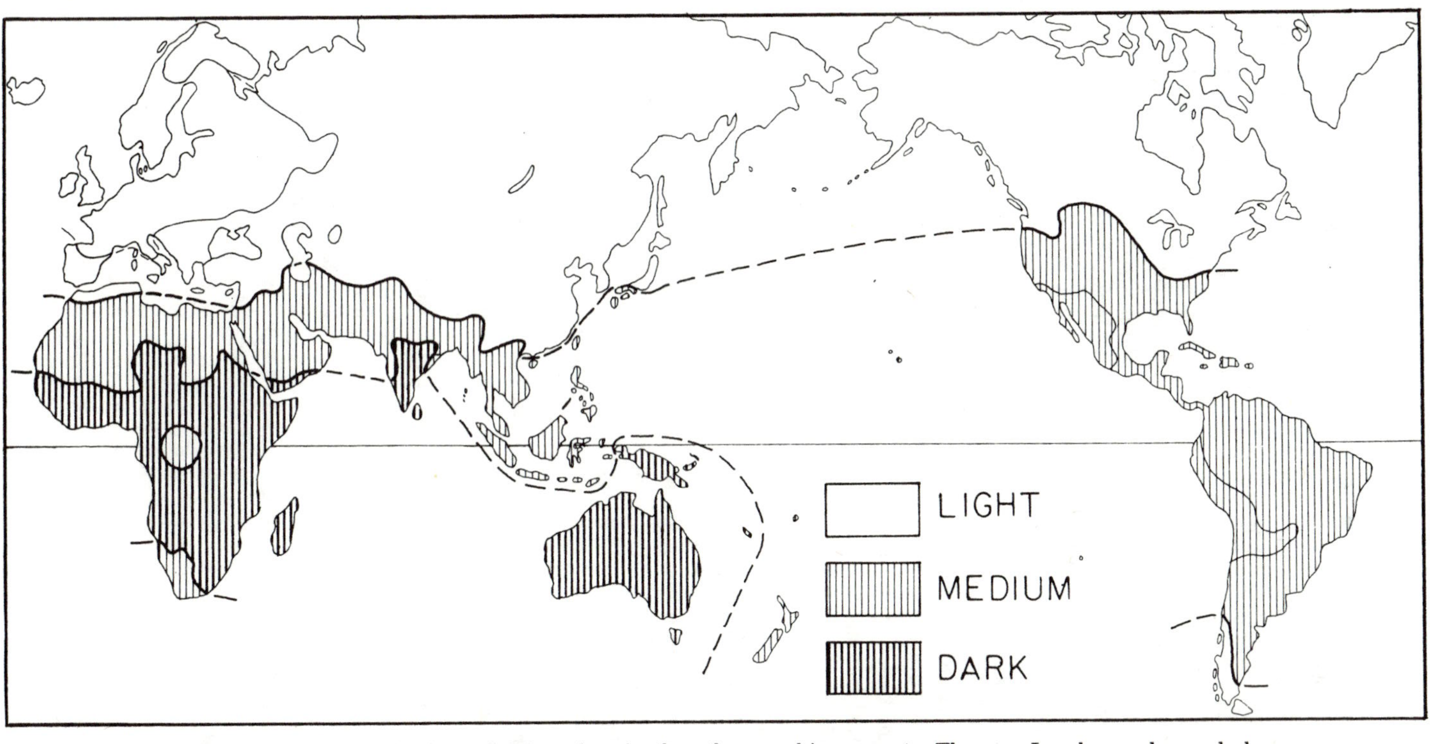

FIGURE 8. Distribution of skin colors in the ethnographic present. The von Luschen color scale has been simplified here to just three major categories, colors 1 through 14 are called light, colors 15 through 23 are called medium, and colors 24 through 36 are called dark. In addition, the lightest part of Europe is set off by a separate line, as are two areas of darker medium in the Americas. (Modified from Biasutti, 1957.)

though some deep sea fish have large amounts. What is abundant is the pre-vitamin D chemical, dehydrocholesterol, which occurs in many plants, all animal meat, and is especially common in fish oils. If these foods are dried in the sun in order to be stored for winter consumption, the supply of vitamin D is more than assured. It is not the fish that is so important to all northern peoples, but the fact that it is sun dried.

Given this dietary source of vitamin D one of the selective pressures on skin color is relieved, that for very light skins in the winter season. At high latitudes basal skin color is best suited to the spring and fall seasons, tanning takes care of the summer, and sun-dried fish takes care of the winter. The general trend of lighter untanned skin-colors away from the equator takes a slight turn toward the darker in many areas of the far north. This anomaly now makes sense, though it used to puzzle anthropologists and it caused some to argue that sunlight intensity cannot be the cause of skin color variations.

Two major anomalies in the color distributions of 1500 A.D. are accounted for by recent movements of large numbers of agricultural (or pastoral) people into high-sunlight areas from homelands farther to the north. They brought their lighter skins with them and they also brought enough clothing and housing practices to ameliorate the effects of selection in their new environments. These are the Arabs and Berbers of northern Africa, and the southern Mongoloids of southeastern Asia and Indonesia. In the case of the southern Mongoloids it has also been noted that much of southern China, at the same latitude as the Sahara, is not a desert and is much more cloud covered. This tends to make selection for darker skins much less intense than in many other areas equally close to the equator.

It should be evident that it is not the sunlight by itself that is selective for color, but rather more precisely just how much of it actually reaches the human skin. Cloud cover reduces the intensity of ultraviolet (but not infrared). Clothing and housing also block out radiation, and natural vegetation can do the same thing. In central Africa the tropical rain forests provide a considerable shield for the Pygmy hunters and gatherers. They rarely spend much time in open sunlight and are, not surprisingly, much lighter than their neighboring farmers. If they are to synthesize enough vitamin D in their skins their melanin level must be reduced just as if they lived much farther north. Forest cover alone is not the measure of adaptive skin color, but how committed the people are to a life within it. Frequent, or daily, excursions out into the sunlight would be enough to require very dark skins, even if the vast majority of the time is spent in shadows.

The Bushmen of southern Africa are another major anomaly with a very different explanation. The stratum corneum of the Bushman skin is unusually thick, thus increasing the layer of dead cells with their included melanin granules on their way to being discarded. Evidently the concentration of melanin is not important, just its total amount, however it may be distributed. The Bushman skin produces much less melanin in the stratum germinativum than does that of the Negro, but it is retained longer in their thicker outer layer, thus giving the same ultraviolet stopping power as would a thinner but denser layer. The surface of the Bushman skin has less melanin in relation to keratin, or dead cells, and so is lighter in color. This lighter color, by definition, is reflecting more of the visible wave lengths and absorbing less heat from the sun's total radiation. The reflective value of Bushman skin is about midway between that of black African and white European skins.

This would appear to be the most advantageous kind of skin for a desert dweller if radiation were the only consideration. The thicker stratum corneum also carries with it a disadvantage in terms of the sweat-cooling system. Man's thin epidermis serves to transmit the heat of the dermal blood into the sweat on the surface which is evaporating. If the stratum corneum is unusually thick it will tend to insulate against this heat transfer. Only very small people with a large surface to volume ratio can afford this specialization. But more on this subject later.

American Indians show little of the skin color variations by latitude as are seen in the Old World. Several explanations have been offered to account for this uniformity, one of course being that skin color has nothing to do with sunshine. It has been suggested that something like the thicker stratum corneum of the Bushman is also present throughout the so-called Mongoloid stock. If so, they would be paying a price in the form of a less effective sweat-cooling mechanism. I have not seen any direct evidence whether this is, or is not, the case. Another explanation would have to do with the recency of occupation of the Americas by people who had passed through the Arctic filter.

There is no doubt now that the source of the Native American population is from northeastern Asia into Alaska and then southward. Their ancestors must then have been fully adapted to Arctic conditions at the time of passage. This adaptation is of the northern fringe type, beyond the vitamin D line, so sun-dried meat and fish was part of the diet. Their skin colors would have been in the light range, as these far northerners are today, but not as light as most Europeans. This skin color was then inherited by all their descendants down to the equator and then on to Tierra del Fuego. It may simply be that not enough time has passed since this great immigration for mutations to accumulate, and selection to fix, significantly darker colors.

Something of a paradox occurs here. Because skin color is very important it is selected for within narrow limits, all extremes being disadvantageous. The genetic load of raw material of variation is thus minimal. When conditions change significantly there does not exist in the gene pool the kinds of variations that are most suitable. Adaptation must wait upon the appearance of suitable new mutations, and this may take a very long time. In contrast, another trait of less adaptive significance will have a greater range of variation preserved, and selection for the best adaptation can be much faster.

A variation on the Arctic filter concept is that such peoples were very adept in the manufacture of clothing and housing. These same skills could be maintained to some degree for protection against solar radiation instead of just against cold temperatures. These skills would not prevent selection for more suitable skin colors, but they may have somewhat slowed the process. Which of these factors is the most important may be quite important in terms of how long these Americans have been here. If it is a simple case of not enough time to develop significant adaptations then a comparison between the Old World and the New World is very important in timing the origin of modern races. The amount of skin color variation in the Old World is easily ten times as great as in the New World. Genetic mutations and selection presumably work at a fairly constant rate at all shades of color (disallowing mixtures with people already at the desired color). It follows that in terms of skin color variations the Old World differences have been at least ten times longer in developing than they have been in the New World. Even the most recent estimates, with which I agree, would place the immigration south from the Arctic at 12,000 years ago. Ten times this figure, or 120,000 years ago, in the Old World would long antedate man of the modern type. This must say something about the time of origin of at least one racial variation.

Color gradients in India are of two kinds, geographical and social. To the northwest are found the lightest untanned skin colors, which grown progressively darker as one moves away from there. In southern India there can be found people who are as dark as any in Africa. At the same time there is a color gradation from lighter among those of high caste to darker as one moves down the social scale. Each caste tends to darken to the south. Part of the social color scale represents the relative amount of time spent unshaded in the sun. It seems impossible to entirely eliminate tanning from skin color evaluations.

Part of the social color contrast would also stem from invasions of large numbers of people into India from the northwest where lighter colors were environmentally normal. This invasion is usually ascribed to the "Aryan" horse-chariot peoples of just over 3,000 years ago who seem to have conquered the region. I am inclined to think these people were numerically insignificant and that the really important influx of people was some 2,000 years earlier with the first cereal-grain farmers. In any case, both invasions would have added to the social stratification of color which is still with us today.

The Polynesians are another example of misplaced color. They straddle the equator but are not especially dark. The largest and best-known populations are from Hawaii and New Zealand which are well away from the equator. Their recency of occupation, coupled with an origin perhaps on the south China coast, might account for their medium to light skin color.

There are three other natural sources of skin color variation in addition to melanin. One of these, already mentioned in the Bushman skin, is keratin. This is roughly the same substance as hair, fingernails, and the horns of other animals. The keratin in the stratum corneum is usually described as having a light, yellowish-brown color. I doubt this because unpigmented hair and fingernails are white or gray. Probably the reported color of skin keratin derives from the small amounts of melanin which are present in the skins of all but albinos.

Carotene is a crystaline hydrocarbon of yellow, or reddish color which may be ingested from certain foods and is deposited mainly in the subcutaneous fat. Its presence will be visible only in people with so little melanin in the epidermis that light can pass through it and be reflected from the carotene underneath. It is especially abundant in carrots, and I well remember three cousins who drank large amounts of carrot juice as children. They were quite healthy, but always had a slight yellowish tinge of color in their skins. Carotene from animal fats may be responsible for some of the yellowish tinge in northern Mongols, but it is difficult to distinguish this from small amounts of melanin. Again, this pigment, like keratin, is probably of little significance in determining human skin colors.

The last pigment is the red hemoglobin of blood. In very light-skinned individuals the light can reflect from the capillaries of the dermis and pass twice through the epidermis. This gives a pink color to the skin and its intensity can vary greatly with the amount of blood in the dermis. This increases with temperature as part of the heat dissipating mechanism and also with certain emotional states. It is a misnomer to call northern Europeans white, as comparison with a piece of writing paper will easily show. The "pink race" would be a slightly more correct designation.

There are many other sources of skin color variation which are not properly racial traits, but which can interfere with color designations. Diseases, such as anemia or yellow jaundice, can be misleading.

Unusual items in the diet, in addition to carotene, may affect skin color temporarily. External application, deliberate or accidental, of artificial chemicals and dyes is fairly common and usually referred to as cosmetics. Simple dirt in the skin adds color and was once used to explain why Bushmen were so nearly the color of the dirt in their desert environment. While Bushmen rarely have enough water to wash the body, when they do it is still the same color. Artificial stimulation of melanin production with certain commercially available suntan creams will darken the skin. Whether this should be classed as natural or not is a moot point. It can usually be recognized for being out of season, but if it is in the appropriate season it should make little difference whether it was the sun or a chemical that stimulated the melanin production.

Measurement of skin color must have a certain degree of precision to be useful. Sailors accustomed to seeing black Melanesians will remark on how light-skinned the Polynesians appear. Others, who have just been in Japan, will be struck by how much darker these same Polynesians are than the people they had most recently visited. One of the oldest and still best known absolute color scale is von Luschan's set of 36 glass color blocks. These range from white to black, with three yellow shades as well, and are simply compared with the subject's skin for the best match. World distribution of skin colors based on von Luschan's scale are given in a simplified version in Fig. 8 (see page 68).

Fifty years ago the color top was a measuring device favored by a few anthropologists for its simplicity. Discs of black, white, red, and yellow paper had center holes punched out and a slit from there to the edge. These were then interleaved to show any desired proportion of those colors on the upper surface. A pointed stick was pushed through the center and it was spun like a top, serving visibly to blend the colors. If the color combination did not match the subject's skin it was simply reset with new proportions showing and spun again. The paper colors were not well enough standardized or pure and some would fade over time, but these technical problems could have been solved eventually. The color top failed mainly because of the time it often took to set and reset the colors before a suitable match could be found. I tried once to solve this by blending the colors in a rotating mirror so they could be shifted without stopping the apparatus each time, but this got too cumbersome and was never successfully used.

Color photographs are useful at times but these may be processed in different ways and this can make comparisons invalid. Other color scales of paper or plastic have been used with varying success. The most promising one now is the Munsell color chip system developed for commercial paint color matching. It is already being used by geologists for naming dirt colors, and a skin color selection of chips may soon be in general use for those few anthropologists who do this anymore.

More "scientific" electronic equipment has been used to measure and record the reflected light by quantity at various specific wave lengths. While this can give insight into some of the phenomena that we don't see, it adds little of value to standardizing the more usual observations. Exact as such machines may be, their expense, bulk, and power-supply requirements have so far ruled them out of general use. If one cannot get a detailed world survey of such standardized measurements, then what is obtained is of limited value to race studies.

In addition to the problem of what measuring scale to use, there is also the problem of just what and where on the body you are measuring. It has become a convention that normal, or tanned, skin color is taken on the forehead, barring some obvious problem of cosmetics or covering. The back of the hand would do about as well, except for the possible influence of blue color from the veins. To get a dependable measure of untanned color is quite another problem, as it is necessary to examine a patch of skin that is not normally exposed to direct sunlight. Getting certain people to remove any clothes at all can be difficult. The most workable solution has been to measure the inside surface of the upper arm. Other regions of the body will be more dependably lacking in tanning, but none of these can be easily observed in most populations.

There has been much speculation on the genetic basis of skin-color inheritance. The fact of inheritance is obvious, but the number of genes involved is not. Simple observation of crosses between mulattoes shows that more than one pair of alleles is responsible. To take the simplest theoretical case, one might assume blacks carry two alleles for dark color and whites carry two alleles for light color. When these mate all their offspring will inherit a dark and a light allele. Assuming no dominance, they will be middle-brown in color. If two of these hybrids are mated to each other, one-half will inherit the same combination as the parents, one-fourth will receive two dark alleles, and one-fourth will get two light alleles. In other words, half of this generation will exactly match the color of one or the other of the grandparents. Only three shades of color would occur. Since this is manifestly not the case we must assume that more genes are involved.

If there are two such color genes, alleles at two chromosomal locations, then five color combinations can result in the third generation of the crosses described above. Each grandchild may inherit anywhere from zero to four of the color-producing alleles. In this case one-eighth of this third generation will exactly match one or the other grandparent. Again, the actual situation does not fit this description. With three genes there will be only seven degrees of melanin concentration, and one out of 32 should exactly match a grandparent. When we consider four genes with nine color categories it becomes at least possible that we have the real situation, and one in 128 will match their grandparents. Most opinion would take this one more step to five genes as the most probable number involved. Even this picture assumes each allele produces exactly the same amount of color in the original dark grandparental generation. If this is not exactly true then color gradations would not be so clear-cut and maybe four genes are enough. At present this is about as much as can be said on this aspect. Although skin color is inherited through the genes, we don't know exactly how. Even if we did know, it would still be classed as a classical variation as opposed to a genetic one in the sense that these terms are used in this book.

The origin of human skin color variations probably goes back about a million years to the appearance of *Homo erectus*. One of the most outstanding features distinguishing this species from its australopithecine ancestor is the addition of big-game animals to the diet on a regular basis. There were no good projectile weapons available and cooperative hunting would require skills and brains not evolved until much later. Evidently the major method used by *erectus* was to walk and run their game to exhaustion, a method still used by recent hunters on occasion. Such persistence hunting not only requires a large brain for its mental time span, but also a body with an exceptionally effective cooling mechanism. The human body is cooled mainly by evaporation of moisture from the skin surface. We have a greater number and variety of sweat glands for this purpose than any other animal. In order for this water to cool the body it must evaporate directly from the skin surface. Drops of sweat evaporating on hair or even farther away will draw their 540 calories per gram from where it doesn't do the body any good. That which evaporates on the skin will draw heat from the blood directly underneath in the dermis. A covering of hair will enclose a dead air space which will quickly reach 100% humidity and permit no further evaporation there. Surplus sweat will then pass uselessly to the surface of the hair covering or beyond. Our nearly hairless condition is to ensure that as much as possible of the evaporation will occur on the skin surface. In order for heat to pass easily from the capillary blood to the surface our insulating epidermis must be very thin. This then sets the stage for ultraviolet rays to penetrate the human body in dangerous quantities and makes the melanin content of the epidermis so critical. The hair covering and/or thicker epidermis of other animals makes their skin color irrelevant in this regard. Skin colors usually tend to approximate the hair coloring, but if an ape happens to have light skin under his hairy coat it is of no particular consequence.

We will probably never recover direct evidence of human skin colors from the distant past, but we can at least make some informed speculations now that we know the reason for the variations. If we assume our *erectus* ancestors did a great deal of persistence hunting it would follow that our nearly hairless condition also dates back to around one million years ago. We have the locations of many *erectus* bones and many more sites where they lived and left their food debris and tools. The amount of sunlight that falls on these various locations, then as now, gives us a rough measure of the amount of epidermal melanin that was necessary for their survival. Our present knowledge of such sites and their dating indicates our earliest ancestors were quite dark and only later did they expand so far to the north as to develop lighter skins.

Another area of speculation regarding skin color merits some mention before closing the subject. This is the possibility that the various colors serve as camouflage. While this may be true in certain instances it was never likely the major selective factor. Dark skins are useful in order to stay hidden from vision-oriented predators at dusk and dawn in all environments, not just the equatorial ones. By day a modern hunter usually wants to be concealed, but the early persistence hunter would rather be as conspicuous as possible, and so the same colors would not serve both purposes. Only the Bushman is noted for having the same color as the terrain in which he is usually found. Negroes and Australians are not surrounded by especially dark colors. European skins approach the color of their terrain in the winter season, but at such times few people travel about naked. Gloger's rule in zoology notes that in moist and shaded environments the animals tend to be darker colored. In man, the darkest people are in the brightest sunlight where it is often quite dry. In any case, the reasons for human skin color follow from a special anatomical adaptation not found to nearly this degree in any other animal.

EYE COLOR.

Human eyes, or more properly their irises, may be any of a number of different colors. These may for convenience by simply divided into light eyes and dark eyes. Eye color has long been noted as a human racial variation and for that reason it is included here among the classical traits. The inheritance of the major variation is well known, a recessive allele for light eyes and a dominant one for dark, so it could logically have been included among the genetic traits. Since my distinction here rests ultimately on the factors determining the traits' distributions, eye color seems to fall into the classical category as determined by climate, but that is not exactly clear either.

Variations in the color of the human iris depend on the amount and distribution of melanin, the same pigment as in the skin. On the inner layer of the iris of human eyes there are malanocytes producing this pigment (See Fig. 9). If there is no melanin in the more forward part of the iris it will usually appear blue. This is because the light passing through the translucent front part scatters the blue wave lengths much as sunlight is scattered to form blue skies. The pigment in the feathers of the familiar blue jay is also brown and the bird appears blue for the same reason. When pigment is present in the forward part of the iris it will appear brown to black according to the amount that is present. If the amount of melanin is minimal, what is there may be distributed in both layers, or it may be only on the back. This distinction is inherited by a single gene. Other interesting variations follow from how melanin tends to cluster around the muscles that open and close the pupillary aperture in the center.

In albinos where no pigment is produced the distinction between light and dark eyes is lost, regardless of which distribution allele the person happens to inherit. In very dark-skinned people this distinction may also be lost because there is so much pigment in the iris (as well as in the skin) that some will be in the front layer in any case. Where we get the distinction most clearly marked is among certain of the light-skinned populations in Europe.

The function of melanin in the iris is to block the transmission of light into the eye from all but the central opening, or pupil. There is a rough correlation between the amount of melanin in the skin with that in the iris. It may be that given only a small amount it is a more effective light blocker if it is distributed in two layers instead of just one. In like-skinned siblings the blue-eyed ones seem to suffer more from glare than do the brown-eyed ones. On the other hand, it has been noted that blue-eyed people can see better in dim light, especially at great distances.

The geographic distribution of eye color supports the idea that selection favors dark eyes in all areas of bright sunlight or with much reflected glare, which is most of the world. The largest area in the Old World where such selection would be at a minimum would be in most of Europe, which is just where light eyes reach their maximum frequency of almost 50% (See Fig. 10). What is not so clear is whether the European climate actually selects for light eyes or if relaxed selection simply permits great numbers of light-eyed people to survive unhin-

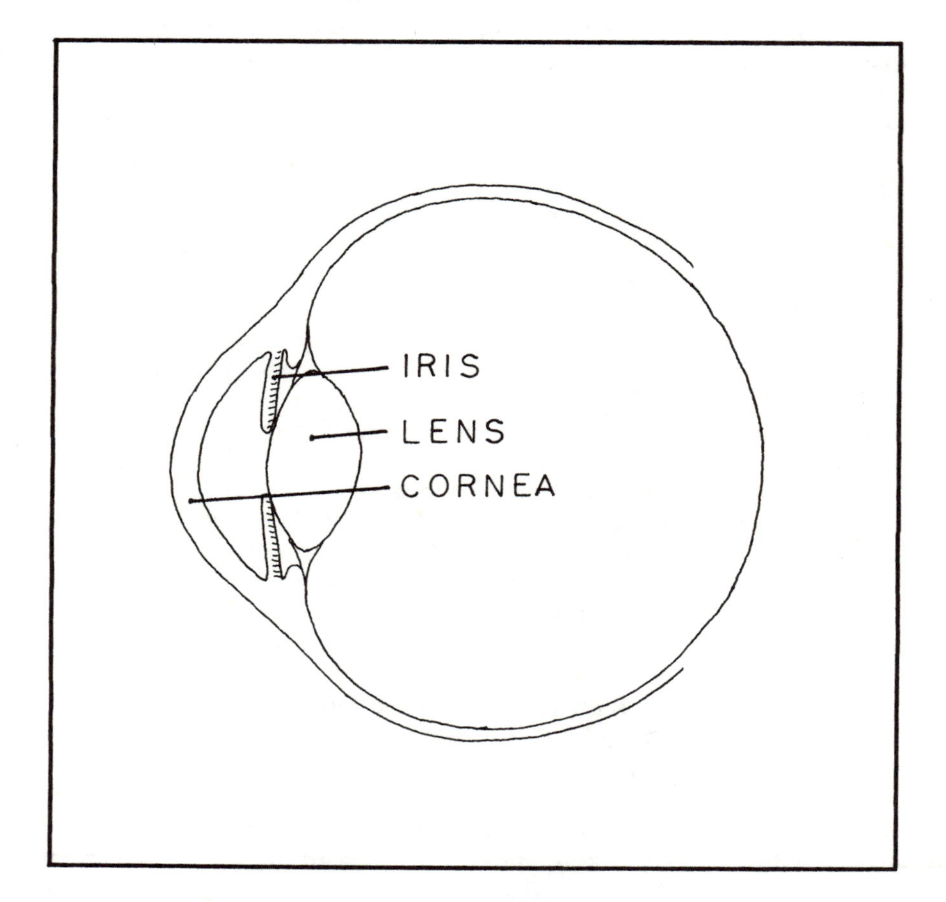

FIGURE 9. Section through the eye showing iris color layer. Melanin blocks passage of light through all but the central opening or pupil. The melanin may occur only on the back of the iris, as illustrated, producing a light color, or it may be on both front and back producing a dark color.

dered. This is not a trivial distinction and many such cases will be dealt with in the section on genetic traits. Chance alone should not cause light eyes to occur in half the population. Given enough time and no selective pressure, chance would make light eyes either the rule or it would eliminate them altogether. There will not be a selective pressure that works on only half the population. A very likely answer to the problem is that light eye color was once the rule in all or most of Europe (by selection and/or drift) and that a substantial influx of dark-eyed peoples has occurred since. At present there may still be a settling out of this mixture with the distribution now reflecting the different degrees of selection against light eyes in different areas. The problem is not so much how the light eyes are distributed today, but how any substantial numbers of them ever got there in the first place.

In Mongolia and parts of Siberia there are also some individuals with light eyes. While history records numerous invasions of Europe by horsemen from Asia, the earliest such movement was by the Kurgans in the opposite direction. This and a still earlier expansion of non-horse pastoralists may well have brought in the genes for blue eyes. Other Caucasoid traits would have been quickly selected against in a mixed population, but eye color may not have been very critical and some remains. The Caucasoid-looking Ainu would not be part of this Kurgan expansion as their culture is of a simpler sort. The earlier pastoralists are a possibility, but in my view a very remote one. Also, it is an extremely long process to eliminate a recessive gene which this one is. Elsewhere in the world light eyes are absent except for what might be called rare anomalies, perhaps original mutations.

Within Europe itself the distribution of light eyes centers on the North Sea between England and Denmark. In all the areas surrounding that sea light eyes are found in about half the population. Their frequency dwindles in all directions from there so that when one reaches the geographical boundaries of Europe, light eyes have all but disappeared. Curiously, the center for blond hair is a bit to the east of this with the Baltic Sea being its major focus.

Melanin is also found in the sclera, or "whites" of the eyes in some people with a very high level of pigmentation elsewhere in the body. There is no indication of a function for such flecks of color. Melanin on the retinal surface inside the eye is also very closely correlated with the amount of skin pigmentation. Here the function in relation to variations in sunlight intensity seems obvious, as this pigment absorbs the light that might otherwise reflect about inside the eye and confuse visual images. A mismatch of retinal pigment with sunlight intensity is not, however, a serious matter as many Europeans in the tropics can testify to. A mismatch of skin pigmentation is far more of a problem.

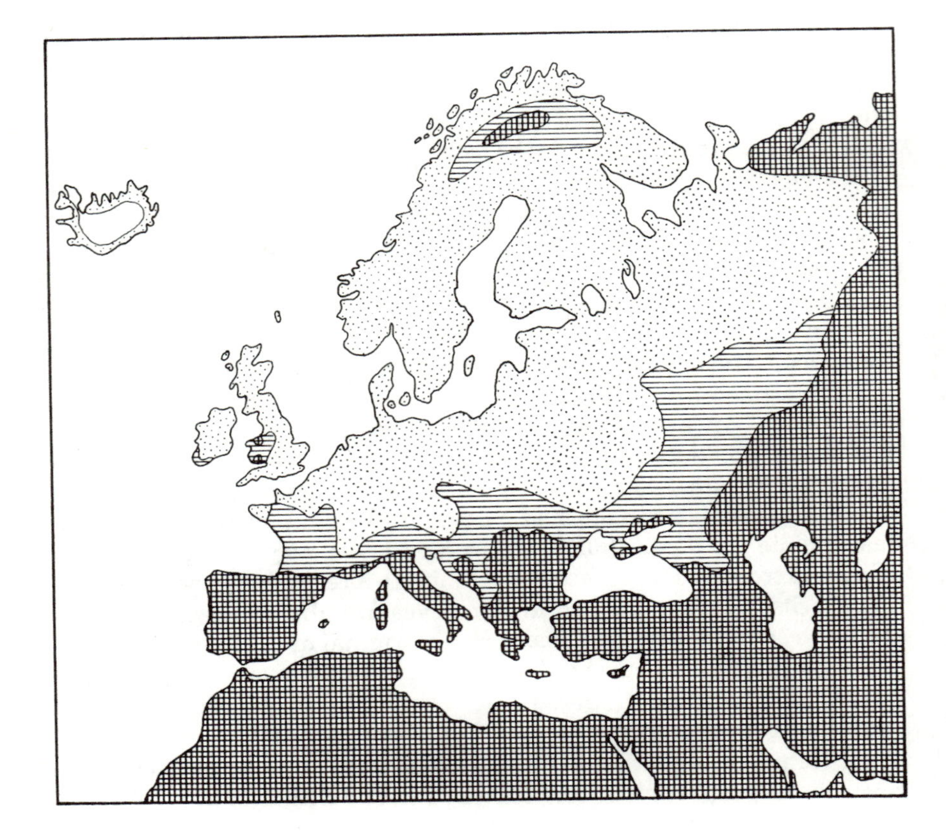

FIGURE 10. Distribution of light-colored hair and eyes in Europe. Blond hair and blue eyes are concentrated in the Scandinavian region (stippled) and decline in frequency (lined, then hatched) from there in all directions. Light eyes and yellow hair each occur in over half of the population in the core area, but the combination of both traits is rarely found in 50% of the individuals. (Redrawn from Coon, 1939.)

Apparently natural selection has worked primarily for the ideal melanin content in the skin, and that of the various parts of the eye simply went along for the ride and functionally agreeing to a slight extent.

Measurement of eye color is also done on a matching basis, though in this case in a much more picturesque manner than for skin color. Europeans have long made artificial glass eyeballs to replace missing ones for the sake of appearances. Since it is often desirable to match colors with a remaining eye, a full range of iris colors is available. Martin's series of sixteen such glass eyes has served reasonably well as a scale for comparing with living eyes. Aside from occasional fake eyes and colored contact lenses, which can easily be identified, there are no serious problems with measurement of eye color.

HAIR COLOR.

Again, melanin is the major source of hair-color variations just as in the skin and irises. Almost the same range of colors is encountered as in the skin though there is usually some discrepancy where the hair is darker than the skin. For the most part the following discussion will deal with that part of the hair covering most noticed and commented on, that on the head.

Hairs grow from follicles which might be described as deep indentations of epidermis which are pushed well into the dermis layer. Much of the follicle around its tip is a specialized and active version of the stratum germinativum, in this case germinating a hair rather than just a bit of epidermis. The hair itself is analogous to a section of epidermis that has held itself together and grown out as a vertical column of cells to a ridiculous height. The germinating part of the follicle is around its innermost tip and the beginning hair shaft grows from there, slowly sliding out the tube of the follicle to the surface of the skin and beyond. Immediately away from the follicle tip and well below the skin surface the hair becomes a column of dead cells, and just like the stratum corneum, without blood vessels or nerves. (See Fig. 11.)

The germinating tip of the hair follicle contains melanocytes which are generally much more productive than in the regular epidermis. They add large quantities of melanin to the hair which would otherwise be described as a shaft or tube of keratin. In cross section the hair may be round or oval and may or may not include a hollow center called the medula, or fusi. The major solid part of the hair, or cortex, contains the melanin. There is normally an outer cuticle of one layer of unpigmented cells.

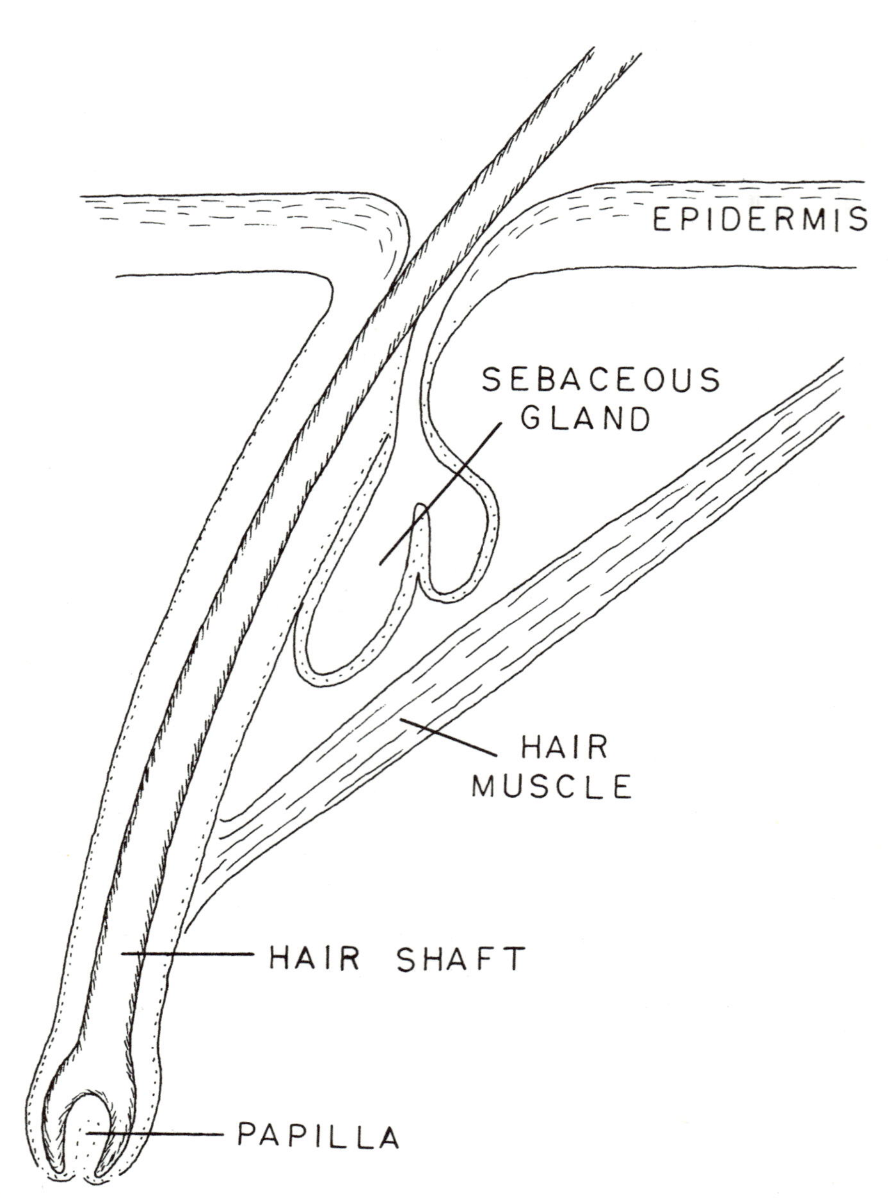

FIGURE 11. The growing hair. The hair follicle begins deep in the dermis as an inpouching of epidermis-like tissue. The hair itself is a tall column of dead cells analogous to an extended piece of the stratum corneum with its included melanin granules. A cross section through the hair shaft may be circular or oval and commonly has a hollow center.

One of the main differences between hair and regular epidermis is that the hair has its main mass of melanin exposed while in the skin most of it is covered by many cells containing only a small fraction of what lies below. Another difference is that the growing source of the hair lies far deeper in the skin and is less influenced by environmental factors. An interesting consequence of these contrasts is the difference in color change in response to sunlight. In people with a modest amount of melanin where the hair is some shade of brown it will bleach to a lighter color after a few weeks exposure to bright sunlight, whereas their skins will darken under the same circumstance. Sunlight will speed up the normal decomposition of melanin that has already been formed. In the skin, this bleaching effect occurs also, but the same sunlight increases the production of new melanin, much faster and much more than it is broken down in the upper epidermis. In the hair the melanin is more exposed to bleaching while its growing source is not exposed to the triggering of new melanin. Not only are the hair follicles protected by the full thickness of the epidermis and part of the dermis, but the hairs themselves add cover from the sunlight. Thus solar radiation both breaks down melanin and speeds its production. In the skin, new production predominates, while in the hair it is overwhelmingly just the breakdown that occurs.

Human hair is too restricted in its coverage to have any significant function in terms of protecting most of the body from harmful radiation. Its location on the head suggests an added protection of this kind only for the most intense sunlight from directly overhead. If this were its major function equatorial people should also have dense hair on top of their shoulders and northern heads should all be bald. Still, to some degree cranial hair does perform this protective function.

If there is no melanin in the hair it is white. Albino skin would also be white if it were not for the blood color that makes it pink. A small amount of melanin in the hair is yellow, more gives various shades of brown, and ultimately black. Additional melanin will have no visible effect as the hair still appears black. Chemical removal of much of the melanin from hair samples which continue to be black shows that dark people can have many times as much melanin as is needed to give a black color.

Because the melanin in the hair is almost directly exposed to view it normally appears darker than the skin where the covering epidermis has a lesser amount of melanin. As most people are fully aware, hair and skin colors do not always correspond even with the regular discrepancy just noted. Part of the reason for this is that very slight differences in low levels of hair melanin are seen easily in terms of color differences. The same amount of variation in melanin in the epidermis causes differences which are not nearly as easy to see.

In addition, there obviously are genetic mechanisms that vary the relative amounts of production between follicles and epidermis. A light-skinned Scandinavian with blond hair has a similar color in each structure, but the hair follicle is clearly producing the lesser amount. Similarly, a black-haired Irishman with equally light skin has follicles producing more melanin than his epidermis. Light European skin with brown hair would be the more normal contrast if melanin production is about the same in each area. These variations in European hair colors occur in about the same absolute melanin range as the previously noted eye-color differences. They are not genetically linked to each other nor are the two kinds of variations structurally related, but the coincidence is striking.

If one were to design ideal hair colors for the world it would be based on reflection versus absorption of solar heat. High sunlight areas should have white, reflecting hair for the best cooling effect, while in low sunlight the darkest colors would absorb the most heat. In general, the structural tie between skin color and hair color production goes against this ideal situation. Selective forces working on skin-color variations are by far the strongest. Some discrepancies between skin and hair do approach the ideal in certain parts of the world. In most northern areas where skins are light the hair is much darker, as is ideal. Only the blond Europeans are unsuited to their climate in this regard. Northerners with brown hair are perhaps the best adapted. The brown will absorb a fair amount of heat in the winter season, and when it bleaches to a lighter color in the summer it will reflect more. Like the Bushman skin color, this is the ideal compromise for hair color. Why this hair color is not more common in the north is something of a problem; perhaps it used to be in the past.

Some Australians of the western desert also have a major discrepancy in having blond hair with almost black skins. This contrast is far greater than any in Europe, so different genes are involved. Australian blondism may be permanent, or just temporary and darken with adulthood. This suggests a difference between inheriting two alleles for blondism or just one. For a high sunlight area this is by far the best adaptation. The limited distribution of this trait suggests that the responsible mutation was a very recent one. Since these Aborigines were among the last people exposed to the agricultural revolution this particular adaptation is as good as lost.

In general then, hair color parallels skin color but at a darker level for developmental and structural reasons. The resulting colors are not particularly adaptive except for the light skin-darker hair contrast in the north. The ideal sun bleaching effect among some Europeans is probably fortuitous. The only clear adaptational variation is that of some Australians toward blondism in the tropics.

Reddish colored hair occurs in varying degrees and is mostly confined to the area of Europe around the North Sea. It is never very common except in small populations. A distinction has been made between two kinds of melanin, eumelanin producing the normal range of colors, and phenomelanin producing red color. This red is confined to the hair and shows only when eumelanin amounts are not so much as to overwhelm it. There is no known function for this variation.

Facial, axillary, and pubic hair tend to follow cranial hair in their color, but not totally. Often, among Europeans, these hair patches are a more neutral color, not as dark nor as light as the cranial-hair color extremes. For most of the world, hair is hair and it's all black. The fine covering of body hair also follows the same rule of being similar to that on the head.

Measurement of hair color can be done crudely with the skin-color blocks or other skin-measuring procedures. The Saller-Fischer scale made from actual samples of human hair has not been widely used. The resultant lack of precise data on hair colors is of significance only in those limited areas of the world where any variation occurs. For the most part it is also only among Europeans that much deliberate hair-color changes are made. Bleaching, dyeing, and wigs are mostly restricted to the more affluent parts of a population and are generally ignored by anthropologists who are studying real people. Noncranial hair is rarely reported on.

HAIR FORM.

Again it is on cranial hair where the emphasis will be placed here. The amount of curvature to the hair shaft is the major variation and is variously described as straight, wavy, curly, spiral, or peppercorn. Hair curvature can be measured in terms of the radius of arc that a hair tends to follow, but this is rarely done. More commonly it is described in terms of the average cross-sectional shape. Some hairs are perfectly circular while others are flattened to various degrees. This flattening can be expressed in terms of the ratio of maximum and minimum diameters of an individual hair shaft, the two measurements being taken at right angles to each other. A circular hair will have an index of 100, but if one diameter is only half of the other the index of flattening is 50, and so on.

Several sets of categories have been proposed and I will here use only the simplest. Indices from 100 down to 80 are circular, or nearly so, and the hair will be straight. Indices from 80 to 60 are oval and range from wavy to curly. Those below 60 curl so tightly they are referred to as spiral. These are commonly equated, not quite accurately, with the supposed three major races of mankind.

Not every individual hair will curl in exact proportion to its index. To get an accurate sample about 20 hairs should be taken, measured, indices calculated and averaged. After doing all this you get a good idea of the degree of hair curl, something that was no doubt seen at a glance when the subject was first approached. Obviously the more oval the hair shape the more easily it can curl, but this is not to say ovalness causes curl. It is not at all clear why hairs curve the way they do. Additional twists or kinks occur in some of the more tightly spiraled hair forms giving a change of direction to the curl.

The function of cranial hair is to protect the braincase in some manner. Shielding the head against excessive sunlight from above has already been mentioned. A cushion against hard surfaces, expecially blows to the head, would be another function. Little can be said about this since while there is some variation in the cushioning effects of various hair forms, man's tendency to do violence to his fellow man with blunt instruments is about equally distributed over the world.

Thermal insulation is evidently the major factor causing variations in cranial hair, but even here the relationships are not entirely clear. Among the so-called Mongoloid peoples, including American Indians, the hair is round in cross section and is straight. It is also somewhat larger in average diameter than in the rest of the world and there are correspondingly about one-fourth fewer hairs per square cm on the scalp. These hairs also have larger and more continuous hollow centers. In all, this kind of hair would provide the best insulation against cold temperatures. Considering the length of the hair which would blow easily in the wind the addition of some kind of head covering, even a net, would make the Mongoloid hair many times better as insulation.

The hair of the rest of the world forms a continuum from straight to the tightest of curl. This continuum is distributed with some consistency in relation to temperature, getting more curly as the temperature rises. This can be seen best along the line from Europe through Africa where the gradation is almost perfect. It is duplicated in Australia, upside down, where again the curl tightens as one approaches the equator. The major exceptions to this picture are the two groups of Mongoloids who have recently reached past the equator in southeastern Asia and in South America. (See Fig. 12.)

Straight or wavy European hair will cover much of the neck when the body is at rest and will add considerable insulation against heat

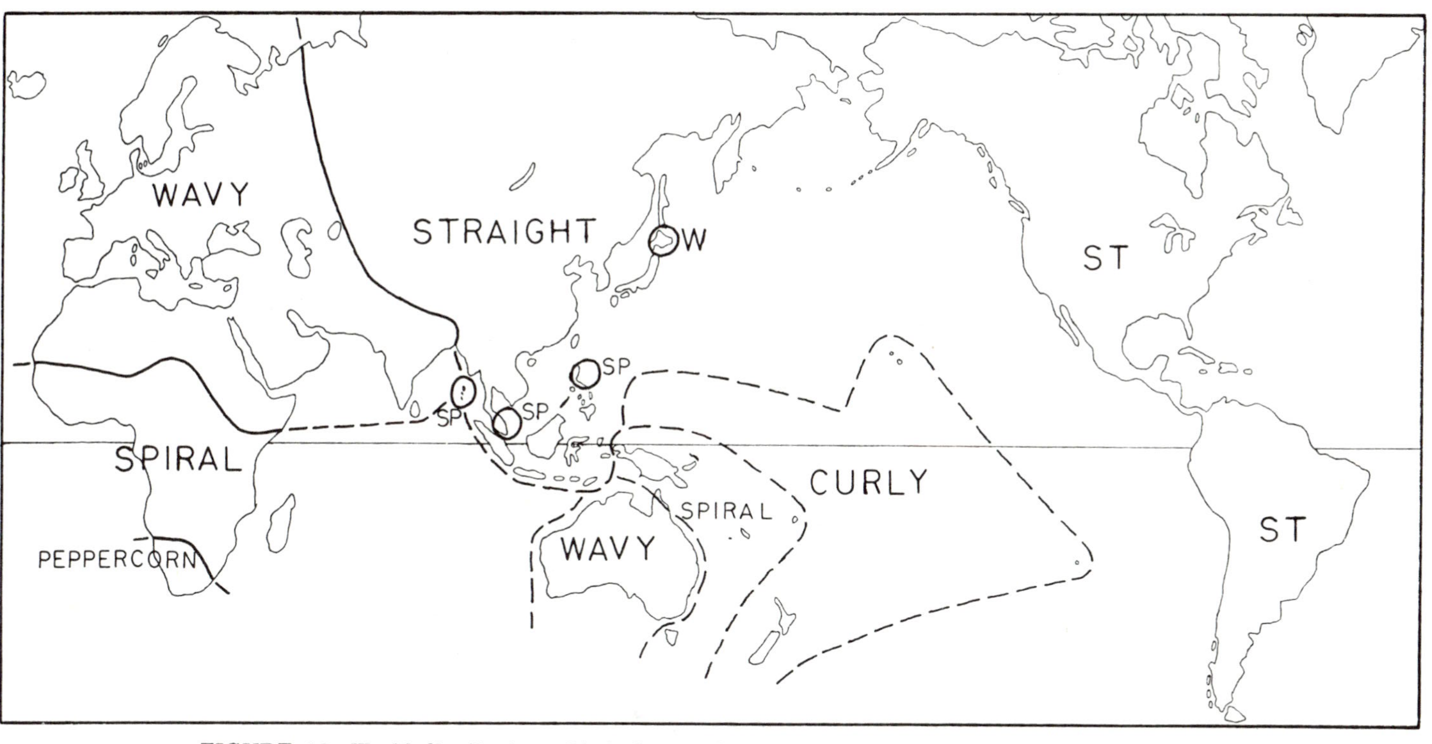

FIGURE 12. World distribution of hair forms. Straight hair shafts are nearly circular in cross section and are larger and fewer in number than the other types. Wavy hair is more oval in cross section, while spiral and peppercorn carry this to extremes. The areas shown here are only approximate and the divisions are mostly not nearly so sharp as the lines suggest.

loss from that area. Males may have the additional benefit of a beard against the front of the neck. This becomes ineffective when one is in rapid motion and the hair flies about, but more body heat is being generated at such times anyway. Toward the south of Europe increasing curliness tends to keep the hair somewhat away from the neck thus reducing its insulative quality. Spiral hair holds itself entirely away from the neck and also does not fall into the face either. Peppercorn hair is so short and tightly curled that it tends to clump into little balls exposing much of the scalp between them. In terms of maximizing the cooling effect this is as much as can be done short of removing the hair altogether. Peppercorn hair, which is common among the Pygmies and some Negritos would appear to be that most adapted to moist heat. Its anomolous occurrence among the Bushmen requires a separate explanation. Ideally, hair curl in northern climates should change with the seasons. Unlike other parts of the epidermis there seems to be no tendency for this.

The spiral mat of hair developed by most Negroes and Melanesians does not seem suitable for any climate. The dead air space is good insulation for the head against cold, but this is not the problem faced by these people. It probably provides the best cushion against impact, but this need is not peculiar to their area. The ideal gradient of thermal design of hair would call for a fairly curly type to occur in Northern Africa down to the edge of the tropical rain forest where a rather abrupt switch to peppercorn should take place. An intermediate zone of spiral hair might have been unavoidable in early times. The tight spiral from the peppercorn area and the greater hair length from the Savannas would spread and mix by gene flow. A narrow band of less-than-perfect adaptation in hair form would not be a serious matter. Later, a major population explosion with agriculture from exactly that area would spread this hair form over much of Africa. The situation in Melanesia may have been similar except that the major mixing of peppercorn with longer hair could have been concurrent with the introduction of agriculture, or even with later advances in cultivation.

By this reconstruction the proper hair form for the open country and deserts of southern Africa should have been curly, just as in other equivalent environments elsewhere. The only mechanism for a change to the peppercorn of the Bushmen would have been a population replacement. The replacement must have been pre-agricultural as the Bushmen are not farmers. A replacement of such antiquity would have to have been total, as any interbreeding would have left curly-hair genes in the resultant mixed population and they would have been selected for. The source of this replacing population would be the Congo forests where peppercorn hair is most adaptive and which is still found among many Pygmies. This leaves us with little choice as to the reason and timing of the event. It was the appearance of *Homo sapiens,* replacing *Homo erectus* in southern Africa. Prior to the origin of agriculture this grade change was the only event that was likely to have given one population so great an advantage over another as to facilitate a replacement of this magnitude.

In general, as I will point out later, the *sapiens* transition was an in-place phenomenon. The final step in the development of human language was culturally passed or diffused around the world and all peoples were then under selection pressure for the changes in anatomy to best make use of this practice. If there should be a significant pause in this diffusion and its development reached a high level of perfection on one side of a geographical barrier, then a later movement across that barrier might bring together two populations so unlike they would not interbreed. Parts of the Congo rain forest which were previously uninhabited consitute just such a barrier.

Another barrier which functioned in the same manner was the water gap which separated New Guinea from Australia. Hard evidence is not available, but a number of items would indicate Australia was first inhabited by *erectus.* The most "archaic" skulls are those of the western desert where the most ape-like wavy hair is also found. In contrast, the Tasmanians were more modern-looking and had spiral hair which could not have been the earliest human condition. It would follow that the Tasmanians were an interjection after the continent was already populated. The simple culture of the Tasmanians rules out any agricultural movement or even sea transport—crafts that would not have been abandoned. Again we find the appearance of *sapiens* as the only remaining force that could cause such a major population replacement. In this case it would appear that the influx of *sapiens* with spiral (or peppercorn?) hair was confined largely to the forested eastern coast and the Tasmanians are a remnant of it, later cut off from the mainland. In the rest of Australia the resident population was sapienized rather than replaced and its original hair form eventually prevailed. The Bushmen and Tasmanians are the only peoples that indicate such a *sapiens* replacement, and both on the basis of hair form. Genetic data given later will support this.

Facial and body hair in man is modest compared with that of the great apes. Although we have about as many body hairs per square cm, they are mostly shorter and finer. In general, all body hair other than on the head is somewhat less developed in Negroes and Mongoloids than it is in Europeans and Australians. Unfortunately, such general statements are most of what we know on the subject. Detailed world surveys of body hair abundance by geographical location are not complete. This characteristic, as many others, is simply described by most authorities in terms of a population that has already been defined on other grounds. What we want to know is whether a scarcity of body hair has the same geographical distribution as spiral cranial hair or dark skins. This may or may not be the case. But when minimal hair is reported as a "Negroid" condition one assumes the answer to the question that is being asked. Many trait distributions, unfortunately, are described in this manner and thus must be viewed very suspiciously.

Since hair and skin colors contrast less in Negroes than in most people, even special statements on their hair quantity are often suspect. Still, it is claimed that most Negroes have less body hair than most Caucasoids or Australians. It has been suggested that a superior adaptation of the sweat-cooling system is here indicated. I doubt it. If the air can circulate freely against the skin, removing any more hair will not improve the cooling effect. Rather than speculate any further at this point I would like to see more data on the actual quantity and distribution of body hair in Africa. It may turn out that we are trying to explain something that does not exist.

With the Mongoloids we are on surer ground in that they do tend to have less body hair than in most of the rest of the world. Here the color contrast between black hair and light skin cannot easily be missed. The explanation may ultimately lie in an Arctic specialization where facial hair is a great disadvantage. Since there is a correlation between facial, axial, pubic, and body hair generally, a selection against any one would tend to reduce them all. The selection against male facial hair follows from exhaling moisture-laden air from the lungs, which then freezes in the cold air that cannot contain it. Ice accumulation in the facial hair is annoying enough, but to have a fur hat freeze to your face (as once happened to me) can be downright dangerous in some circumstances. If the face is frozen to one side of a parka during an ambush wait, and a bear wanders over from the other direction, a hunter and his genes could easily be lost. There may well be other factors involved, but here at least is one selective force that would have reduced noncranial hair in long established Arctic peoples. Their descendants in any other climate would carry this trait on for lack of different selective forces.

Axial (armpit) and pubic hair serve as cushions against the friction of moving limbs that would otherwise leave skin surfaces rubbing together. These hairs, like facial hairs, are not very round in cross section, but often square, rectangular, or various other polygons of shape. Much of the pubic hair is not between the limbs, but other circumstances of skin friction might account for this. There is little difference in such hair around the world, except as noted above. Likewise, the male vs. female contrast, especially in facial hair, is a human constant without geographic variations of significance. Why human males should have any facial hair at all is an interesting question, and it may have to do with aiding in identification at a distance. If the subject has a beard it is an adult male, and one's expectations are guided accordingly; if it has large breasts it is an adult female; if it has neither it is a child and the sex does not matter (except to the child, of course). Perhaps to our distant ancestors these were the only three categories of strange people whose distinction was important.

BODY FAT.

Most of the fat in the human body is located in a layer immediately underneath the skin, and is accordingly referred to as subcutaneous. In more or less normal people this fat amounts to anywhere from 10% to about 30% of the total body weight, with women being near the upper end of this range and men nearer the lower. There is so much individual variation in the amount of body fat that it is difficult to use it as a racial trait. Still, marked differences do exist in the averages around the world. Subcutaneous fat differences are mainly of two kinds: total quantity and distribution over the body.

The functions of subcutaneous fat are for thermal insulation and for food storage. Fat is a fairly good insulator, and a good supply under the skin will serve to help retain some body heat. Its effectiveness depends more on the surrounding skin than on the fat itself because that is the major site from which heat is lost to the environment. If and when the skin's blood supply is reduced to a minimum the insulation effect is at its best. But with maximum use of the skin's blood for dissipating heat, the insulative value of the subcutaneous fat is mostly bypassed. The fact that the skin with its temperature receptors remains on the outside means the individual receives no perception of relief from the cold no matter how effective his insulation may be.

Variations in total fat quantity still show some correlation with average temperatures, but only among some peoples (See Fig. 13). Those in rather cool climates are the fattest, such as Europeans and Alakalufs. Those in warm climates have maybe one-fourth the fat thickness, as among Bushmen. There is also a body size contrast here, which serves as a heat regulator in itself, so it may be difficult to separate the two factors.

The exceptions to the expected rule are numerous, but perhaps mostly explainable. Polynesians have the greatest thickness of fat and

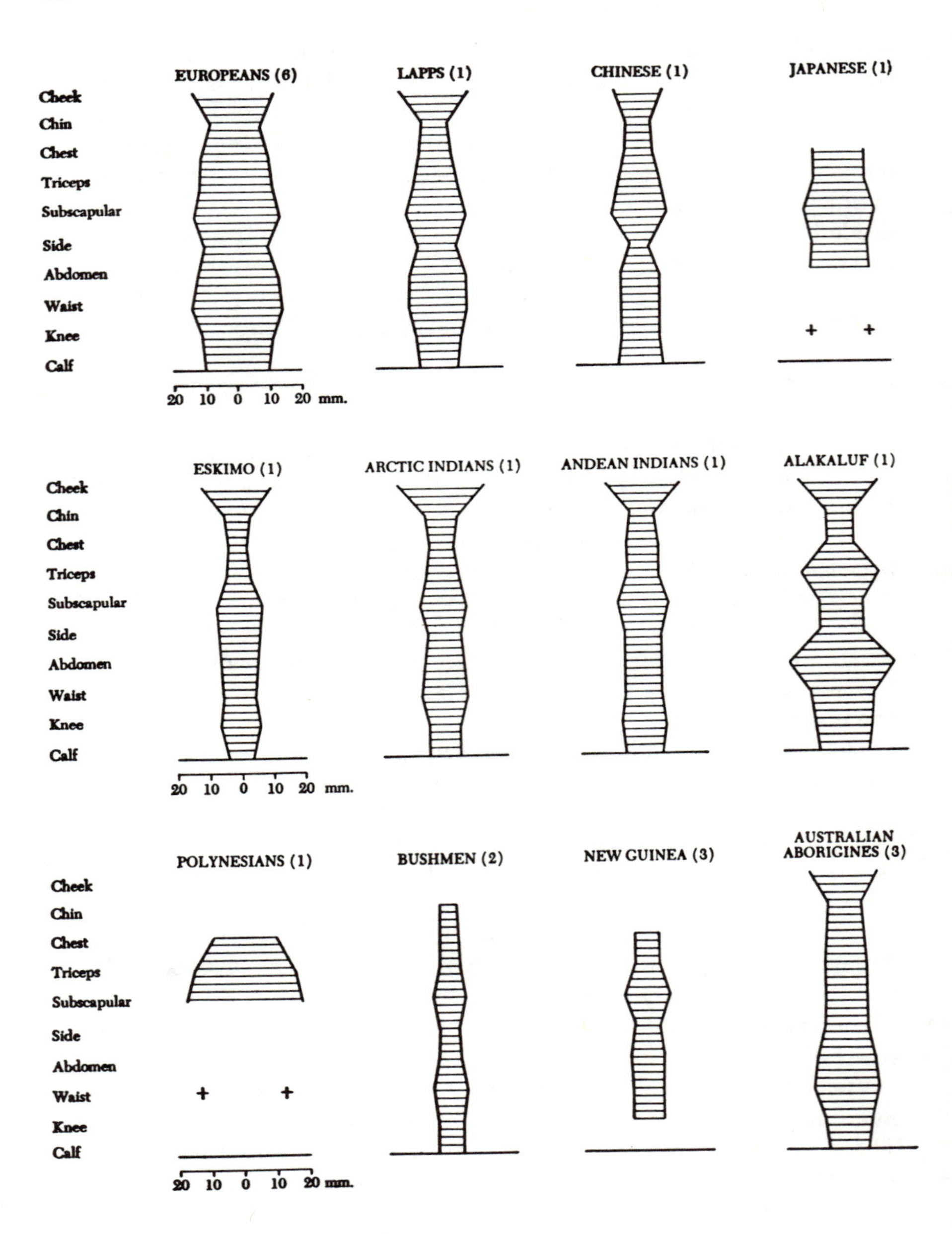

FIGURE 13. Some fat profiles. Each picture represents the subcutaneous fat thickness of the average person, measured at various locations along the body. (Reproduced with permission from *The Living Races of Man* by C. A. Coon, Alfred A. Knopf, Inc., Publisher.)

live in a warm climate, but they are both very large and spend much of their time in water. Australian Aborigines have a medium fat layer and are of medium body size, but they live in a very warm climate for the most part. Natives of New Guinea are much thinner than Australians. Most Arctic peoples (Lapps, Eskimos, and Arctic Indians) have rather modest amounts of body fat except on their faces. In extreme temperatures they must depend on clothing, fat is not enough, but their faces are usually still directly exposed to the cold.

In looking at the limited data available there are a few generalizations that can be made, but with little confidence. Large people tend to have more body fat. People in cool climates, or who swim a lot, have more body fat. People in Arctic climates have only fat faces. Dietary practices, affluence, and other individual variations are too great to say much more than this. If fat profiles were more completely available for all geographic areas of the world (and not pooled by preconceived racial categories) then maybe we could find some more detailed correlations.

Subcutaneous fat is measured by a skin-fold caliper which gives the thickness of a double layer of fat and skin. Pinching the subject between the thumb and one finger amounts to the same thing, except that the caliper holds a constant pressure and gives readings in milimeters. A proper profile consists of a standardized series of measurements beginning on the cheek and running down the body to the calf. Thicknesses of fat on European bodies and Arctic faces run typically 10 to 15 mm. At the other extreme among Bushmen they are barely 5 mm.

Little is known of geographic variations of fat supply in terms of its food storage function. In this case cultural and individual determinants may be pretty much the whole story. Among our Neandertal ancestors a massive deposition of fat may have allowed them to survive the winters. Without projectile weapons and tailored clothing it is difficult to see how they could procure much food in the cold season. Neandertal skeletal differences are clearly designed to move an incredibly heavy body and this may well have been their condition each autumn.

Bushmen and Hottentot females are noted for their protruding buttocks, called steatopygia, which is made of fat and connective tissue (See Fig. 14). This is clearly for food storage and its location makes complete sense. In a hot climate a thin body is desirable for heat dissipation, so food reserve fat ought to be concentrated in a very limited region. It should be located as low as possible so its weight will not complicate balancing problems. The fat also should not be on the legs or arms which would add weight to moving parts. Given another

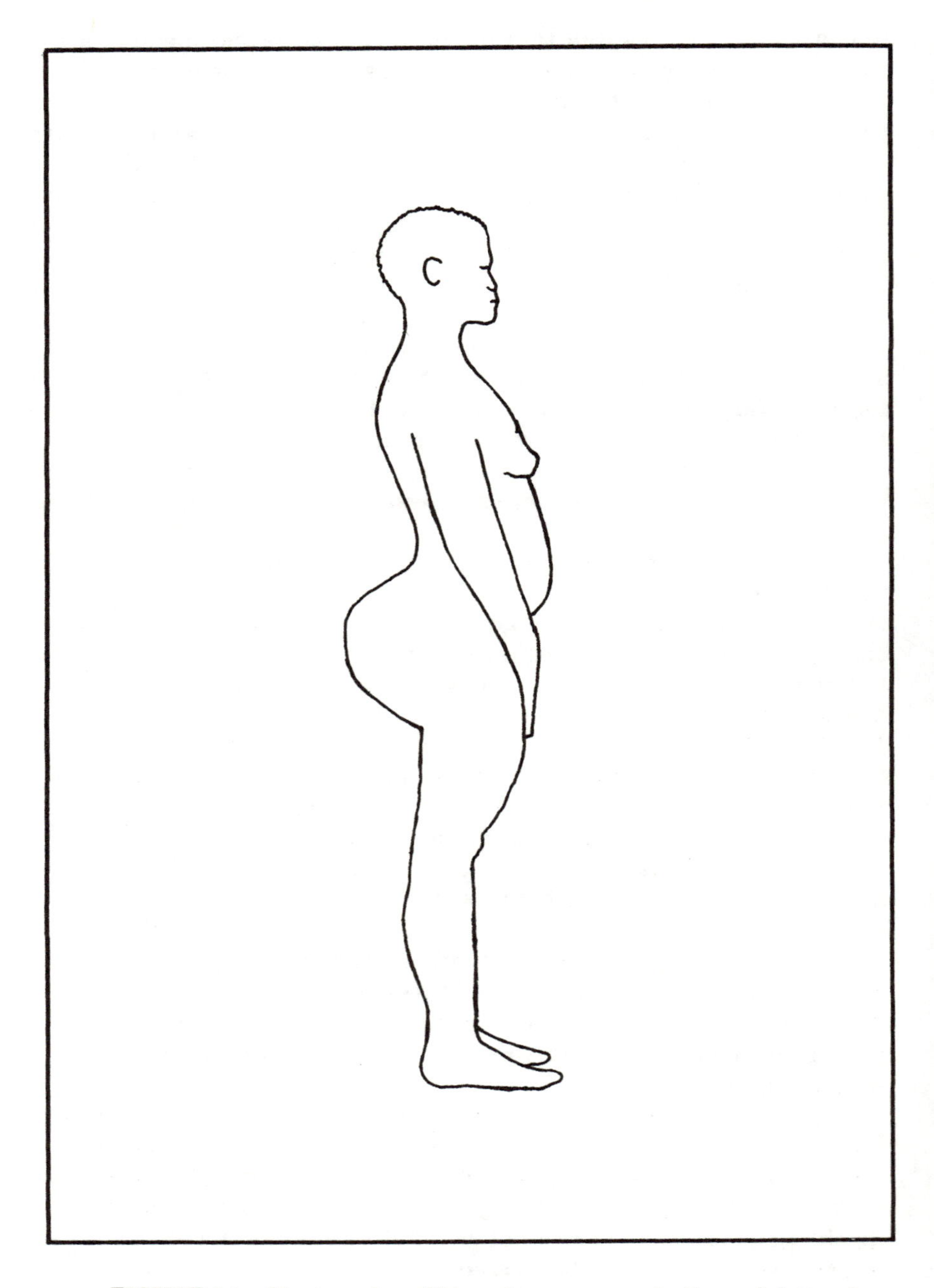

FIGURE 14. Steatopygia. This extreme concentration of fatty deposits in the buttocks is charactistic of Bushman females.

restriction of an interpersonal nature, this leaves the hips and buttocks as the only logical place. Early European art work of Upper Paleolithic times included drawings and carvings of women with enormous fat deposits, largely in the hips, thighs, and buttocks, but the degree of concentration does not match that found in the southern Africans. No special connection is implied as these early depictions can be matched best by some modern European women who have unusual amounts of body fat. Also, this art work cannot necessarily be taken as the normal condition for those times as it may only have been an esthetic ideal.

SIZE AND BODY BUILD.

It has been said that variation in stature is the second most noted of all racial traits, skin color being the first. Unfortunately, stature by itself is not particularly related to anything. Its variations make sense only in conjunction with differences in size and body build. Together these factors determine the amount of area the body presents to the environment in relation to the body's mass. This is a ratio between surface and volume.

Heat is generated by metabolic processes throughout the body. The amount of heat is roughly in proportion to the volume of the body, which in turn is most easily measured in terms of weight. Heat is dissipated into the environment from surface areas, the lining of the lungs and the skin. Heat loss through exhaled air has no variations which can be dealt with here and will be taken as a constant. Heat loss through the skin can be regulated by the amount of blood present in the dermis and by the output of the sweat glands. Generally, the human potential in these regards are also constants, so the only remaining major variable to be dealt with is the size of the skin surface itself. Variations in the surface to volume ratio follow from size and from shape which will be described separately.

Large people have more body mass than small people in which to generate heat. Large people also have more skin than small people from which this heat can be lost. But large bodies have relatively less skin in terms of their body mass; the larger the body the lower the surface to volume ratio. This is a simple matter of solid geometry which can best be illustrated with cubes of different sizes. A one cm cube has six surfaces (top, bottom, right, left, front, and back), each consisting of one square cm, for a total surface area of six square cm. Its volume is one cubic cm, so in these units its ratio of surface to volume is 6:1. If one doubles the linear dimension of the cube to two cm, its six surfaces each now have four square cm, for a total of twenty-four square cm. Its volume is now eight cubic cm (2x2x2), and its ratio of surface to volume has dropped and now becomes 3:1. While both measurements have increased in this simple illustration, the volume has increased twice as fast as the surface. If this is difficult to visualize, imagine taking the two cm cube and dividing it into eight separate cubes of one cm each. The larger cube must be cut in half three times in three separate planes, thus doubling the total surface without altering the total volume.

If one uses any other geometric figure, sphere, pyramid, or human body, the result is still the same. A doubling of its linear dimension increases its surface by four times and its volume by eight times. Whatever factor is used to multiply its length, the square of that factor multiplies its surface and the cube of that factor multiplies its volume.

Human bodies are not cubes but they follow the same rules of geometry. Alakaluf Indians stand 1.25 times as tall as Ituri Pygmies (not a surprising difference). Since they have roughly the same body builds, the Alakaluf will have 1.76 times as much skin surface as the Pygmy, but will weigh 2.2 times as much. For each unit of his body mass the Pygmy has 25% more skin surface from which to expell the heat it generates.

If body shape is held constant, larger individuals tend to retain more heat and are adapted for cooler climates, while smaller individuals expell heat more easily and are suited to warmer places. Size variations among closely related species or subspecies of other animals are distributed according to temperature in this manner. Since 1847 this has been known as Bergmann's rule after its discoverer. Distantly related species do not follow this rule in relation to one another because they can have very different mechanisms for heat control. Following Bergmann's rule alone we would expect the smallest people living in the equatorial zone and getting increasingly larger as one approaches the poles. In many cases this is just what is encountered.

Body shape can also vary in order to present more or less surface area to the environment while the mass or volume is held constant. From the last illustration let us take the two cm cube and redistribute the eight included small cubes into a vertical column. Where before there were twenty-four square cm of surface there are now thirty-four square cm. The ratio of surface to volume has increased from 3:1 to become greater than 4:1.

Differences in human body shapes range from what one might call stout to elongated. Anthropologists have long termed these lateral and lineal body types. Lateral bodies are as close to a sphere as can be constructed; limbs are short, especially the distal segments, hands and feet are thick and fingers and toes stubby, the neck is short, while the body is relatively large and deep from front to back. Lineal types are the reverse, with thin, flat bodies and with all extensions elongated—the farther from the body the more elongated. (See Fig. 15.)

There is little data on actual surface areas of skins with body weight held as a constant. The maximum effect of the extremes (Eskimo vs. Nilotic) would appear to be about the same as with total body size. If either size or shape were much more effective in altering the cooling surface then variations in that one should predominate. Equatorial people are often very elongated or lineal while many northerners are stout or lateral. Again this observation holds for other mammals as well, and since 1877 it has been known as Allen's rule from its formulator.

In man, either Bergmann's or Allen's rule may apply. In equatorial climates people tend to be either small or lineal, sometimes both. In polar climates people are either large or lateral, or a combination of them. Thus stature, by itself, is meaningless. Tall peoples, such as Nilotics or Alakaluf, may be adapted to opposite temperatures, and both the tallest and shortest people in the world live near each other in tropical Africa. There are no distribution maps available of the world's sizes and body builds, either as separate phenomena or combined and expressed in terms of surface to volume ratios.

Variations in size and body build can have an effect on certain technological aspects of culture. These in turn may stimulate selective pressures which act on these same variations. Best known of these is the choice of weapons between the bow and the spear. Archery does not require speed so much as strength to draw the bow which stores energy for the moment of release. The lateral body build is best suited to this because their limb leverage generally emphasizes strength over speed. Had the Neandertals invented the bow and arrow their anatomy would have given them at least twice the bow-drawing power of any people today.

Spear throwing is a more direct action in that the missile moves only as fast as the hand that throws it. Lineal bodies with long slender arms can move the hand rapidly in a long arc, though not with great force, and thus are ideal for throwing spears.

If both classes of weapons are available, all else being equal, there would be an expectable choice by people with each body type of the weapon easiest for them to use. It is thus for an anatomical reason, not a cultural one, that most Africans are spear throwers (in the ethnographic present). Likewise, the fact that the more recent bow and arrow was taken up by the Mongoloid peoples more readily than by

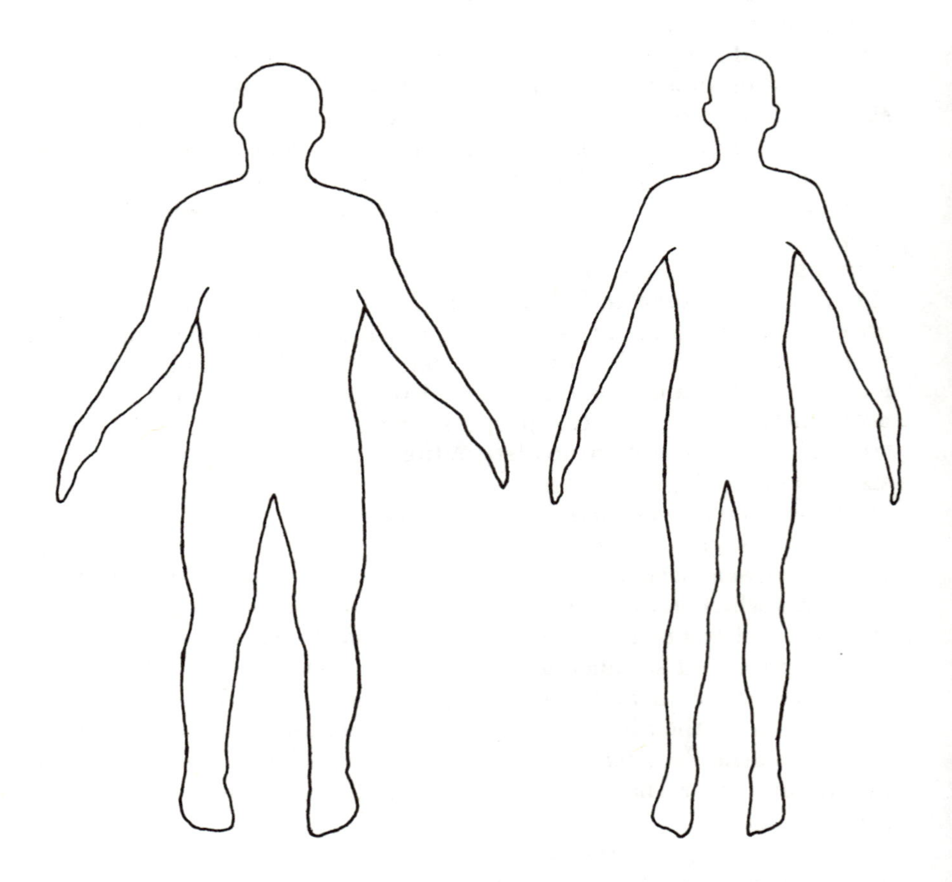

FIGURE 15. Lineal vs lateral body builds. The elongated, thin build common in Africa (right) presents a maximum of skin surface for the body mass. The lateral build (left) is common in the Arctic and has a minimum of surface area.

most others follows from their anatomical pre-adaptation. The obvious corollary is not so easy to answer. Has the use of these weapons acted as a selective factor to exaggerate these same lineal and lateral body builds? The bow is probably too recent to have had much effect of this kind, but I would not be at all surprised if spear throwing has had a slight elongating effect on some Africans over the last few tens of thousands of years.

Many cattle herding peoples in eastern Africa are especially lineal. They do not leap from fast horses and wrestle calves to the ground as do modern American cowboys, but rather tend their cattle in a more gentle manner. A long reach with a light stick, and long legs to walk with the animals are more important to them than brute strength. When this is combined with spears as weapons and placed in a hot climate, the world's most lineal bodies result.

The wearing of heavy body armor for war is emphasized by such large people as Europeans and Polynesians, and by lateral ones such as Mongolians. Given a set of piercing weapons an absolute weight of body armor is required for adequate protection. Some people have the strength to carry such weight and others do not. I doubt there would be much positive selection for appropriate bodies in this case. Among those who could carry body armor there were always returning war heros, but also generally a lot of casualties as well.

In hunting there is need for large and/or strong bodies to wield whatever weapons are used to bring down the game. There is also selection pressure in the opposite direction because the smaller you are the less you need to eat. If game is limited within the hunters' range there is a limit to the biomass of people that can be supported. When people are large there must be fewer of them, and in some cases, too few to maintain a working social unit. These two selective pressures will balance at some optimum size for the local circumstances.

The Bushmen kill large game with tiny poisoned arrows shot from weak bows. This dramatically reduces the selective pressure for large body size and permits the already existing selection for smaller size to prevail to some degree. Pygmies and Negritos also use similar weapons which should help account for their size as well. Small bodies also present smaller targets for an enemy's arrows. Here it would appear that a cultural practice had an important effect on a physical trait. It is not immediately clear how much their small size results from poisoned arrows and how much from temperature adaptation, but both are probably involved.

Considering the small size of Ituri Pygmies, I've often wondered what would have happened if they had access to a large breed of dog such as the Irish Wolfhound. Since they weigh less than half as much as the dog, could they ride them like horses in hunting and in warfare? Such a mount would have unusual advantages in terms of trainability, social attachment, and its own fighting qualities.

Agricultural practices often call for certain feats of absolute strength such as breaking through a given type of topsoil, reaching a branch of a certain height, carrying various products, handling domestic animals of particular strengths, etc. Often small people do not perform well at many of these tasks and at the same time there may be enough food to feed larger bodies. If southeastern Asia and Melanesia were once entirely populated by Negritos, as many suspect, then the first introduction of horticulture may also have introduced selective pressure for a return to larger body sizes. Those populations which maintained the hunting the gathering way of life would remain small and are the Negritos we know today. It is difficult to separate this from the effect of introducing new peoples as well with the first horticulture. Obviously the later intrusion of plow agriculture was accompanied by the bodies of the Mongoloid farmers themselves. But one is hard pressed to find an outside source for the Papuans of New Guinea unless they were Negritos before simple horticulture arrived.

SOMATOTYPES.

Some thirty-seven years ago a different method of classifying body types was proposed by W. H. Sheldon. Based on three extremes instead of two, they were named from the three embryonic tissue layers which lead to different organ systems. Endomorphy is an emphasis on the digestive organs derived from the endoderm. Mesomorphy maximizes muscle and bone which are derived from the mesoderm. Ectomorphy emphasizes the skin and nervous system which develop from the ectoderm. Endomorphy and mesomorphy combined are the old lateral body, while ectomorphy is the same as lineal. Actually, similar three-fold divisions had been made earlier, but this one hit the popular press and has not yet faded from common usage in some quarters.

Each of the three components is measured in its expression on a scale from a minimum of one to a maximum of seven. Each individual is then given three numbers representing his position on the scales of endomorphy, mesomorphy, and ectomorphy in that order. Thus a somatotype of 622 emphasizes endomorphy and one of 444 is about average, and so on.

Somatotyping has gradually fallen into disuse without there ever being a good world survey made. Part of this follows from the rather subjective method of evaluating subjects in which the evaluators did not always rate them the same. More difficulty arose from attempts to equate body types with personality types and the inevitable clash with those who held culture and individual experience to be the formative factors. Even worse was the extension of these correlating attempts to include the criminal type, somewhere between endomorphy and mesomorphy. With this, most investigators abandoned this system of description entirely.

Body designs and sizes in past populations can be determined from just a few postcranial bones. As noted above, Neandertals are noted for their extreme lateral design. Most other fossil hominids are more average in body build, but some differences among *erectus* specimens suggest the same kind of environmental selection as today. Java man was on the lineal side to judge from one femur (the provenience of the others being in doubt). Peking man, guessing from fragments, was lateral, but whether as much so as Neandertals we can't say. A few African *erectus* bones seem nearly average without clear indication of the elongation common there today. There are no very old bones of tiny people, certainly not in *erectus* times, but then we have rather few bones of any size to say much.

NOSE FORM.

After color, stature, and perhaps hair form, noses are the most noticed and most used in categorizing people. Human noses are rather notable in the degree to which they project from the face, though no more so than in the proboscis monkey and the tapir, not to mention the elephant. The height and breadth of the nose have long been measured by physical anthropologists (See Fig. 16) and a nasal index is given of the breadth as a percentage of the height. Observations have also been made about degree of projection, orientation and shape of nostrils, and the profile shape of the nasal bridge. Some very approximate correlations with climate were immediately seen just as with skin color and hair form. And as with these other traits, the exceptions and inconsistencies accumulated to such a degree that the climate correlation was seriously questioned. A tall, narrow nose with a nasal index under seventy was called leptorrhine and is common among Europeans. A short, wide nose with an index over eighty-four was platyrrhine and is most common among Africans. Nasal indices between seventy and eighty-four were called mesorhine.

In order to make sense out of its variations we must first examine the nose in terms of its function and all the other factors that significantly affect its shape. What we call the nose is just an anterior extension of the nasal chamber which functions more or less as a unit

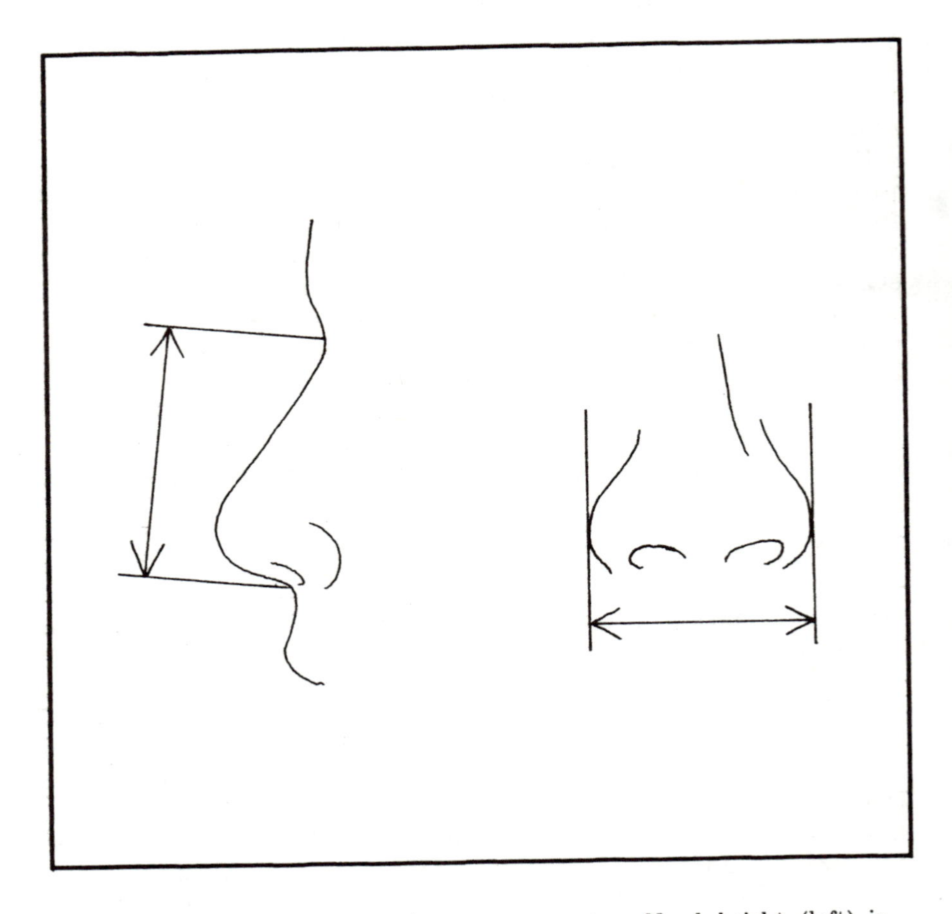

FIGURE 16. Standard nasal measurements. Nasal height (left) is measured from the top of the nasal bones to the lower edge of the nasal septum. The points are vaguely defined and measuring error is common. Nasal breadth (right) is quite precise. The breadth, expressed as a percentage of the height, is the nasal index.

(Fig. 17). This unit prepares the inhaled air for reception by the lungs. The first significant function results from the upward direction of the air inhalation into the nostrils and tends to prevent entry of large particles like rain drops and sand grains which normally fall downward. This is a consequence of the nose length being in excess of the mouth projection and is quite fortuitous. Other animals generally do not select for this discrepancy unless some other nasal function is involved. A second defense against inhaled objects is provided by the hairs just inside the nostrils which I indelicately refer to as the bug filter. Both of these functions can be viewed as constants because there are no known geographical variations that seem designed for these purposes.

The next function is to remove the vast majority of dust particles and bacteria that are being inhaled with each breath. This is accomplished by these particles touching and adhering to the moist mucus lining of the nasal chamber. Again, there may be no significant racial variations in nasal designs for just this purpose, but if there were, it would be difficult to distinguish them from adaptations for the next, and apparently major function.

When inhaled air reaches the microscopic alveoli, or air sacs in the lungs, oxygen from this air is dissolved into the thin water lining of each and from there it passes across cell membranes and into the body for a long and complicated journey to all other cells. If there is no water lining in the alveoli the first step of oxygen transfer will not take place. With each exhaled breath, air leaves at body temperature and fully laden with moisture — 100% relative humidity. This tends to remove the critical water lining. This moisture will be replaced by seepage from the lung cells themselves, but it is far more desirable that it be supplied by the incoming air in the same amount as it is being lost through exhaling.

Under most normal conditions the nasal chamber manages to prepare the air so that it is at least 35° C (95° F) and 95% relative humidity when it enters the trachea. Its incoming moisture content is thus virtually the same as the residual air in the lungs. Should a discrepancy occur more moisture will be lost than is brought in, and while the lungs try to make up the difference a certain amount of reduction will take place in oxygen transfer.

Inhaled air is usually at much less than 100% relative humidity. It is also usually much cooler than body temperature. As air temperature increases, the amount of water it can contain also increases. Thus warmer air must contain a greater amount of water if it is to maintain the same relative humidity. Air inhaled at 5° C (40° F) and 100% humidity contains very little water. That same air raised to body

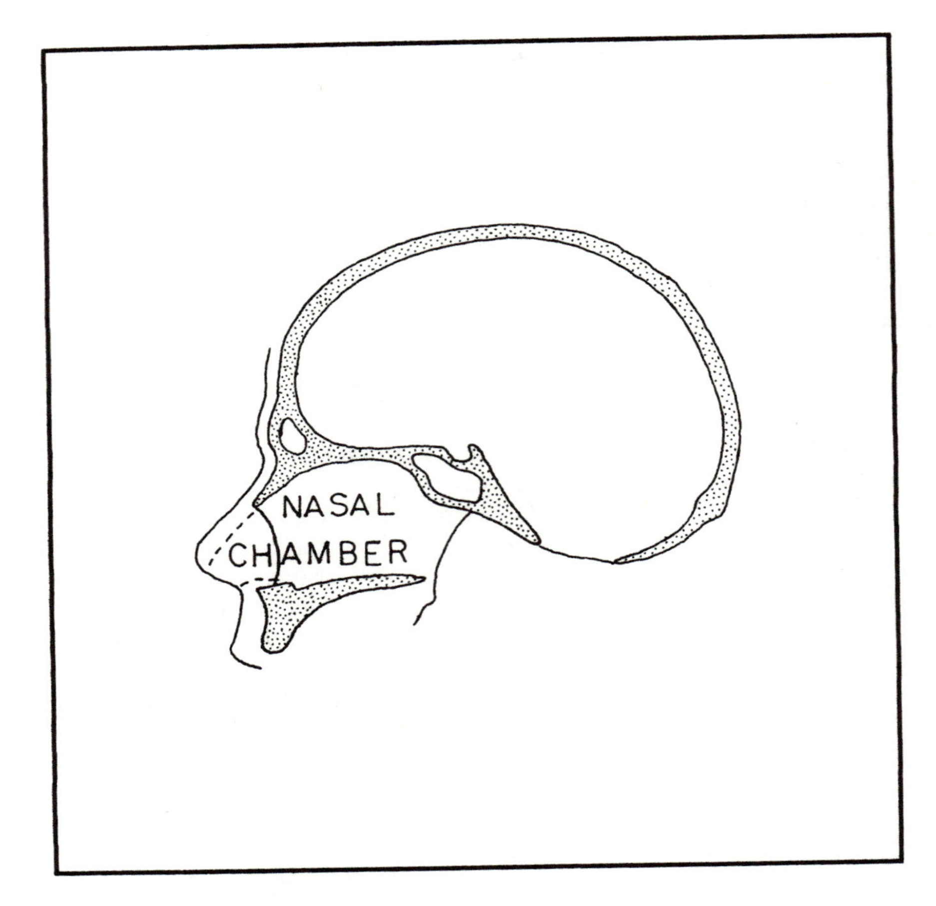

FIGURE 17. The nose and nasal chamber in longitudinal section. The external nose is an anterior extension of the nasal chamber. The entire structure functions as a unit to warm and moisten inhaled air for reception in the lungs. The posterior limit of this chamber is fixed in location, so any elongation is possible only by adding to the anterior projection of the nose itself.

temperature will be at only about 12% relative humidity and its absolute water content must be multiplied by eight times to best prepare it for reception in the lungs. The function of the nasal chamber is then both to warm and to moisten the inhaled air.

The nasal chamber not only has its inner walls covered by the warm, wet mucous lining, but it is also divided by mucous-lined partitions into a series of air columns. The nasal septum divides it into right and left halves for its full length from front to back. In addition, the main part of the chamber is invaded by a number of bony turbinals that reach in from the side walls and descend vertically for some distance. They are also covered with mucous lining. These structures effectively divide the nasal chamber into four vertical air columns and are so spaced that the air passages are nowhere more than about six mm wide. This means that inhaled air will always be within three mm of one of these warming and moistening surfaces. (See Fig. 18.)

Variations in human nose form are merely anterior manifestations of alterations in the design of the entire nasal chamber. If it is advantageous to add much warmth and moisture to the inhaled air these surfaces must be brought closer together. Since the primary orientation of the air columns is vertical, this is most easily accomplished by narrowing the entire structure, air columns included, so that the air passes even closer to the mucous surfaces. In order to maintain the same ease of air flow the chamber must also be made taller, enough so that its cross-sectional area remains about the same. It has long been noted that tall, narrow noses tend to occur in climates with cold and/or dry air.

An additional means of increasing the warming and moistening function would obviously be to lengthen the distance through which the air must pass. There is no obvious way to extend the chamber posteriorly, but anteriorly there are few limits. The turbinals do not extend far into the projecting nose, but the nasal septum does. Any anterior elongation of the nose will provide at least some additional air preparation. Again, it has long been observed that where noses are tall and narrow they also tend to be more projecting. All human noses are tall, narrow, and projecting when compared with those of apes. It's just that some are more so than others. Obviously, this does not show varying degrees of kinship with these apes, just differences in atmospheric conditions to which they are adapted.

Early attempts to relate nose form with the environment showed a modest correlation between nasal index and average relative humidity. It was suggestive, but far from satisfactory. As with any correlation, interest should be centered on discovering the reasons why it is not perfect, and not on congratulating ourselves on the fraction that does

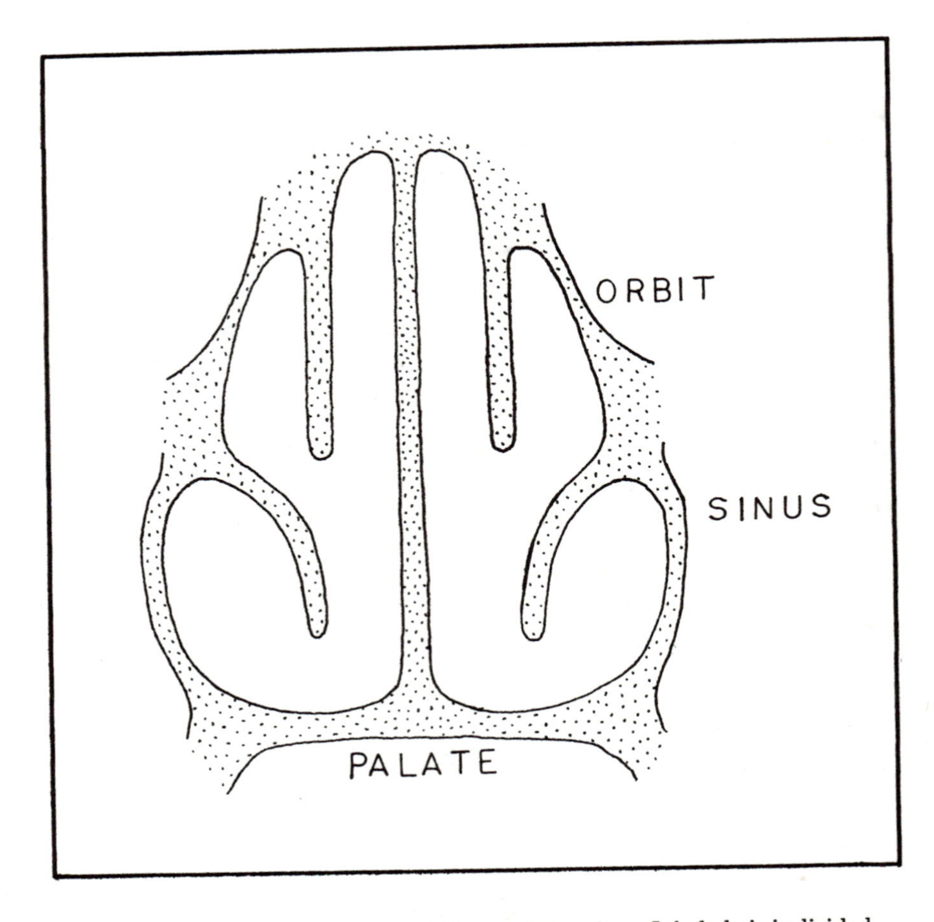

FIGURE 18. Cross section of the nasal chamber. Inhaled air is divided into a series of tall, narrow air columns by the nasal septum and the turbinals which extend into it. These mucus-lined structures will always be within about 3 mm of any incoming air molecules. Dust and bacteria are removed by contact with these surfaces, and the air is warmed and moistened as well.

work. An improvement was found if it was absolute humidity, not relative, that was considered. Obviously, if the inhaled air is all going to reach the same temperature in the lungs it is only the actual, not relative, moisture content of the air that matters.

Finally it was realized that with seasonal variations in temperature and hence in moisture, it was the winter season that was the most important. A tall and narrow nose is little inconvenience breathing the summer air, but a short and broad one is at a great disadvantage when the air is cold and dry. A map of the world showing absolute humidity for January in the northern hemisphere and for July in the southern hemisphere (Fig. 19) now shows the best correlation with nasal indices.

There are still a number of real and apparent exceptions to this simple explanation of nose forms, and most of them can be satisfactorily accounted for here. The breadth of the nasal aperture in the skull is approximately fixed by the location of the roots of the upper canine teeth. These roots do not rise up into the nasal margins but the supporting bone around these roots does (See Fig. 20). Whatever the spacing of the aperture, the rest of the nasal chamber tends to approximate this to some degree. If the chamber is to be adapted for cold and dry air the upper canines ought to be drawn close together. There are several ways to accomplish this.

The spacing of the upper canines is not determined by these teeth themselves but by the incisors which are implanted between them. The upper incisors form a gentle arch across the front of the mouth in normal people, but this arching may be greatly exaggerated (See Fig. 21). This would allow the canines to be closer together without affecting the size of any teeth. Another variation would be to overlap the margins of the incisors to similarly reduce their total lateral extent (See Fig. 22). Both of these might be regarded as moderately pathological conditions.

A total reduction of tooth size, incisors included, would produce the same result but would carry with it the price of an earlier wearing out of the entire dentition. Relatively small teeth are a European characteristic, showing sometimes in the fossil record as well, and is likely selected for to accomplish just this purpose. This may be referred to as the European solution to the nasal breadth problem.

The incisors can be reduced in breadth without sacrifice of size if their flaring margins are folded back. This is simply another picturesque description of what are called shovel-shaped incisors which are so characteristic of the so-called Mongoloid peoples. Here the edges of the incisors, upper and lower, extend backwards into the mouth creating a slight hollowing on their lingual (tongue) surfaces (See Fig. 23). In the past all attention was focused on what shoveling

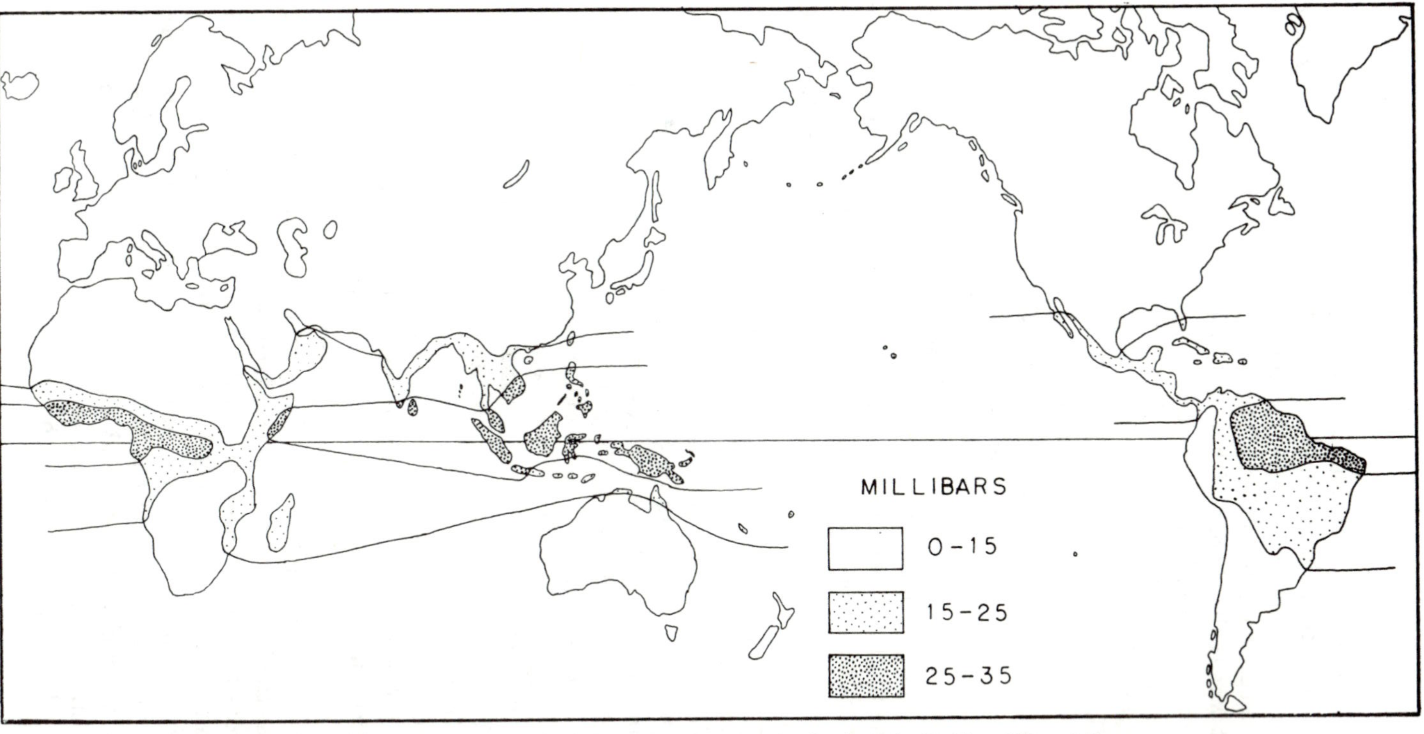

FIGURE 19. World map of absolute humidity in winter. In dry air (0-15 millibars) there are no more than 140 grams of water in the 17 cu. meters of air that an average person breathes in a day; in medium air (15-25 millibars) there are 140-280 grams; and in moist air (25-35 millibars) there are over 280 grams of water. The northern hemisphere is shown for January and the southern hemisphere for July. (Modified from Coon, 1965.)

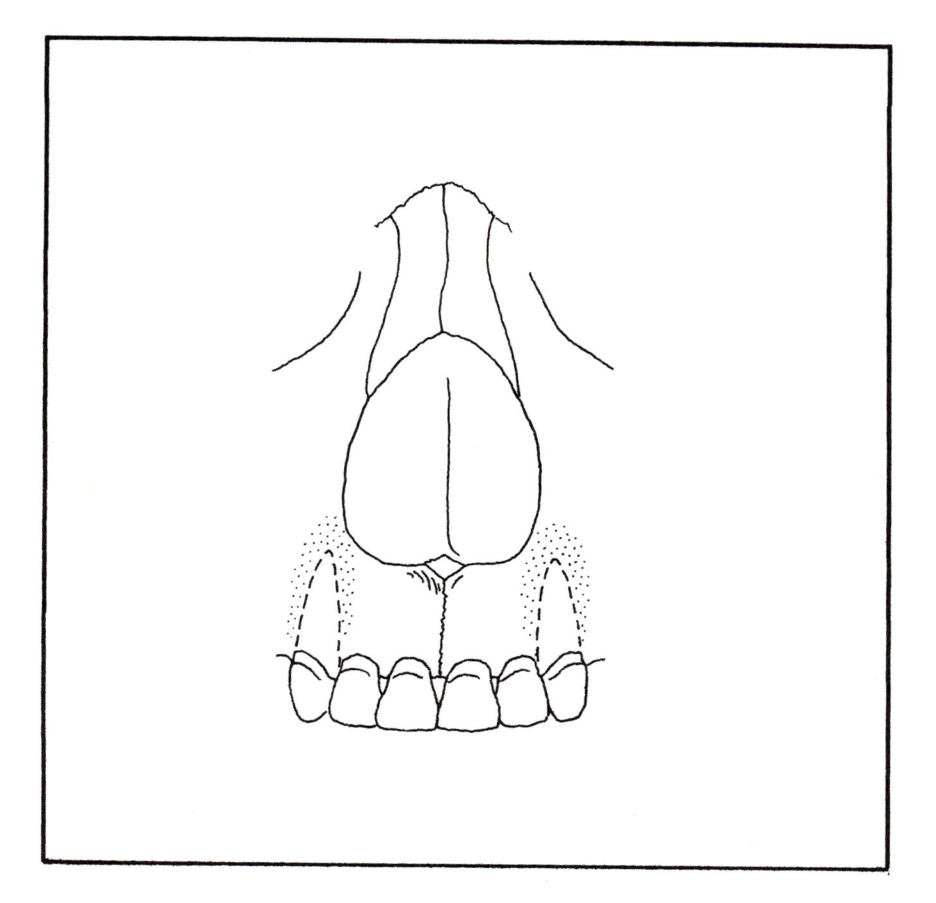

FIGURE 20. Canine roots and nasal aperture. The bone surrounding the roots of the upper canine teeth rises on each side of the nasal opening and puts approximate limits on the breadth of this aperture. This means nasal breadth on the skull is roughly determined by the distance between the canines, or more directly, by the size and placement of the incisors which are between these teeth. There are several adaptations which serve to reduce this space.

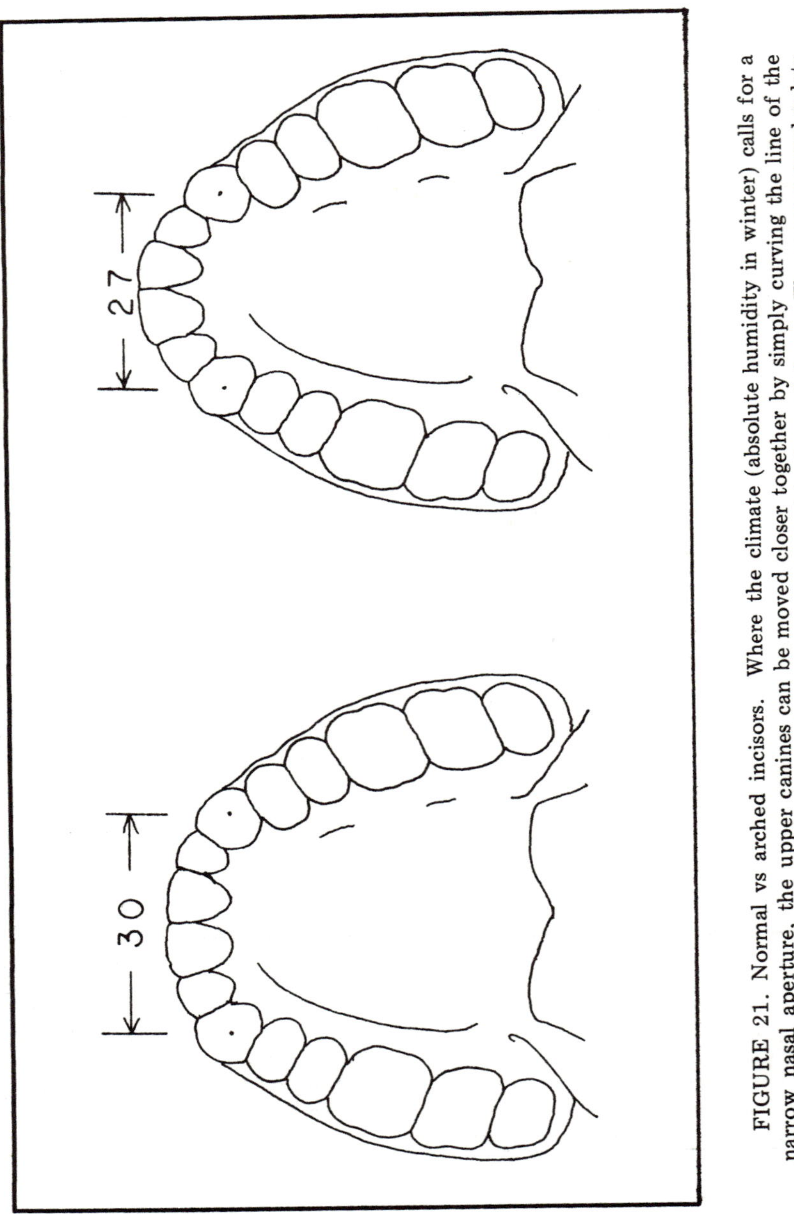

FIGURE 21. Normal vs arched incisors. Where the climate (absolute humidity in winter) calls for a narrow nasal aperture, the upper canines can be moved closer together by simply curving the line of the incisors that separates them. This leaves the incisors unaffected in size and shape. The more normal palate (left) has a distance of 30 mm from one canine center to the other. The same teeth, slightly arched (right), allow the canines to be 10% closer together.

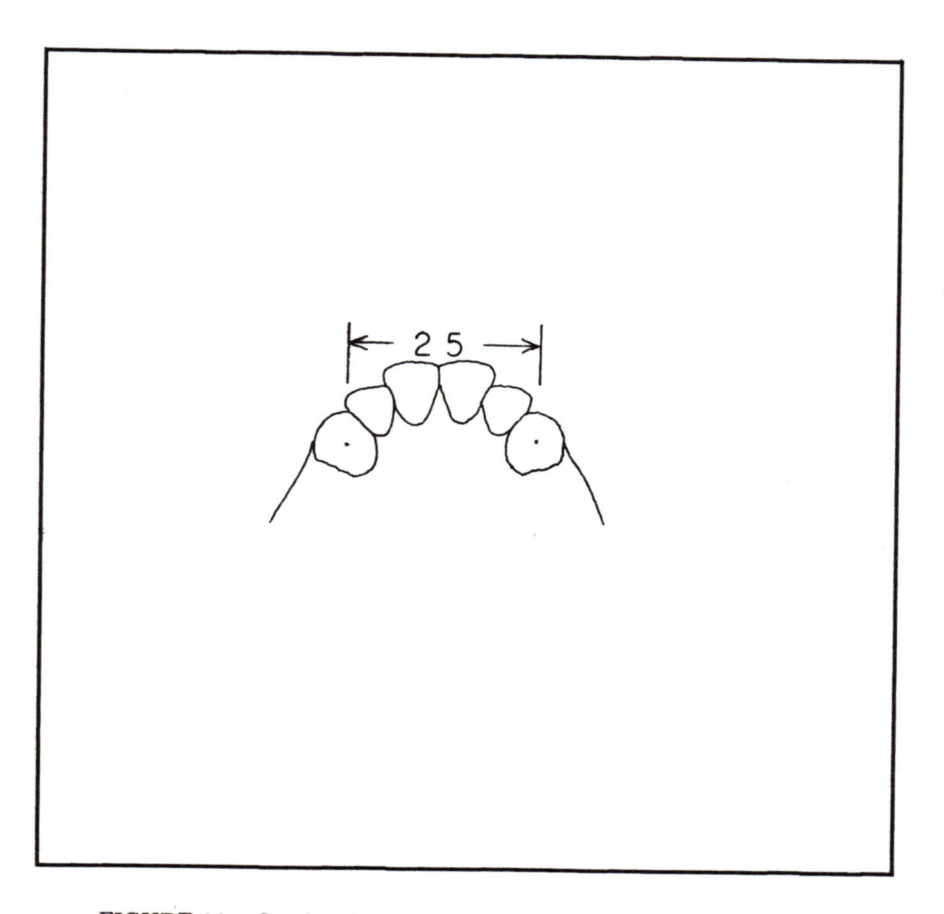

FIGURE 22. Overlapping or staggered incisors. The space between the upper canines may be reduced by partially overlapping the intervening incisor crowns. The symmetrical overlapping shown here is an individual anomaly, not a racial trait. It may be even more pronounced if the medial incisors lap over one another asymmetrically. Removal of one or more incisors will still further increase this effect as the remaining teeth will move in to partially close the gap.

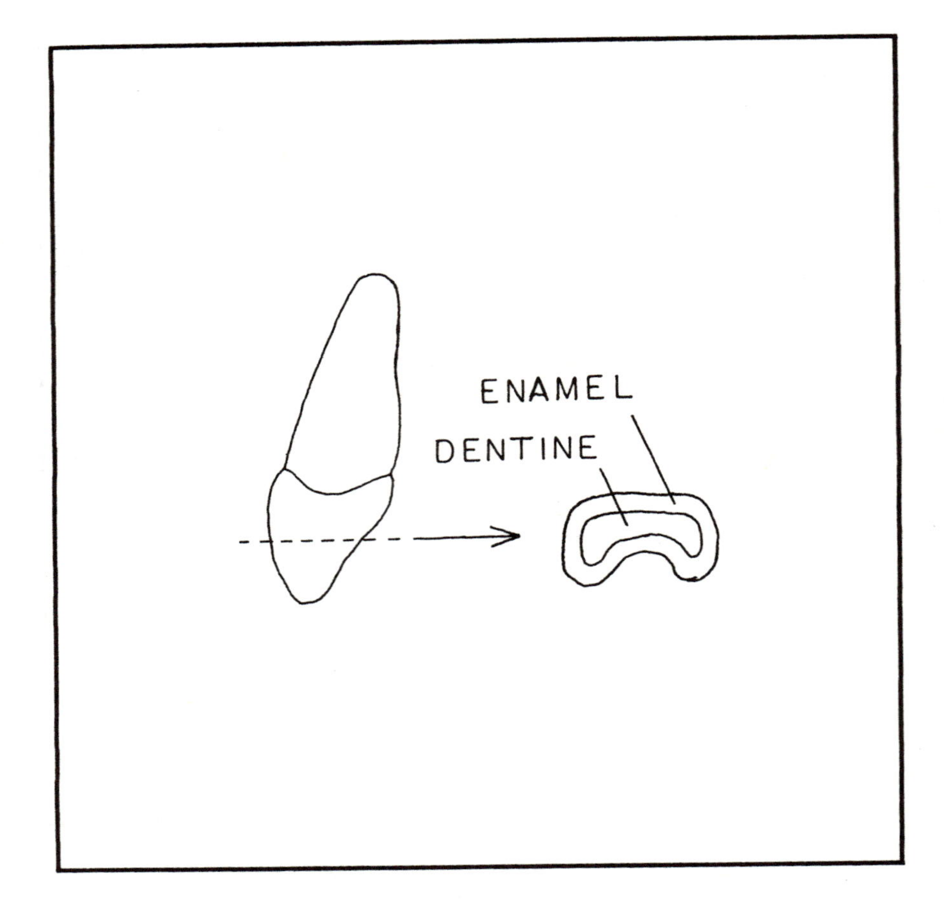

FIGURE 23. Shoveled incisors. There are various possible reasons for this design, but one consequence is to shorten the intercanine space without reducing the chewing surface. In this sense one can regard them as very large incisors with their edges folded back and forming a hollow on the rear face. Pictured above is an incisor as seen from the side and a cross section of its crown as it appears when well worn.

created, the hollowing. Now it appears more likely that what it removes, namely part of the breadth, was a more important reason for this development. We might refer to this as the Mongoloid solution to bringing the canines closer together. It is genetically probably a more complicated process than the European solution, but then it does not exact any price in terms of reducing chewing capacity.

Another fascinating possibility in this connection is the removal of two or more upper incisors as part of initiation ceremonies into manhood. Such tooth evulsion is still practiced in northern Africa (I have seen it done on film only) and was also done as far back as the Capsian culture times, some 10,000 years earlier. I have examined these Capsian skulls and found the gaps from the missing teeth were partly closed together and the upper canines were substantially closer than they would otherwise have been. Their nasal apertures were also much narrowed. I doubt these people had any idea they might be improving one adaptation while they were messing up another. Still, with all the possible ways to mangle young men it is curious that this one should have lasted so long in an area where it would not be a total liability.

Very large teeth in general can also have an effect on the nose. In tropical climates where wide noses are acceptable, perhaps even desirable, teeth can be very large. There are limits to where these teeth can be placed in the mouth and the major free space, as with the nose itself, is to extend the dental battery forward. There may not be a corresponding anterior projection of the nose beyond the upper lip. Since one visual measure of nasal projection is simply to note how far its tip extends beyond the upper lip, a certain amount of such projection will thereby be masked. This front-to-back shortening of nasal projection will also minimize the space available for the nostrils, and as a direct consequence they expand or flare to each side. The so-called flat nose of some people is thus partly a result of their large teeth. Of course, thickened and everted lips will even further exaggerate the nostril flare and apparent lack of projection of the tip.

Another major visual estimation of nasal projection is how far the nose tip is located in front of the cheeks. One of the most characteristic features of eastern Asian and American skulls is that the malars, or cheek bones, are set forward by about one centimeter. The obvious result of this is a reduction in the apparent anterior projection of the nose. Most northern Mongoloids have nasal chambers with front to back lengths comparable to Europeans, but the nose does not stand out nearly so far because their cheeks are set forward somewhat also. Comparison with the upper lip does not clarify matters either because the relatively small teeth of the European give an exaggerated impression of their nasal projection.

In extremely cold climates frostbite enters as a possible determinant of nasal features. Where cold and dry air argues for a very projecting nasal tip, adequate circulation to avoid its freezing argues against it. In terms of gross anatomy the anteriorly set cheeks will help warm the Mongol nose and the lack of tooth reduction leaves the upper lip reasonably close too. Even so, there is a balance between the needs of air processing and of frostbite avoidance, so actual nasal projection is halted at about, or slightly less, than in Europeans though it's appearance is quite a bit less.

The Mongoloid cranial design includes a number of features of an anterior emphasis in the masticating apparatus. Two of these, shoveled incisors and anterior malars, also relate to extreme cold adaptations. One wonders if they are the cause of the rest of this anterior emphasis or whether the relationship is purely fortuitous.

The very low nasal bridge of most Mongoloids is also worth mentioning. Much of this is an artifact of the anterior cheek bones which also bring forward the outside rim of the optical orbit and, to a degree, the eye itself. There still seems, to this observer at least, some degree of lowness of the nasal bridge that remains unexplained.

Body size variations can also affect noses in two ways. The warming and moistening effect of the walls of the nasal passages depends on the absolute distance from the air molecules to the mucous lining. In very large people more inhaled air is required and the nasal passages should be correspondingly larger. Because they cannot increase much in width without impairing function, the major effect of large size must be a heightening of the nasal passages instead. This will affect the external nose too, and an increase in height without a corresponding increase in breadth will result in a lower nasal index. Thus the lower nasal index of Europeans is exaggerated for yet another reason.

The converse of this is even more revealing as it partially accounts for the otherwise inexplicably flat nose of the Bushman. Their nasal chambers are of about normal width for a desert climate, but because they are so small in body size their nasal heights are much reduced, thus giving them the fairly high nasal index that seems so out of place.

The other effect of large body size follows from the large volume of air that uselessly occupies all the space between the nostrils and the alveoli of the lungs. Some of this air simply moves back and forth, neither yielding its oxygen nor reaching the outside air for replenishment. For this reason very shallow breathing (short draughts in and out) will yield little oxygen because it mainly shifts this dead air. If air is to move at a fixed rate past the mucous lining, the longer air passages of the larger person require that he take longer and deeper breaths to move the dead air sufficiently. As each inhalation is warmed and moistened this will cause a cooling and drying of the nasal chamber. This effect will be greatest at the anterior end which receives the raw air first. A zone of cooling and drying will progressively move back into the chamber, the longer the inhalation the shorter the remaining effective nasal chamber becomes. Larger people tend to have more projecting noses simply to compensate for this shortening effect. The already projecting European nose thus adds another reason to project still more.

Again, the converse of this size effect applies to the Bushman. With his small body he breathes more shallowly and does not dry out or cool his nasal tip so much with each inhalation. His need for an elongated nasal chamber is disproportionately reduced. Bushman noses now make sense.

The amount of physical labor that is engaged in will have the same effect as enlarging the body. An Eskimo will avoid exertion in cold temperature to avoid sweating, but it also relieves his nasal chamber of an additional burden that may also cost him the tip of his nose. With their poisoned arrows, Bushmen probably also engage in somewhat less exertion, even in relation to their size, than do most people. This would only give more reason for a flat nose. Aside from these and perhaps a few more cases, physical work is probably too much of a cultural variable over time for it to have any long-term evolutionary trends that we can see.

Living at high altitudes means breathing thin air with fewer oxygen molecules in a given volume. One response to this is larger lungs among the peoples in Tibet and the Andes Mountains. This means longer and deeper inhalations which will cool and dry the anterior part of the nasal chamber just as in big people. Again the response is an elongation of the chamber and a projection of the nose. In spite of the masking effect of their anterior cheek bones these mountain people have some of the most projecting noses in the world.

By applying all the factors affecting nose shape which have been described here we can reasonably well account for the kinds of noses that are found almost anywhere in the world (See Fig. 24). Climatic variations, either directly or indirectly, are the source of most of these differences. In all climates natural selection will work on nose shapes by reducing the frequency of the nonadaptive extremes.

Simple observation in any part of the world will show a great variation in nose shapes, no matter what the local adaptive average may be. Noses vary a great deal more than aboriginal skin color. If common sense had not already told us, this observation would; selection pressure on noses isn't very strong, certainly not as strong as it was on skin color which varied within narrower limits. While averages move

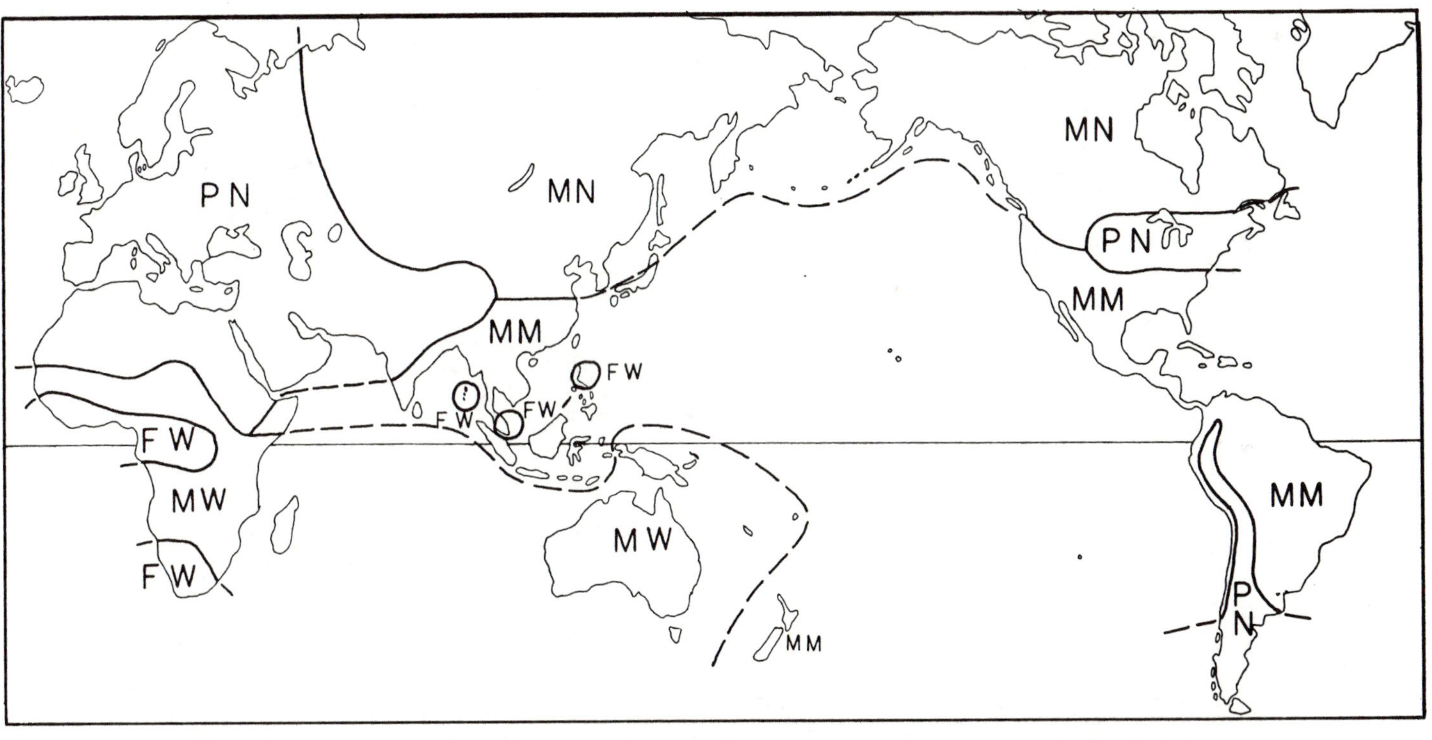

FIGURE 24. World map of nose forms. The various designs of external noses can be described in terms of projection and width. In the two-letter designations on the map the first is for projecting (P), medium (M), or flat (F); and the second stands for narrow (N), medium (M), or wide (W). The dividing lines are rather arbitrary and broad transitional zones are the rule. A fair correlation can be seen between broad noses and moist air, and between narrow noses and dry winter air (Fig. 19). Exceptions to this correlation are explained in the text.

with climatic adaptations, most individuals will manage to survive with their various noses, though at times with some difficulty. One might think that nasal adaptation to the environment would be a slower process than with a more important trait such as skin color. If the American Indians are a valid example just the reverse is true.

The original populating of America was by a single population. These immigrants had Arctic-adapted skin colors and noses. Since then, and it makes little difference how long ago that was, the skin colors of their descendants have acquired little variation, but their noses show perhaps half of the range of adaptive differences as are found in the Old World. The contrast is accounted for by the availability of variation in the gene pool for these two kinds of variations. The range of skin colors was narrow and there were no other people to mix with, so anything new depended on the appearance of very specific mutations. The range of nose forms was greater because it was not so tightly selected, so the genetic load for variation was also greater. In addition, there are so many more possible anatomical variations that can affect nose shape that the genetic raw material was not in short supply.

Nose forms can be determined in fossil skulls if the appropriate parts are preserved. We cannot see lip eversion and thus lose some measure of nostril flaring, but otherwise, reconstructions can be made rather accurately. Early hominids, the australopithecines, had very flat noses, rather like those of the great apes. One could conclude they did little work of any kind, certainly no hunting that would involve long distance running or even much rapid walking. About the only exertion would be the short and rapid dash to safety when a carnivore threatened, and the body's stored oxygen level would be enough to handle that.

Given the advent of big-game hunting, especially if persistence hunting were the major method, elongated nasal chambers would become adaptive. This is evident in a number of *erectus* skulls where at least the root of the nose is preserved. In the australopithecines the nasal bones had little projection, sometimes even lying entirely behind a line drawn across the front of the cheek bones (malars). In the *erectus* skulls of Chellean and Peking man there is enough of the upper ends of the nasal bones to show a projection of about average modern proportions. I suspect the nose of the Peking reconstruction should have been even higher-bridged than Weidenreich made it.

The contrast in dentitions which serves to narrow the gap between the upper canines seems to be evident very early. Peking teeth clearly have the shoveled incisors like modern Mongoloids. The earliest European dentition in the Heidelberg jaw is already notable for its small teeth relative to the jaw itself and also in comparison to other *erectus* dentitions of comparable date. Each of these cases foreshadows the later *sapiens* conditions in their respective areas which allow for a narrowing of the nasal apertures. In China, the even earlier Lantian jaw is missing its third molar and this may, then as now, be part of the general picture of anterior emphasis in mastication which involves some nasal anatomy as well.

Neandertal dentitions do not fit the European continuum from Heidelberg to the modern inhabitants. For various reasons they look like a foreign interjection, a possibility that will be discussed later. Neandertal incisors are not only shoveled but are quite broad as well. Correspondingly, the skulls had quite broad nasal apertures in spite of the presumably dry winter air. At least two possibilities come to mind to reconcile this apparent contradiction, both of which can be checked against tangible evidence. A vegetarian diet with no serious hunting activity could reduce the need for warming and moistening the inhaled air. To some degree this may have been the case, but only during the critical winter season when it is difficult to see how they could have done much hunting for food anyway. Seasonal distinctions in kill times for big game would settle this issue if such determinations can ever be made.

The other solution for Neandertals would be to increase the front-to-back elongation of the nasal chamber to a remarkable degree. The better preserved skulls show that indeed this was the case. The entire nasal margin is pulled well forward in relation to all adjacent structures giving them what has long been referred to as a muzzle. The nasal bridge is also very high and set well forward. This last point was long overlooked because of faulty reconstruction of the missing nasal bones in the famous La Chapelle skull. These were restored as low and flat and could possibly be fitted into the empty area, evidently on the assumption that they were supposed to be ape-like.

It has recently become the fad to say that Neandertals would pass almost unnoticed on the street if they were shaved and dressed. I doubt this, because of their noses if nothing else. These noses were as broad as most Africans, as high-bridged as most Europeans, and probably more anteriorly projecting than any found today.

In general, early *sapiens* nose forms indicate much the same kinds as are found in their respective areas today. One blank spot is the lack of Pygmy or Negrito skeletons of any great antiquity. This may be partly because this body size has no great antiquity, and it may also be from the lack of many excavations in the areas where they would most likely be found.

EPICANTHIC FOLDS.

About one-third of mankind has long been popularly known to have sloping eyes, but this is not true. The so-called Mongoloid eye is often set forward to some degree but otherwise it is oriented in its socket just like all others. The confusion results from a different design of upper eyelid which covers the inner corner of the eye and lowers its apparent position.

Epicanthic means above the canthus, or corner of the eye. An epicanthic fold is a thickening of the area above the upper eyelid which extends downward over that eyelid, especially at its inner corner nearest the nose (See Fig. 25). The pink, fleshy spot seen in non-Mongoloid eyes at this inner corner is covered and the dividing point between upper and lower eyelids is shifted downward. A line drawn from inner to outer corners of the eye opening thus often appears to slope up to the outside.

The epicanthic fold is composed mainly of fatty tissue and its major effect is to greatly thicken the upper eyelid. A comparable thickening which occurs in the lower eyelid generally goes unnoticed. At least two functions have been suggested, both relating to climatic situations in Arctic climates, the evident homeland of most of the Mongoloid adaptations.

The upper eyelid, even more so than the lower, is a thin structure exposed to the environment with only a modest amount of blood and internal heat generation. The fluid content of the eyeball itself generates no heat. It has been suggested that in extreme cold the eye fluid may cool down and leave the thin eyelid vulnerable between there and the cold exterior. In order to protect it from freezing it is provided with extra thickness of heat-producing and heat-retaining flesh. Against this it can be pointed out that fat produces relatively little metabolic heat. It would require measurement of the internal temperature of the eyeball to verify this idea. In favor of this explanation Mongoloid skiers tell me they don't get ice particles on their eyelashes as their Caucasoid companions do.

The other explanation for the epicanthic fold is that it helps retard the entry into the eye of unwanted radiation, particularly the reflected glare off snow and ice. Ideally, the only light entering the eye is through the pupil, but actually light can pass directly through the eyelids in very lightly pigmented people. Caucasoids are the least protected against such light entry. They can test this simply by closing both eyes, then covering one with a hand and noting how it becomes sensibly darker than the other one. Squinting has a similar effect of cutting down such light entry. People adapted to northern climates

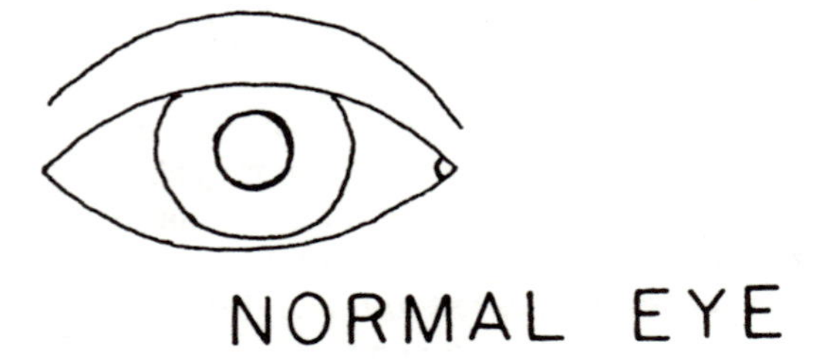

MONGOLOID EYE

FIGURE 25. Epicanthic eye-folds. The thickened upper eyelid adds some insulation and reduces light transmission into the eye. In section, the lid appears thickened with fat and connective tissue, and it droops down to the level of the eye-lashes. In frontal view the free upper eye-lid all but disappears. The inside corner especially is covered and appears lower in position.

will have light skin colors and may need such extra protection for the eyes. An additional complicating factor for light-skinned people is that visible radiation also reflects from the sides of the nose and tops of the cheeks into the eyes, whether open or closed. Caucasoid athletes will sometimes darken these patches to cut down on this reflection. Eskimos, who have some of the best epicanthic folds in the world may find even this protection inadequate. They will sometimes wear snow goggles which cover the eyes with only a horizontal slit to see through.

The epicanthic fold is well developed at the medial and usually in the middle part of the upper eyelid. It does not always extend all the way across to the outside corner in less developed examples. In contrast to this there is the so-called Nordic fold which is a similar down-folding of flesh over the upper eyelid which is common in northern Europe. The Nordic fold mainly covers the central or the lateral part of the upper eyelid, sometimes both, but never the medial part. This kind of eyefold evidently serves the same function and it also occurs commonly among lightly pigmented desert dwellers of the Sahara. A strong occupational selection for Nordic folds has also been evident among Hollywood actors who work under bright lights. The reverse slope it can give to the eye opening is often noticed.

Another contrast between the two kinds of eyefolds is their timing. Epicanthic folds are present in infancy and remain throughout life. Nordic folds generally develop with maturity and get more pronounced in later years, especially among those individuals who consume large amounts of alcohol.

Non-Mongoloid infants often show good epicanthic folds which disappear as they grow up. It has been suggested that the growing nasal bridge pulls up the skin and thus removes at least the inner corner of this fold, and the persisting low bridge of Mongoloids preserves the fold. I have observed two European women with low nasal bridges and good medial epicanthic folds. In each case a simple pinching up of a bit of skin at the root of the nose caused the fold to disappear and the caruncle to be seen. This explanation can apply only to the innermost corner of the fold, and in any case it obviously does not apply to most Africans with low nasal bridges who have no folds at all. This anatomical explanation also will not account for some Mongoloids, such as Plains Indians, who have very prominent noses and sometimes good epicanthic folds as well. At best, the low nasal bridge is only part of the story, the rest is in the eyelid itself.

It might be noted that fat is not notably opaque to visible light and will stop only a small amount of radiation. In response to this it may be pointed out that there seems to be little else structurally available for the purpose, and a little protection is better than none.

The distribution of epicanthic folds is continuous over the northern Mongoloids from Asia to North America. As one follows these people to the south, especially in America, the fold fades out to a less frequent structure but there is usually at least some hint of its presence. This decrease in development is in contrast with the coarse, black hair, the anterior cheek bones, and shoveled incisors, all of which maintain their original intensity as far south as the equator in Asia and far beyond in America. One could assume there is some disadvantage to having an epicanthic fold in the tropics.

There is nothing in the skeleton that directly indicates whether an epicanthic fold was present. Other Arctic adaptations like shoveled incisors and anterior cheeks only suggest a good possibility of the fold, but only if it had evolved by such times. Low nasal bridges, as noted above, are also not good indicators of eyefolds, but in an Arctic environment they would be suggestive. Nordic folds are also not indicated in the skull. Overhanging brow ridges suggest a similar function but this could be taken either way. Given a need for glare protection we could assume that all means, brow ridges and eyefolds alike, would be developed. Or, lacking any kind of eyefold modifications, low brow ridges would be the only mechanism available to reduce the vertical field of vision in manner similar to built-in snow goggles.

COLD ADAPTATIONS.

In addition to the more obvious anatomical variations that relate to cold temperatures there are physiological mechanisms as well. Since these do not involve visible structures they should perhaps not belong here among the classical traits. On the other hand, they do not fit any definition of genetic traits either. Their heredity is unknown in detail and they are not distributed in continental areas as if by drift and founders effect. Physiological cold adaptations are distributed in the appropriate environments and undoubtedly by natural selection.

Such internal modifications have been intensively studied in recent years and much is known about them in certain selected people. Unfortunately for the purposes of this book the world-wide distribution of such variations is very poorly known, so little will be said about them. Internal anatomy requires dissection of many cadavers to learn what the variations are and where they occur in the world. Physiological variations are mostly detected by intensive data collection procedures and by the use of expensive apparatus applied to the subjects. Limitations in money, qualified scientists, and time are obvious deterrents to gaining a world picture of the variations involved.

We do know there are two main categories of cold adaptation, calorie conservative and calorie expensive. In the conservative kind the adaptations are just for moderately cold environments such as those faced by southern Australian natives during winter nights. Such temperatures rarely go below freezing. Blood flow to the extremities is reduced, allowing them to cool off while maintaining the body's core heat. There is also a heat exchange system between the outgoing and incoming blood. Arteries and veins are located close together allowing a transfer of heat from one to the other. This means the outgoing blood is not as warm as it might otherwise have been and so it offers less heat to the extremities. Conversely, the returning blood has picked up some heat from the arteries and is not as cool as it would otherwise be.

These systems decrease heat loss by reducing the temperature gradient from the person's extremities to the environment. It is the most economical way to adapt as long as the cold is not too severe and the risk of frostbite is not there. It also helps if one is not too sensitive about physical discomfort. The calorie-conservative system is found among Australians, Bushmen, and Lapps, but little more is known about its occurrence. For the Australians and Bushmen the adaptation seems obvious for their environments. For the Lapps it seems inadequate for the much greater cold they can encounter. This would argue that the Lapps originally lived to the south in a milder climate and only recently moved to the far north.

The calorie-expensive system is best known among Eskimos, but it also occurs among other northern Mongoloids. Here the body makes the opposite response of sending more blood out to the extremities, when they cool down, in an effort to maintain their temperature as well as possible. This means a great loss of body heat to the environment which must be made up for by metabolizing greater quantities of food. This adaptation is clearly for very much colder climates than the calorie-conservative adaptation could possibly handle. Again, the world-wide distribution of this adaptation is too little known for us to use it as a regular racial characteristic. It is often assumed that it coincides with the Mongoloid race, but this has not been demonstrated.

HEAT ADAPTATIONS.

In addition to the classical anatomical traits there are other physiological adaptations to high temperatures. These are even less understood than the cold adaptations. It is clear that people who live in hot climates, whether damp or dry, are more comfortable than temperate-climate people who move into such areas. This is true even if they have essentially the same obvious physical characteristics. To some degree one can become adjusted to heat, just as to cold and to high altitude. Growing up in a hot climate may also add some adaptations that cannot be acquired later. But we are concerned here only with inherited variations and it is not at all certain which these are. In fact it is still possible that there are no such racial variations.

HIGH ALTITUDE ADAPTATIONS.

Some studies have shown a number of adaptations peculiar to people living in very high altitudes, this meaning generally above 2,500 m. The problem here is simply that of thin air and is solved in a number of ways.

The nasal adaptations were discussed earlier and are clearly inherited traits, but they do not apparently differ from adaptations to cool, dry air at lower altitudes. Enlarged lungs are a different matter and are unique in high altitudes for obvious reasons. There is also a greater volume of blood with far more red corpuscles and a larger heart to pump it. Here we are less certain which are inherited and which are developmental for someone growing up in that environment. Sometimes both may be true in that certain people may develop such traits if they grow up there, and others will not.

Perhaps the only data on this subject that can truly be called racial relates to the problem of oxygen transfer to the fetus. With a low oxygen pressure in the lungs to begin with, each tissue crossing lowers it still farther. The growing fetus is at the far end of the oxygen transfer scale and is the most likely to suffer if it doesn't work perfectly. In the Andes Mountains the native Indians reproduce about as effectively as anyone elsewhere in the world. European women living there generally cannot carry a fetus to term. Indian-European mixtures often can reproduce, and people with only a small fraction of Indian ancestry often can too. Clearly some inherited traits are involved and they have been selected for very powerfully. Still, Indians continue to dominate the racial make-up at high altitudes. At the other extreme it is reported that Negroes cannot reproduce there under any circumstances, and can rarely even live at such high altitudes at all.

The trouble with this kind of racial data on high altitudes is that it is already pooled into the three major races as previously defined. Do all Indians adapt to high altitudes? Do all Europeans have difficulty? Where in Africa did the Negroes come from who couldn't survive? The sources of the information I have drawn from here simply took it for granted that all members of a major race will be as much alike in altitude adaptations as they are in nose forms or skin color. It is just this assumption that is being challenged here. If we had world data on these adaptations this assumption could be tested.

A second source of data on high altitude people is said to largely confirm the observations made on Andean Indians. This consists of examinations made in India on refugees who left Tibet after the Chinese take-over in 1950. One difficulty is that the examinations had to be conducted at lower altitudes and some of the physiological responses may have already become greatly altered. Another possible problem with these studies concerns the ultimate genetic source of the people in question. These refugees included a disproportionate share of the wealthy and politically dominant class of Tibet and who had significant cultural ties to India. It should be established whether some of them might also trace a large part of their biological ancestry to India rather than to the native Tibetans.

SOME ODDS AND ENDS.

It should be obvious that I have been saving the worst for the last in this chapter on classical traits. Many more traits could be discussed, but like those immediately above, our data base on them does not permit serious comparisons with other traits on a truly geographical basis.

Lip eversion is a well-known human variation normally attributed to the Negroids. There are two measures of this, outrolling and exposure of the mucous membrane of the mouth, and thickening of the lips making them stand forward from the teeth. I have been unable to find any serious suggestion as to a possible function for such eversion, nor for its absence. Protruding lips are characteristic of apes, but outrolling is just the opposite of the apes whose lips are thin. Lip eversion is common among African Negroes, but varies greatly from place to place and is less pronounced among Pygmies and Bushmen. Melanesians hardly show it at all. In general, lip eversion is a warm and/or moist climate trait, but its preponderance in Africa has no explanation at present.

A mandibular torus is a thickening of bone on the inside of the lower jaw just under the premolars. This may bulge inward a few mm or much more, almost closing off the space for tongue muscles. It is commonest among Eskimos and other northern Mongoloids and shows in their presumed ancestor, Peking man. But it also occurs among Scandinavians fairly often and I have seen two European students who have good cases of it. There is obviously some connection with Arctic environments and perhaps there is an additional tendency for it to occur among people with an eastern Asiatic ancestry. Beyond that we can say nothing.

Eyeball sizes have been measured in a few cases and it was found that Africans had the largest, Europeans intermediate, and Japanese had the smallest of the three groups. Male eyes were also larger than females' in each case. A not surprising correlation is obtained with lineal body build having the largest eyes and lateral build having the smallest. Temperature adaptations of the ancestral type in each case may also be important. Without a data base along geographical lines no more can be made of this.

Variations in tooth numbers occur in certain populations, at least with certain frequencies. Failure to develop one or more third molars (wisdom teeth) occurs in about 30% of eastern Asians, in about 10% of Europeans, and very rarely elsewhere. Eruption of a fourth molar is a rare event anywhere (I've seen one in a student), but this is commonest among Australian Aborigines. The first wave of eruption of the teeth begins in the front of the mouth with the baby, or milk teeth, and continues eventually through what are questionably called the permanent molars. In each half of each jaw this first wave usually consists of eight teeth, the last one being the wisdom tooth which erupts at 18 years or later. It is a common anomoly for this wave to stop short by one tooth or, more rarely, to continue for one more. Likewise the second set, or replacement wave, begins at the front of the mouth at age seven and runs through five of those teeth in about four years and then quits. This second wave can also stop one short (and we call it a retained milk tooth), or it can go on one more place (and call it a third set of teeth because the tooth it replaced is dubiously called a permanent molar). There are almost surely a number of geographical variations in all this that might prove interesting in their distributions.

Anatomists have noted that certain peoples are unusual for such things as heel projection, depth of hip socket, the "Mongoloid spot" over the sacrum, attached or free ear lobes, freckling, muscles of facial expression, straightness of femur shaft, and many more. Unfortunately these are not known with the kind of data that we could use here. Either too little data is available, or else the data has been pooled into supposed racial categories already.

5.
CLIMATIC RACES

SUMMARY.

The classical traits described in the preceding chapter may be combined in geographic areas to delineate general types of climatic adaptations. In the modern world, and even in the ethnographic present, some of the world's populations have made such major expansions as to badly disrupt much of this correlation between race and climate.

A new base line of about 10,000 years ago is used to describe the natural condition of man prior to agriculture. To establish the distributions of peoples at that time all known and suspected migrations are pulled back to their sources, all relict peoples are expanded as far as seems reasonable, and other blanks filled in by what we know of climate-trait correlations. Rigorous application of some generalized climatic distributions then are seen to delineate nine rather clear-cut climatic races. Variations in temperature, sunlight, and humidity are the major climatic determinants.

The nine climatic races are: Caucasoid, Saharan, Pygmy, Bushman, Mongoloid, Ainu, Negrito, Australoid, and Veddoid. These are mostly well known in spite of the small numbers and limited distributions of some of them. The Saharan is largely a new reconstruction here which had a morphological mix of what are usually thought of as Caucasoid and Negroid traits. Actually the recent Negroids derive mostly from the southern fringe of this climatic race, some mixture with Pygmies, and a good deal of selection since then. An estimate of the numbers of people in each climatic race 10,000 years ago shows Mongoloids were the most numerous, especially with their just-completed populating of the Americas. Between then and now some major alterations in numbers have occurred, with Caucasoids gaining and all others losing in relative standings.

Hunting peoples do not move freely from place to place in large numbers, except into uninhabited areas. When climatic races shifted boundaries during natural times this would have been a process of gene flow and selection. The classical traits themselves can move into new areas but the human base that carries them remains more or less stationary.

Prior to the natural condition, the sapienization process occurred and was evidently an in-place development for the most part. In southern Africa and in eastern Australia there seem to have been exceptions to this rule where fully evolved modern man actually overran large areas of the preceding type with little or no intermixture. Since then, about 40,000 years ago, there have been no differences between human populations where one could be called inherently superior.

Climatic races can be pushed back into pre-*sapiens* times with only a modest degree of confidence and a great deal of shuffling. Skin color variations would have been just as marked among *erectus* populations as today. Variations in body design and nose form existed but were not so extreme as now. Hair-form variations were in the process of developing. For other traits we can only speculate. Racial continuity in terms of classical trait distributions over the last half million years is an approximation only.

ADAPTATION AREAS.

The distributions of the classical traits are all clinal in the sense that they change gradually over distance. The degree of expression of each can be graphed along a line in any direction and it will be found to slope one way or the other. Nevertheless, there will be plateaus and steep places along these clines where trait expression is nearly constant over a great distance and then alters much more rapidly over a short distance. These plateaus are, in effect, what people generally call races and the steep inclines are what may be called race boundaries.

There have been two major forces in the past which have created these plateaus and steep clines, climate adaptations and population expansions. Basically these two have no inherent relationship to each other, but their influences on classical trait distributions are essentially the same. The problem now is to try to separate these two forces and their effects.

For now the effects of population expansions will be removed by the simple expedient of describing the world's trait distributions prior to the development of agriculture. This might be called the "natural" distribution of peoples. This means establishing a new base in time, similar to the sliding concept of the ethnographic present, but much earlier. Approximately 10,000 years ago is the time-line if one wishes to put a date in years on it, but this can vary. For the few remaining hunters this time is still the present. For others it was passed at various dates in the past when they either adopted agriculture or had their lives seriously disrupted by those who had adopted it. By disruption I mean any major change in their locations or in the contents of their gene pools by intermixture.

The date of 10,000 years ago was chosen mainly to exclude the agricultural revolution that began in the eastern Mediterranean area and which has had the most far-reaching effects on human distributions. The natural distributions of people would be their locations before this cereal-grain agriculture had any impact on them. The agricultural development in southeastern Asia, properly called horticulture, may have begun even earlier, but its effects were less dramatic. Root-crop farming increased population levels but it does not appear to have had the same tendency to cause geographical spreads of people. A major reason for this difference lies in the degree of transportability of the agricultural produce. Cereal grains are highly concentrated and nutritious foods that can be stored for years if necessary and transported from place to place. Root crops store poorly as a rule and transporting them includes moving all the water they contain as well. With cereal grains the food is also the seed for a new crop which can be grown in a wide variety of environments with little care. Many root crops are not so easily propagated and are more restricted in where they will grow. The modern practice of carrying dehydrated foods for traveling is only a modest improvement on the cereal-grain principle.

The 10,000 year date also must be adjustable in terms of the retreat of the last glacial ice sheet. Large areas of land were made newly available to human occupation as the ice melted. While the end of the last glaciation is usually put at a thousand years earlier, the full withdrawal of ice cover took somewhat longer in some areas. It could be argued that the natural distribution ought to be placed at the last glacial maximum because of the human movements that took place immediately following it. Such movements included the occupation of areas such as Scandinavia as they became inhabitable. It also included the occupation for the first time (I believe) of most of the New World when the ice barrier across Canada opened to permit human passage. These movements are too recent to have allowed anywhere near full adaptation of the people to their new environments. In the following discussion I will treat these populations differently because of this. The Lapps will be located in Scandinavia but with due allowance for the fact that they are rather recently there. The Americans will be treated as an extension of the Siberian-Alaskan population with only modest adaptations to their new environments.

The natural distribution of man must also take into account a number of cultural adaptations, mainly technological, which have permitted human occupation of certain new environments. Had the base line been placed even earlier, some of these innovations would have to be ruled out and the range of human adaptation would be somewhat less. It is thus somewhat arbitrarily that I have accepted tailored clothing as part of the natural condition of man and have treated tilling the soil as a modern disruption. Actually one could map human racial adaptations and distributions at a number of different times, each illustrating the consequences of a major cultural adaptation that triggered new distributions of people and new physical modifications.

Classical traits are adaptions to the physical environment. Mainly they relate to variations in sunlight, temperature, and humidity. These three climatic features vary somewhat independently of each other and the traits that adapt to them also vary independently. Natural selection will work on the available variation within each local breeding population without regard to whom their distant relatives may be. In terms of classical traits there should be no tendency for broad geographical unity except where the climatic factors themselves tend to be uniform. There are exceptions to this, as will be seen, where the available variation is somewhat governed by connections outside the local gene pool.

For any given trait there will be steep places in its cline of distribution which can be used to mark arbitrary race boundaries. If two or more traits show abrupt changes along the same line the race boundary is all the better and more distinct. These will not be sharp lines simply because climates do not change along sharp lines, but in terms of a world map they are quite sharp enough in most cases. It must be emphasized again that populations located on such transitions are just as natural as those located on each side. The intermediacy resulting from local climatic adaptation does not imply interbreeding between races that are any more real.

These boundaries can be extended until they enclose a large geographic area which may then be termed a climatic race. The traits used to define the boundary can change from place to place, separating by skin color on one side, by hair form on another, and by body size on still another side. The only test of validity applied here is that the people within the racial area tend to be more or less similar and can be distinguished from those found in major areas elsewhere. This does not mean identical expression of the classical traits but merely a relative consistency compared with the range of variation found in the world at large. This means an arbitrary classification which could have its parts combined or split by another observer without doing violence to any biological principle. In short, the climatic races are made by the observer and have no basic biological reality as units.

Climatic races are not gene pools or breeding populations. They need not have any high degree of inbreeding or common ancestry. Their members simply look alike. Why they look alike is from natural selection for the same or similar climatic adaptations and the other considerations are irrelevant in this context. Members of a climatic race may be inbred, but they don't have to be. They may have a common ancestor, but this isn't necessary. They may constitute a gene pool, but few are small enough to do so and it makes no difference anyway. In its simplest terms a climatic race is what most people think of, at least superficially, when they think of race. The first and foremost question to be dealt with is just that—why do the various kinds of people look the way they do?

There is a three-step procedure for reconstructing racial distributions as of 10,000 years ago. This involves withdrawing all known movements, expanding relict populations, and filling blank spaces by analogy with known adaptations.

(1) Correcting for known and suspected population movements of significance since 10,000 years ago (and before the ethnographic present) is largely a matter of pulling people out of areas where their classical traits don't fit the environment and putting them back to where they do fit. The major examples will be summarized here.

Southern Mongoloids in southeastern Asia and Indonesia must be moved to the north into Arctic climates of central Asia and/or Siberia. Most of the population of China and Japan must also be returned to central Asia. The Arabic people of northern Africa are not original there and should be moved back to perhaps the eastern edge of the Mediterranean. Much of India's lighter-skinned population should go back some distance to the northwest. The entire Bantu people must leave southern and central Africa to a homeland in the northwestern corner of their present area. Then these original Bantus and all others of western Africa should probably move northward about 600 km to a location just out of the rain forests. A major element of the European population should move home to the eastern Mediterranean, but here the racial difference is minor enough that it can almost be ignored. The Polynesians, Micronesians, and Melanesians (in part) must go back to the Asian mainland. All this will strip much of the world bare.

(2) Small populations could not have evolved their climatic adaptations with their present numbers. They are relicts of once larger populations which had both the time and the numbers to become what they are. When recent intrusions of other people are removed the next step is to expand such relicts so that they contact one another and fill

the intervening spaces. One then can theoretically expand them still farther until they fill the entire climatic zone in which they are found and to which they appear adapted.

The clearest example will be the Negritos who can be expanded to fill all the Indonesian area and a fair amount of mainland southeastern Asia. Larger Papuans fill the areas vacated by the removal of the true Melanesians, but this involves little change. A greater change would be the physical reduction of these Papuans to Negrito body size before agriculture. This would appear to be a logical step, although one is reluctant to take it without corroborating evidence.

In Africa the equivalent expansion of Pygmies would fill the central forest area, and by logical extension they should also be postulated as the natural inhabitants of the western African forests as well. To the south, Bushmen would be expanded to fill the entire southern part of the continent and probably the east horn area as well.

In Europe the Lapps should occupy all of Scandinavia, at least. The rest of Europe was probably not affected enough in terms of classical traits to require any adjustment. In eastern Asia, where the climate is similar to that of Europe, the Ainus must be expanded to fill areas vacated by the Japanese. By climate analogy they must also expand into Korea and into the eastern half of China as well.

Veddoids would probably be the natural population of India and Bangladesh, as well as Ceylon (Sri Lanka). Pakistan could remain part of the western area of Caucasoids. There would be no population adjustments in the Americas simply because the contrasts in classical traits would be too small to be noticed.

(3) Filling in further empty spaces does not prove to be a major problem in most of the areas discussed above. In all cases there was a relict population in or adjacent to the places that would be vacated by migration withdrawals. The relict could be expanded to fit the entire area in question with reasonable adherence to the ideas of which traits are adapted to which climates.

There may be some surprise over the concept proposed here of the greater Ainu climatic race occupying so much of eastern Asia. Implicit in this is the assumption that Ainus are not a Caucasoid interjection that somehow migrated to Japan as many people think. All the basic climatic conditions in this part of eastern Asia are essentially the same as those which are found in most of Europe. Given enough time for local adaptations the natural population should have come to acquire basically the same classical traits in each area. The modern Ainu live within the area in question and have traits that are rather Caucasoid in their superficial appearance. If they actually are Caucasoid intruders from the European area then they must have replaced a population that looked pretty much like themselves anyway.

In the rest of the greater Ainu area it is difficult to say exactly what the people should have looked like, but light skins and lots of wavy hair are easy to predict. No epicanthic folds would be expected and bodies ought to be medium to large with neither extreme of lineal or lateral build. Noses would be fairly prominent, but only as narrow as tooth size would permit. Light hair and eyes would be possible and would be interesting if they occurred, but lacking any good corroborative evidence for them I would not seriously suggest it. The northern and western boundaries of the greater Ainu would grade into the true Mongoloid peoples with their extreme cold adaptations. The southern boundary would grade into the Negrito type as skins became darker, bodies smaller, noses blunter, and hair more curly. From somewhere along the China coast the ancestors of the Polynesians could easily have been drawn with the appropriate classical traits.

The natural inhabitants of the Sahara and Arabia are the biggest blank spot in this whole scheme. In spite of suggestions there is no solid evidence of a Bushman population for this area. By the rules given here the natural classical traits can be predicted. They would be tall and lineal in build, skins would be very dark or black, hair and eye color would also be dark, and hair form should be curly. Noses ideally should be fairly tall and prominent, and also narrow if the tooth size permitted, as I suspect it would to some degree. People fitting this description can be found in parts of eastern Africa, and many of the characteristics are common along the southern fringe of the Sahara itself. The most novel part of this description is the combination of Negroid skin characteristics with a mainly Caucasoid skull, topped with curly hair, and put on a very lineal body. Actually this trait combination should be no surprise for this area in view of what is known about climatic adaptations. What is surprising is the nearly total demise of this type under pressure of agriculturalists from both north and south.

Since there is only modest direct evidence to support this Saharan climatic race it should not be taken as a proven fact. The evidence for a native Bushman type has been presented by Carleton Coon and cannot easily be ignored. While I cannot see a Bushman adaptation at an early date in northern Africa, an intrusion of their type shortly prior to agriculture remains a distinct possibility. In general, the Bushman adaptations are unusual and therefore would be more recent than those of the Saharans as postulated here. I would expect that if given enough time these Bushman adaptations would spread, by gene flow and selection rather than invasion, into all accessible environments where they would be useful. Only the fact that the most direct descendants of the Saharans live in eastern Africa makes one doubt that the Bushman type could have made major inroads through just that area.

None of the other relict expansions and population reconstructions seem to pose any great problems. There are many fine points in this picture so far that I have run over rough-shod. Some of these will be touched on later and some will not. Many details will be ignored simply because there is no possibility of treating comparable details over the whole world with the same degree of care. The intent here is to draw the picture of climatic races in broad outline, and carry it only a short distance toward the detailed end of the scale, and stop at a uniform level.

WESTERN RACES.

A somewhat systematic and graphic approach will now be followed in presenting the correlation between race and climate. For the first step the western half of the Old World, consisting mainly of Europe and Africa, will be looked at in terms of climatic differences along a north-south line. This line is drawn from Lappland to Capetown and passes through all the major climatic zones and, presumably, the climatic races of the two continents. It might be referred to as the western axis (See Fig. 26).

This western axis is divided into a series of roughly equal sections named after various major geographical features, both physical and cultural. From north to south they read: Scandinavia, Europe, Mediterranean, Sahara, Sudan, Congo, Angola, and Kalahari. Along this axis three graphs of climatic features can be drawn, showing temperature, sunshine, and humidity (See Fig. 27). These are the three most influential in determining classical traits. Steep places on these climatic clines should correspond to steep places on trait clines in the natural distribution of 10,000 years ago. If some reasonably good agreement between even two of the three clines can be found on which to draw race boundaries, then there would be some descriptive reality to races drawn on these lines.

The temperature graph (Fig. 27a) is shown as two lines, one for summer and one for winter. I suspect the winter temperature would be by far the most critical determinant of body size and shape, especially in the higher latitudes. Towards the equator the summer temperature becomes the more critical but there is little variation in this area. There are no very steep places on this graph. Although the extremes are greatly different, any race lines based on this would be rather arbitrary and there would be a strong clinal distribution of body size

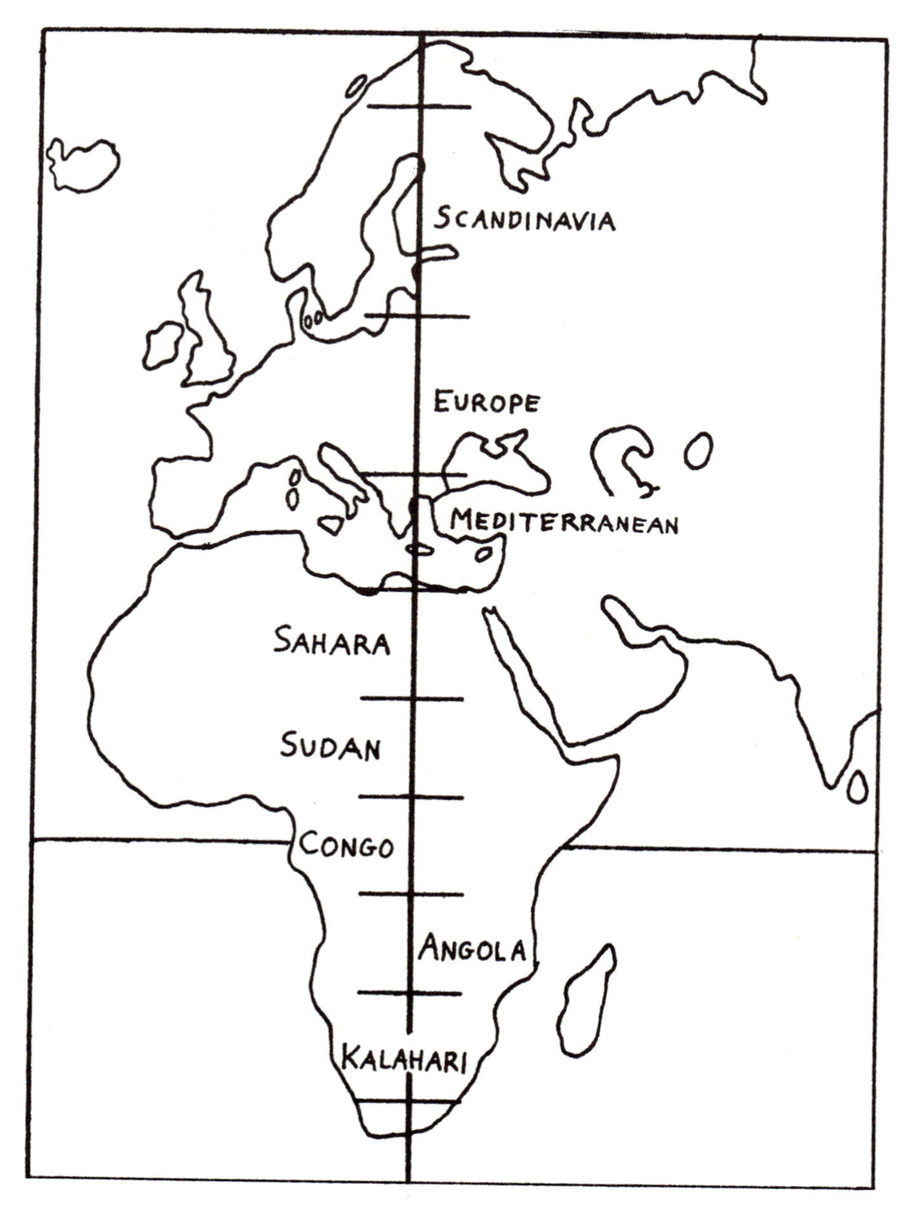

FIGURE 26. Racial axis in the western Old World. Along this north-south line from Scandinavia to South Africa are plotted the climatic curves of temperature, sunshine, and humidity (Fig. 27) which largely determine the variations in classical traits. The axis is divided into eight equal zones of 12½ degrees latitude which are named for notable geographic features. The four climatic races occupy regions along this axis, each consisting of from one to three of the geographic zones.

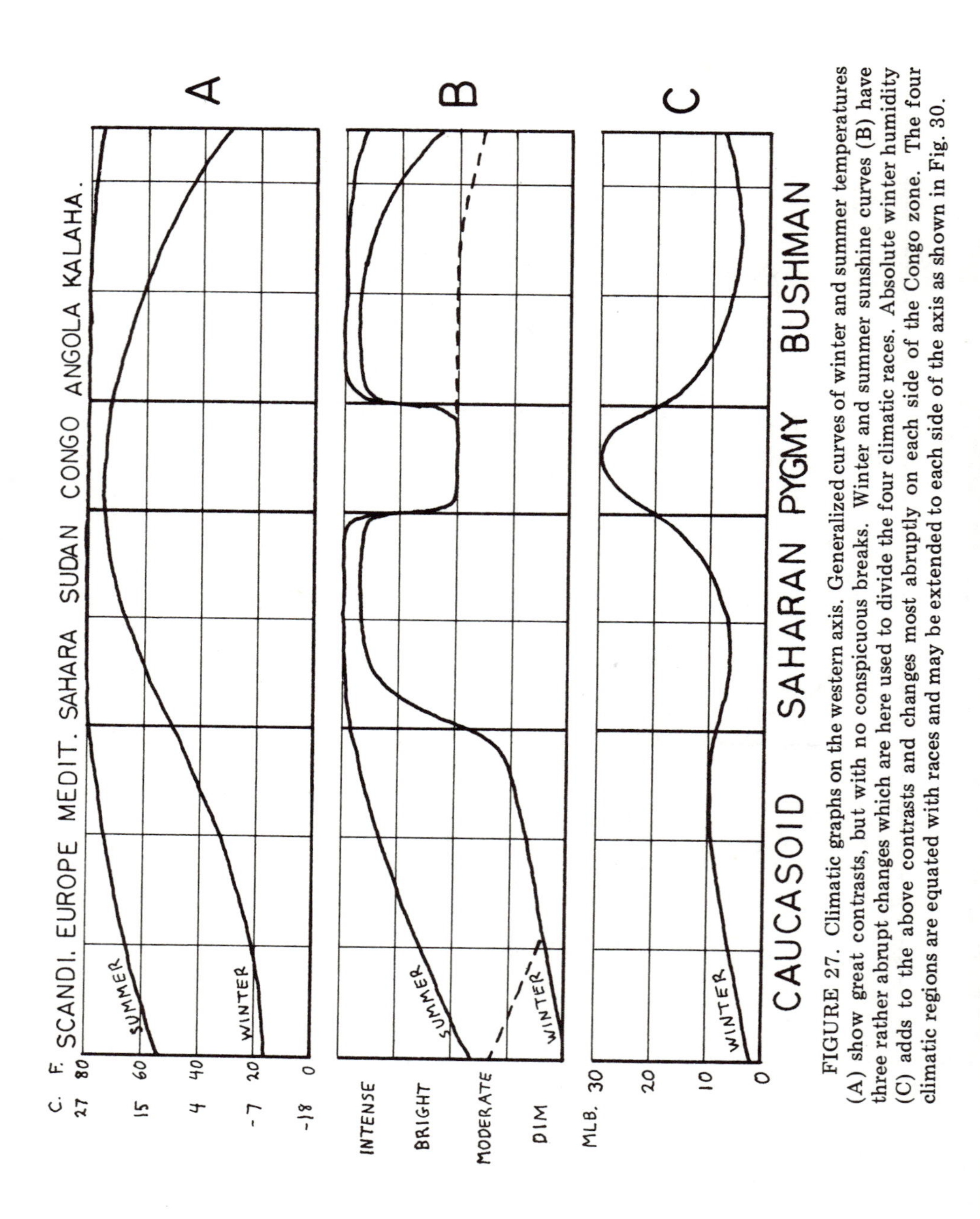

FIGURE 27. Climatic graphs on the western axis. Generalized curves of winter and summer temperatures (A) show great contrasts, but with no conspicuous breaks. Winter and summer sunshine curves (B) have three rather abrupt changes which are here used to divide the four climatic races. Absolute winter humidity (C) adds to the above contrasts and changes most abruptly on each side of the Congo zone. The four climatic regions are equated with races and may be extended to each side of the axis as shown in Fig. 30.

and/or shape within any such races. This graph will also have some bearing on nose shapes but a later one will be more critical. Hair form should follow the temperature line, but again it calls for no especially clear breaks by itself. While no race lines can be based on this temperature graph it can serve as descriptive support for races delineated on other criteria. The pertinence for including it will also become evident when it is compared with its equivalent graph for the eastern axis.

The graph of sunshine intensity shown in Fig. 27b is also divided into winter and summer lines. These are scaled rather subjectively into categories of intense, bright, moderate, and dim, and are very generalized. They are based, in part, on the theoretical maximum of sunlight at each latitude in each season, and further modified by two local conditions which are rather outstanding. One of these is the winter cloud cover that affects much of the north, down to and including the Mediterranean area, and abruptly stopping there. The other is the dense vegetational cover in the tropical rain forest area which drastically reduces sunlight intensity at ground level in that region throughout the year. All other areas receive roughly the expectable amount of sunlight.

These sunlight curves also indicate ultraviolet intensity and human skin colors may be expected to follow them. The theoretical ideal would be a base level of melanin production paralleling the winter radiation curve and a tanning capacity that will make up the difference from that to the summer curve. To a large degree this is indeed the case. The quantity of tanning in the three northern zones is the greatest, and it has long been noted that this reaches its maximum around the Mediterranean.

The amount of sunlight reaching the ground in the tropical forest is actually lower than indicated on the graph. People living in such dim light would nevertheless be exposed to direct sunlight at least on occasion and a compromise skin-color expectation is about where the line is drawn. The Pygmies of Africa have the melanin level that seems most reasonable for this region as long as they spend the vast majority of their time well shaded.

The Pygmy color line is extended through the next two zones to the south as a dashed line which represents the actual melanin level that occurs there. Here the explanation is entirely different, as it is the thicker stratum corneum of the Bushman that permits a lower-than-expected melanin level in the skin. If it weren't for this local specialization their skin colors would have to have been much darker, just as they are to the north. The similar melanin level in both Pygmies and Bushmen may suggest an extension of the Pygmy type in some kind of mass expansion to the south. This has already been argued quite independantly on the basis of hair form. Although Pygmy and Bushman skin colors differ in other respects there may be some support here for a central African origin of the native southern Africans. This cannot be pushed too far because body sizes don't work out.

The earliest *sapiens* in southern Africa were full-sized people, and they are the presumed replacing population with peppercorn hair. Yet the thicker stratum corneum with its greater insulating qualities is an adaptation which we presume only rather small people can well afford, especially if they don't have to work very hard. The small size is recent, and if poison use was a factor, so is the relief from wielding powerful weapons of the hunt. If the earliest, full-sized Bushmen did in fact have modest melanin content in their thick skins, this alone would have introduced a selective pressure toward smaller size (or linearity) quite independently of the kinds of weapons they used. At the moment this uncertainty will have to remain.

The darker base line in the far north, though little applicable to Europeans, is indicated by the dashed line coming out of the winter sunshine curve and rising as it moves northward. When vitamin D can no longer be obtained from sunlight-triggered synthesis then it must be added to the diet in the form of sundried meats which are stored for winter consumption. This then permits a rising base level for winter melanin content. It leaves the summer ideal color unchanged.

This sunshine graph has three conspicuous steep places on its clines that serve to separate four major regions of skin-color adaptation. The first three zones, Scandinavia, Europe, and Mediterranean are very similar in their adaptation. Base level melanin is low and tanning ability is very high in all of them. This serves as the first delineation of what might be called the Caucasoid climatic race. Within it there is a strong north to south gradient, but that is insignificant when compared with the abrupt change in base color at its southern border.

For the zones of Sahara and Sudan the basic melanin level is high and the tanning margin is minimal. This drops off abruptly at its southern edge. These zones may be combined to constitute the largely theoretical Saharan climatic race.

The Congo zone of tropical rain forest is a major region by itself. It has a low intensity of sunlight at ground level and is demarcated both north and south by the higher intensity of radiation in more open country. The name Pygmy will be retained for the climatic race of its natural inhabitants.

Angola and Kalahari combine to form a region with a sunshine level about the same as that of northern Africa. At some distant time in the past its inhabitants were likely the same color as the Saharans, but more recently they have had a yellowish-brown coloration. The Bushmen serve as the model for this climatic race. It is not known, however, when they acquired their unusual skin-color adaptation. Interestingly, the region has now returned to its presumed ancient skin color as a result of the Bantu expansion based on agriculture.

The northernmost zone of the Caucasoid climatic race, that of Scandinavia, is interesting for the expected reversal of the skin-color cline. It could be argued that another climatic race should be based on this zone. I would prefer not to do so on the basis of the degree of change involved. Natural Scandinavians would be no darker in basic skin color than the Mediterraneans who are also included in the Caucasoid climatic race. If the adaptation ideals of the Scandinavian zone were more extreme, and if people had lived there long enough to develop them, then a separate climatic race would be justified. This is just what happens at the northern end of the eastern axis.

The humidity curve shown in Fig. 27c is also very useful although its divisions are not so abruptly marked as in the sunshine graph. In this case only the minimum season of humidity is shown, January in the northern hemisphere and July in the southern. This is a graph of absolute humidity only, which is expressed in terms of millibars of water vapor pressure. All else being equal, the nasal index will vary directly with this atmospheric water level. Since all else is not equal, this graph is only an approximation of the index.

Natural nose forms would appear to divide themselves into three regions, broad noses in the humid center with narrower noses to both the north and south. The dividing lines are not very sharp because the clines slope gently. There is no distinction here between the Caucasoid and Saharan climatic races, but there might be if other factors were considered. The northern zones of colder temperature have led to larger bodies and an additional task for the nasal chamber to warm the inhaled air. Both these factors would lead to relatively narrower and more projecting noses in the Caucasoid region than in the Saharan, in spite of what this graph alone would suggest. Even so, no sharp dividing line would appear, and it is the skin color more than anything that locates this line.

The humidity change in the Congo zone is the most marked here. Even if the natural inhabitants of this equatorial region were of normal body size their noses would be notably broad and nonprojecting. This is the case with the modern Negro peoples who live there. The Pygmy nose form takes this to an extreme because of the added influence of very small body size.

South of the Congo zone, the Angola and Kalahari zones can be combined and here would call for more projecting noses. As with skin color and hair form one could postulate as very ancient population that used to fit these climate-dictated predictions. In this case some late *erectus* skeletal material supports the predicted nose type along with the large body. The rather broad and flat Bushman nose follows from their small body size. To what degree they owe their smallness to Pygmy connections remains uncertain, but we do know that if they entered as the first *sapiens* the small size had not yet been evolved.

Four climatic races have now been postulated from the three major climatic variables plotted along the north-south length of the western axis. Their lateral extent to the west and east can now be drawn on the map by simply following these same major climatic variables as closely as possible. It should now be more than obvious just how sharply these climatic races are bounded from each other. While they differ profoundly in classical traits between their centers, and tend toward some uniformity within each, their boundaries grade only gradually into one another.

Before giving a general summary of the major classical traits of these four western races it would be best to follow this same procedure in the eastern half of the Old World. With this, and a little filling in between, we will have a picture of all the climatic races as of 10,000 years ago.

EASTERN RACES.

The eastern axis can be drawn from north to south through eastern Asia at about the longitude of Manila as far as the equator, then it shifts east by 10° to run the rest of the way south through Australia (See Fig. 28). This puts the line over water along much of its course but our attention and descriptions will concentrate on the adjacent land masses, mainly to the west of the line. The geographic zones are named here, from north to south: Siberia, Manchuria, Northern China, Southern China, Philippines, Indonesia, Carpentaria (from the Gulf of), Australia, and Tasmania. These are divided to correspond exactly with the latitudes of the zones along the western axis. The only differences are that the Siberian zone extends somewhat farther to the north, and an additional zone is added at the southern end.

The winter and summer temperature curves shown in Fig. 29a give a picture similar to that along the western axis, except that they tend to be a bit lower. This is especially evident in the winter temperatures to the north which are much colder. There are no particularly steep places along these clines, but over considerable distances the effects of temperature adaptation will be extreme. As in the west, this will affect body size and shape, hair form and type, and nose shape to some degree.

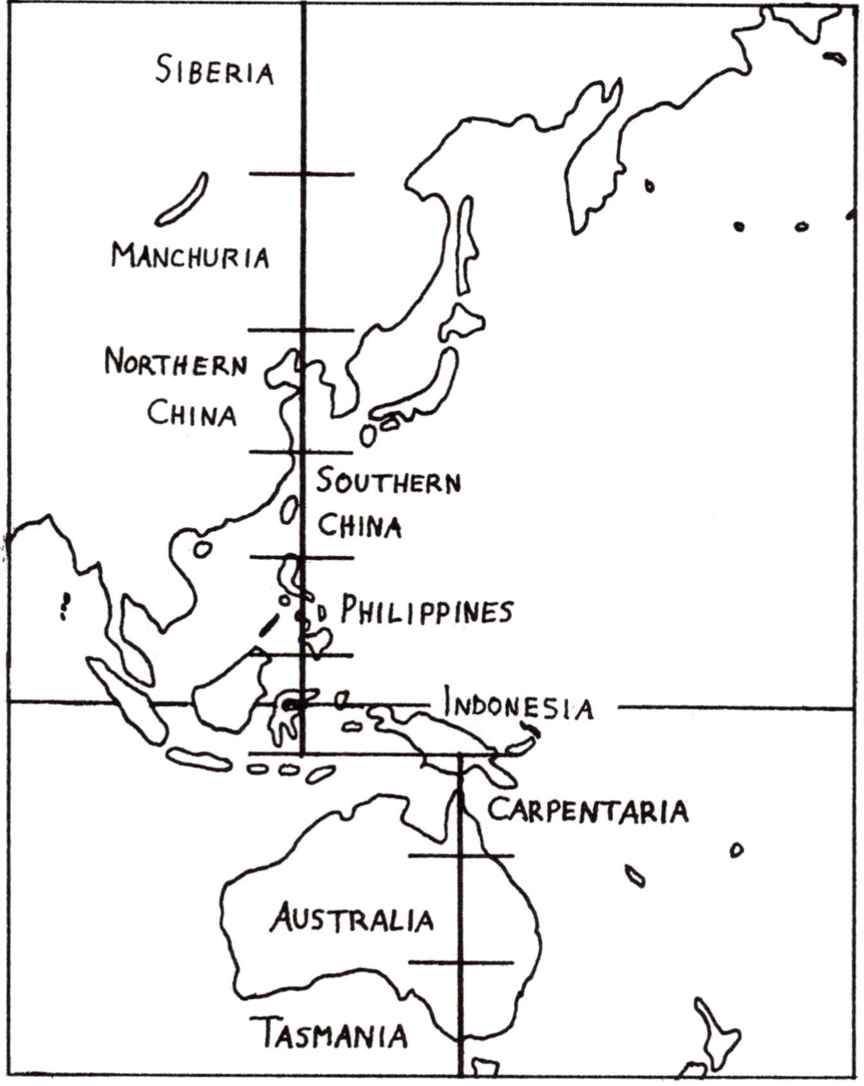

FIGURE 28. Racial axis in the eastern Old World. Along this north-south line from Siberia to Tasmania are plotted the climatic curves of temperature, sunshine, and humidity (Fig. 29) which largely determine the variations in classical traits. The axis is divided into nine equal zones of 12½ degrees latitude, one more than in the west, which are named from notable geographic features. The four climatic races of the eastern world occupy regions along this axis, each consisting of from one to three of the named zones. The axis is shifted to the east in its lower part in order to include Australia. It is drawn in part over water, but refers mainly to the adjacent land masses.

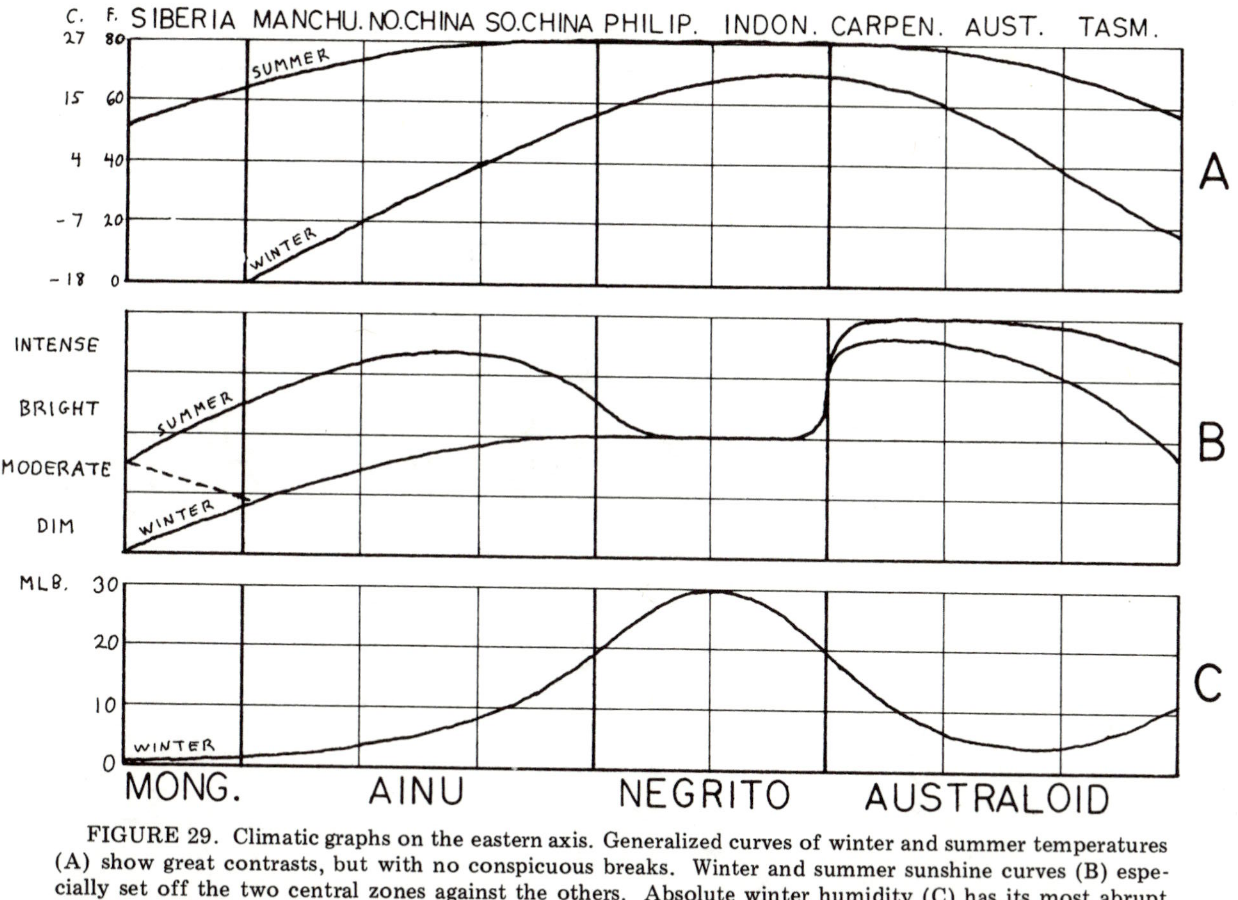

FIGURE 29. Climatic graphs on the eastern axis. Generalized curves of winter and summer temperatures (A) show great contrasts, but with no conspicuous breaks. Winter and summer sunshine curves (B) especially set off the two central zones against the others. Absolute winter humidity (C) has its most abrupt changes bordering the same two zones. The four climatic regions are equated with races and may be extended to each side of the axis as shown in Fig. 30.

In Fig. 29b the summer and winter solar radiation curves show only a partial similarity to those along the western axis. The major difference follows from the fact that there is no desert on this line that compares with the Sahara. This means there isn't a high intensity sunlight zone north of the equator that lasts all year.

The Siberian zone has the same dashed line added to the winter sunlight line as in the west. This represents the addition of vitamin D in the diet and the cessation of selective pressure for the lightest skin color. This zone was apparently inhabited for a much longer time in this area than it was in Europe because it was not entirely covered with ice during the last glaciation. Adaptation to this condition, and also to the greater extreme of winter cold, has led to enough physical distinctions here for us to treat it as a major region whose natural inhabitants will be called the Mongoloid climatic race. This race has far greater geographical extent than would appear from the single climatic zone given to it here. The interior of much of Asia to the west and southwest has much area of high altitude, and a continental climate that also provides comparably cold winters and which elicit the same or similar adaptations.

The next three zones, Manchuria, northern China, and southern China can be united into a single region. The expected base level of melanin would be medium to light and with a high degree of added tanning ability. These three zones have only a modest amount of change within them, with summer sunlight peaking in the center zone, and winter sunlight gradually increasing toward the south. The natural inhabitants of this region 10,000 years ago ought to have looked rather similar to the Caucasoids in many of their classical traits, because the climates are so similar. This eastern region extends a full zone farther south, while the European region includes a zone to the north, but they overlap by two full zones, or 25° of latitude. In the east the base level of melanin should overlap that of Europe, but should average somewhat more. Tanning ability would be comparable. With the exception of the Ainus of northern Japan this entire region is now inhabited by peoples obviously not originally adapted to this climate. The inescapable implication is that these Ainus are just a small remnant of a climatic race that was once much more wide-spread. Accordingly, this is called the Ainu climatic race and the people will be referred to at times as the greater Ainu to distinguish them from their modern descendants.

The next two zones, Philippines and Indonesia, together show a strong similarity to the Congo zone of the west. There is the same reduced sunlight over most of the region from the tropical rain forest, though here it is not so continuous as in Africa. Summer and winter show no significant difference in sunlight intensity except on the northern boundary where it grades into the Ainu region. It might be noted that this boundary is a full zone north of where it is in Africa and it grades into a European-like climate directly, without the intervening region of desert as in the west. To the south the border is more like in the west where both winter and summer sunshine increase sharply in the open desert conditions. Negritos represent the natural inhabitants of this equatorial region as of around 10,000 years ago, and they constitute a climatic race very similar to their counterparts in Africa, the Pygmies.

The last three zones of Carpentaria, Australia, and Tasmania, have a sunlight pattern like that of southern Africa and inversely like that found in northern Africa. The expected skin colors are encountered here, a dark base level of melanin tapering off somewhat to the extreme south, and with a high level of tanning throughout. Actually this is the only one of the three such desert areas that now shows the "proper" skin colors. In southern Africa the Bushman's special skin superseded whatever may have been there earlier. In northern Africa only part has the "proper" color and the rest has been recently overrun by people of lighter color who are able to shield their skins from the sunlight with clothing. These last three zones can be combined into the Australian region and its native inhabitants called the Australoid climatic race.

As suggested earlier, the forested east coast strip of Australia was evidently once overrun by Melanesian peoples as far to the south as Tasmania. These have been largely absorbed except for the Tasmanians themselves, who were cut off when rising sea levels separated their island from the mainland. This invasion was presumably by early *sapiens,* just as the equivalent invasion in southern Africa, and it occurred prior to the body-size reduction that later characterized the Negritos. This left a population rather badly out of place in terms of the climate to which they were originally adapted. Temperatures were lower, but sunlight intensity was not far off since they came from a shaded tropical rain forest in the first place. Body design, hair form, and nose form were not proper. But the area was so small and contained so few people that suitable mutations had not appeared before they were discovered and exterminated by Europeans.

The curve of absolute humidity in the minimum season is shown in Fig. 29c. Just as in the west, this one serves mainly to demarcate the equatorial region, here inhabited by Negritos with their very high nasal indices. The slopes of this cline are also not very steep, so sharp limits can not be set on this basis alone.

In the Siberian zone the air is drier than in Scandinavia and the

Mongoloid noses there are narrow. In the greater Ainu region of three zones, noses should show increasing width toward the south. Skeletal evidence of early peoples would agree with this expectation, and the recently arrived Mongoloid invaders also show adaptation to this humidity with broader noses than in the north.

Negrito noses are broad not only because of the humidity, but also because of their small body size. The Australian region should show broad noses in the north, grading into narrow ones in the extreme south. They actually remain fairly broad throughout, with only a modest change toward the south, evidently because the teeth are too large to permit much narrowing of the nasal aperture. Noses do get more prominent in the south as might be expected.

We now have four climatic races along the eastern axis of the Old World, which are defined by methods similar to those used in the west. The races are not the same, only the Pygmy-Negrito equation is really close. The Australoid race is somewhat similar to that reconstructed for northern Africa. The Caucasoid and greater Ainu overlap in some traits. The Mongoloid is unique to the eastern area as its Lapp equivalent scarcely exists. The Bushman is almost totally unique.

The geographical extent, west to east, of the four races along the eastern axis can be drawn following the climatic zones as closely as possible. These are shown in Fig. 30, along with those in the west, and of course some boundaries are problematical as well as vague. The Tasmanians don't seem to belong anywhere, except possibly with the Papuans of New Guinea who may have been both reduced in body size and then grown large again since the Tasmanians separated. In any case, the Tasmanians are not of small size, and so represent a proto-Negrito type. Whether the eastern coast of Australia belongs in the Negrito region as of 10,000 years ago is also unclear, even if we had some way of knowing what the people there looked like then. For now I will leave it all labeled Australoid. Just how far to the north on the Asian mainland the Negrito line went cannot now be determined. On the basis of climate I'm giving them Indochina, Thailand, and Burma. They should also have a claim to Taiwan and the southern China coast, but these are small areas and the overwhelming numbers to the north would provide so much gene flow that modest selection pressure might not have been enough to maintain the type there. The Negrito extent to the west has been arbitrarily cut off at the modern boundary of India. Had they extended into India the similarity of environment is such that they should have occupied most of that land and would have left their remnants today. There are no such remnants, nor are there elsewhere on mainland southeastern Asia, except in Malaya. It is fairly certain that Negritos did not reach

India, but whether they even approached that border may never be known.

The boundary of the greater Ainu region is fairly straightforward, even if fuzzy in its exact position. It stops to the west and north where winter temperatures get severe. Beyond this is the region of the Mongoloid homeland, the largest of the climatic races in terms of total area, because it includes most of the heartland of Asia.

OTHER RACES.

There are some parts of the world which are not adequately covered by the eight climatic races described along the two north-south axes. There are also some small populations which exist but cannot easily be fitted into the scheme so far. Only one of these will here be ranked as a climatic race of its own, but a case could possibly be made for others.

Bringing the western and eastern climatic race boundaries together in most of Asia is no problem. Caucasoids and Mongoloids meet on a broad front and merge rather gradually, making the placement of the dividing line somewhat arbitrary. To the south, in India, the situation is quite different. Caucasoid types which anatomically border on being Saharans will extend through Pakistan and stop there. Negritos from the east may have been the type as far to the west as Burma, but no farther. This leaves the Indian peninsula unaccounted for. The most obvious answer is that the Veddas are the remnants of the natural inhabitants of the region. In terms of classical traits they form something of a bridge between west and east, as might also be expected from their location. They are too dark, too small, and too broad nosed to be included among the Caucasoids. They are too large, too straight haired, and too prominent of nose to be Negritos. Some have called them dwarfed Australoids, and this may be closer to the truth than merely descriptive. The Veddoids would then be race number nine which now completes this inventory of climatic races of 10,000 years ago.

If another climatic race were to be added it would be the native Americans, or Amerindian. As of the ethnographic present their distinctions from the Mongoloids are fairly clear, but are only a matter of degree. They show the Mongoloid cold-weather adaptations for the most part and can thus be considered merely a massive geographic extension of that climatic race. It was just a fortuitious circumstance that the first connection from the Old World to the New World was from the tip of Siberia and not from Europe or from somewhere else.

The Mongoloid character of the Amerindians was probably clearer 10,000 years ago than it is today. Some of the cold-weather adaptations have been toned down in the new climates of the Americas while selection for them was progressed in the original direction among the Mongoloids proper. The dividing line today puts the recently intrusive Eskimos on the Mongoloid side and all Amerindians in the other group. The Mongoloid-American distinction is reminiscent, in terms of degree, of that which distinguishes the Lapps from the Caucasoids. Also it is not logically possible to call the Amerindians another climatic race, because there is not one climate to which they all show adaptations. Given enough time they might have developed into a number of different climatic adaptations, but this was cut short much too early, one hundred thousand years too early at the very least. About all they share in common, aside from their Mongoloid affinities, is that these Mongoloid affinities are not all as clear-cut as might be desired. It does not seem advisable to define a climatic rate on some degree of lack of adaptations.

The inhabitants of Oceania have been given major race status in some classifications, but that is not possible here because they mostly did not exist at the time-line in question. Micronesia and Polynesia were occupied only in the last few thousand years. Melanesia is partly recent and partly ancient, and here the distinction between Papuans and Melanesians may be important. Papuan is mainly a linguistic distinction of the non-Austronesian speakers in New Guinea and some of the larger islands to the east. The Melanesians, linguistically, are an overlay of sea travelers who are related to the other Oceanic peoples, and who have occupied most of the coastal regions. They have so mixed with the original Papuans as to be physically almost indistinguishable from them today. Although we generally use the term Melanesian for this physical type today, it is really the Papuans who are the source of it. Only these Papuans have any great antiquity in the region. They are not treated as a separate climatic race but are just the eastern-most extension of the Negritos. It is assumed here, without clear evidence, that the Papuans were reduced in size along with the other Negritos before the introduction of agriculture.

RACE DESCRIPTIONS.

A summation of the characteristics of the nine climatic races as of 10,000 years ago is given here for the sake of direct reference. Their geographical ranges are shown in Fig. 30.

(1) Caucasoid: Skin color was light with a high tanning capacity, and graded to medium in the south. Light eyes and hair were common and possibly universal. Cranial hair form ranged from straight to wavy, and body and facial hair was relatively abundant. Bodies were large,

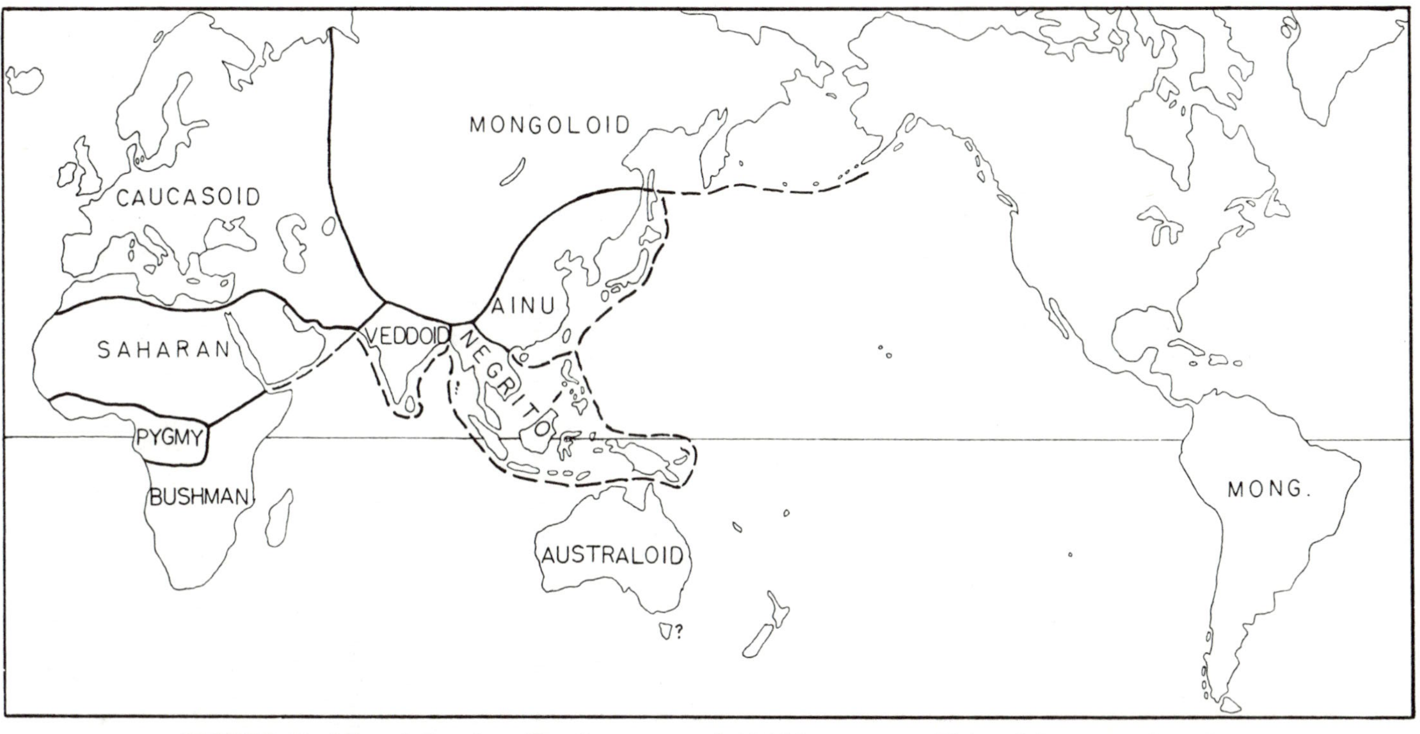

FIGURE 30. Map of the nine climatic races as of 10,000 years ago. Eight of these races have been defined from the climatic regions shown in Figs. 26 and 27 for the western part, and in Figs, 28 and 29 for the eastern part, of the Old World. The Veddoid climatic race was added to fill in the central gap. These nine races handle the major variations in classical traits in their areas of adaptation prior to the development of agriculture.

especially toward the north, and body build was about medium. Noses were tall, narrow, and prominent. Nordic eye-folds were common in the north.

(2) Saharan: Skin color was very dark with a medium fringe on the northern edge. Dark eyes and hair were universal. Cranial hair was wavy or curly with tight spiraling only in the extreme south. Body and facial hair were probably scant. They were fairly tall with lineal body builds. Noses were generally tall, narrow and prominent. Larger teeth to the south probably masked some nasal prominence and led to wider flaring of the nostrils. Everted lips may have added to this. There was no development of eye-folds.

(3) Pygmy: Skin color was mostly about medium, depending on local vegetation cover. Eyes and hair were dark. Cranial hair was all peppercorn. Facial hair was scant, but body hair may have been fairly well developed to judge from some recent observations. Stature was the shortest in the world, and body build about medium. Noses were short, very broad, and projected little. Prognathism and some lip eversion led to exaggerated nasal breadth. There were no eye-folds.

(4) Bushmen: Skin color was medium, often yellowish-brown with a thick stratum corneum. Eye and hair color were dark or black. Cranial hair was peppercorn, and facial and body hair were scant. They had small bodies, but not as small as the Pygmies, and body build was medium. Noses were short, broad, and flat, but again not so extreme as with the Pygmies. Eye-folds were common, epicanthic and Nordic were both evident, but not extremely developed.

(5) Veddoid: Skin color was generally medium to dark depending on local vegetation cover. Eye and hair color were dark. Cranial hair was wavy or curly, and facial and body hair about medium. They had rather small bodies, like Bushmen, and medium body build. Noses were fairly broad and short, but more prominent than in Bushmen or Pygmies. There were no eye-folds.

(6) Mongoloid: Skin color was light, but not extremely so. Eye and hair color were uniformly dark. Cranial hair was straight and of larger diameter than others, making it stiffer. Facial and body hair were much reduced. Body sizes were fairly large but with short stature and a lateral build. Noses were tall and narrow, but projection was largely masked by anterior cheeks. Epicanthic eye-folds were well developed. Amerindians are a toned-down version of this race.

(7) Ainu: Skin color ranged from light in the north to medium in the south. Eye and hair color were presumably all dark, but this is not certain. Hair form was generally wavy, but probably was curly in the south, and body and facial hair were abundant. Noses were about medium in all respects, but were narrower and more prominent to-

wards the north. Probably they had no development of either kind of eye-folds, but this is uncertain.

(8) Negrito: Like the Pygmies they had medium skin, dark in some areas, dark eyes and hair, and peppercorn hair form with little hair on the body. Size was as small as Pygmies, at least in some areas, and body build about average. Noses were short, wide, and flat, but usually not so extreme as in Africa. There was no indication of eye-folds.

(9) Australoid: Skin color was dark but ranging toward medium in the south with more tanning ability. Eyes were uniformly dark, but blond hair may already have become common in the desert areas. Cranial hair was curly in the north and wavy in the south, and facial and body hair were rather abundant. Bodies were full-sized and had a lineal build in the north and a more average build in the south. Because of their large teeth, their noses were quite broad, but were also rather prominent, especially in the south. A deep nasion notch was one of their distinctive traits. There is no reason to think they had any eye-folds.

These nine climatic races will reasonably well encompass the world's people in what I have called their natural condition. They may be compared with the major racial stocks as delineated by Kroeber with which this book began. Since Kroeber was also using classical traits any differences between us should result from how we differ in lumping vs. splitting them. It is clear that Kroeber is the lumper here and that I am the splitter.

Krantz	*Kroeber*
Caucasoid Ainu Veddoid	Caucasoid
Mongoloid	Mongoloid
Saharan Pygmy Bushmen Negrito Australoid	Negroid

Another contrast of perhaps even greater interest is that of total population numbers between 10,000 years ago and the modern figures based on the census of 1973. For the nine climatic races the estimates are based on the all-over average for hunting peoples of about 4 per 100 square km. It is hoped that there is enough environmental variety in each area to make these figures average out about right.

1.	Caucasoid	652,400 people
2.	Saharan	604,000
3.	Pygmy	116,000
4.	Bushman	388,000
5.	Veddoid	124,000
6.	Mongoloid	2,467,100
7.	Ainu	255,000
8.	Negrito	178,600
9.	Australoid	297,500
	World total	5,082,600

The Mongoloid figure is exceptionally high because it includes the Asian area of 846,600 people, those of North America numbering 935,900 people, and the 682,600 inhabitants of South America. Only the Australoid population is based on a direct estimate of numbers of native hunters, and it may apply to northern and southern Africa as well. The European and Ainu areas might have had greater populations considering the probable biomass of game that was available to them. The equatorial forest areas and the Arctic may have had smaller populations than are indicated here. If better estimates become available they could be substituted, but this will have to do for now.

If these figures are then lumped into categories corresponding to the modern races, allowing an Australoid race to be added to Kroeber's list, we get the following comparison:

	10,000 years ago	*1973 census*
Caucasoid	652,400	2,044,138,000
Mongoloid	2,722,100	1,264,216,000
Negroid	1,108,000	280,068,000
Australoid	600,100	10,845,000

In this case the Ainus were combined with the Mongoloids; the Saharans, Pygmies and Bushmen became Negroids, and to the Australoids we added the Negritos and Veddoids.

Perhaps even more revealing is to translate these population numbers into percentages of the world's total at that time and compare them with the modern percentages.

	10,000 years ago	*1973 figures*
Caucasoid	12.8% of world	56.8% of world
Mongoloid	53.6	35.1
Negroid	21.8	7.8
Australoid	11.8	.3

The relative changes since the natural condition are quite remarkable. The Caucasoid category has multiplied its share of the world's total by more than four times its earlier percentage. The others have all lost ground roughly in proportion to their earlier holdings, the smaller the share the greater the relative loss. If the natural condition were set back just two thousand years more the Mongoloid share would be reduced dramatically by the loss of most of the Americas. The Caucasoids would also lose much of northern Europe to glaciers. Alterations in land areas are left out here as it is uncertain whether equatorial sea levels were lower or perhaps higher during glaciations. The percentages at about 14,000 years ago would become, approximately, Caucasoids 16.2%, Mongoloids 33.9%, Negroids 32.4%, and Australoids 17.5%. To hear many Europeans talk today one gets the impression that they think of the world's racial proportions as being similar to those of twelve or fourteen thousand years ago.

NONMIGRATION.

In an earlier chapter I described some of the factors which led to the conclusion that hunting and gathering peoples are not able to move into or through the territories of other hunters in large numbers. Some more data on this subject and the application of the principle to specific cases is pertinent at this point.

Individuals and small family groups can and do frequently move from one hunting tribe's territory into another. Sometimes there are cross-tribal kinship connections or just friendships which facilitate this. Sometimes the movers are stragglers or refugees from some disaster. In either case they pose no threat to the receiving tribal population or to its territory. When cross-tribal movements are of a major sort, involving so many people as to threaten actual conquest and destruction or absorption of the resident population, then resistance will occur. The forces are normally about balanced on each side and the tribe defending its own territory will have an overwhelming advantage.

There are certain circumstances under which territories can be conquered, even over vast distances and involving great numbers of people. One of the best measures of such conquests is the language spoken by the people in question. Recent civilized societies have often made conquests which resulted in the adoption of the conqueror's language where it had political and/or economic advantages. Such language changes do not represent a real change of population. This kind of change will normally occur only when there is a widespread political or economic system under a centralized power.

Prior to the early civilizations this did not occur, by definition.

Under more natural circumstances a change in language means an actual population replacement. People learn their speech from their parents, mostly from their mothers. While language can be learned from other people, and new languages can be added later in life, the fact of the matter is that this is rare. Just because a thing can be done it does not follow automatically that it is regularly done. And what may be done by individuals cannot as easily be done by whole societies; where, for instance, do all the teachers come from? For noncivilized people, language affiliations are usually as good an indication of ancestral connections as are blood types.

If one people is to prevail over another people and to replace them over vast areas, there must be some means by which they can regularly overcome the advantage that residents in an area always enjoy. In short, there are only two ways in which noncivilized man can do this—inherent superiority or overwhelming numbers. Technological advantages and new methods of resource exploitation may lead to minor shifts of populations but these innovations are quickly transmitted and conditions are soon stabilized again.

The last instance of inherent superiority of one human population over another was probably when *Homo sapiens* appeared and replaced *Homo erectus*. This event will be described in a later chapter in some detail. For the most part the *sapiens* revolution was a development in place, a nearly simultaneous selection in many populations for those anatomical variations that best facilitated a new cultural behavior. This behavior was phonemic language which spread rapidly by cultural diffusion and resulted in the same anatomical modifications appearing world-wide. There was no necessary movement of people, not even much movement of genes by flow, and only selection need have been involved. As the new behavior spread, a gradual development of the new anatomy spread as well. Degrees of sapienization would spread concentrically from the source, even though the changes were all local accomplishments. Each adjacent population would differ only to a slight degree in this new adaptation while the change was taking place.

If a geographical barrier were interposed which temporarily halted the diffusion of phonemic language, those on one side of that barrier could complete the transition before those on the other side even began it. When the barrier is then crossed by fully modern people the contrast between the two types would be a large gap in evolutionary grade. Such an inherent superiority is what evidently facilitated the Bushmen to totally replace the original *erectus* inhabitants of southern Africa. This kind of superiority also evidently facilitated the spread of peoples from New Guinea down the east coast forests of Australia and into Tasmania, but was not enough for them to completely overrun the continent. There does not seem to be any other instance where this kind of movement occurred. One could argue for an early population of *erectus* in the New World, though evidence is meager, which was overrun by incoming *sapiens* 12,000 years ago. If the earlier inhabitants held out long enough for modest interbreeding only in California this could account for some peculiar skeletal traits and excess hairiness found there.

Since the *sapiens* condition of the world has become universal there have been no differences in evolutionary grade. All of modern mankind has the same culture-bearing capacity. Still, one can read about many supposed migrations of hunting peoples, even repeated waves of migrations over continental areas. Some of these are so commonly accepted and are used to account for natural human distributions that they must be commented on here.

The populating of the Americas, and of North America in particular, is generally described in terms of a series of waves of immigration with each one eliminating large areas of the ones that went before. Language phylum distributions are used to show the supposed remnants of these various waves. The Eskimos are a legitimate intrusion as they had the technology to exploit the Arctic coasts which were either unoccupied or underutilized by the earlier native Americans. Otherwise the populating of the Americas follows simply from a single intrusion which expanded to fill the continents.

Some of the language-family distributions in western North America do not, at first glance, seem to make sense in such terms. It must be remembered that while individuals and families can move themselves and leave empty spaces behind, larger units of people normally do not do this. When they move, it is with an advancing front like an unrolling carpet, occupying new territory but leaving no empty space behind. As the first immigrants expanded into and through the ice-free corridor in western Canada they would fan out with their natural rate of population increase and gradually cover the continent. At all times a frontier-feeding zone of maybe 200 km depth would provide the new recruits and those behind this zone would not know a frontier even existed.

North America would not be occupied by a single, concentric wave of expansion because many delays and barriers would impede the flow of people. Paramount among these were the still-glaciated mountains in the west. The human tide would pass through only a few accessible openings between the major barriers. After centuries of slow advance they would meet again as somewhat distinct peoples beyond these barriers. This process automatically begins a division into several separate human groups whose distributions coincide remarkably well with the proposed language phyla of the ethnographic present. Later adjustments would result from depopulations during dry climates followed by repopulations from the unaffected areas. Some technological advances would also cause small shifts in linguistic boundaries before stabilization is again achieved. By such procedures the distribution of hunters can be well accounted for without proposing any additional waves of immigration.

The popular three-wave theory of the populating of Australia is also impossible as it is usually presented. There is no mechanism by which a second wave of *Homo sapiens* hunters could eliminate most of the first wave of the same species. The proposed third wave is even more impossible. Actually, the second and third waves are to account for the differences between southern and northern natives which are climatic adaptations and need no such explanation. The first wave was supposedly the Tasmanians, but their origin is more easily accounted for here. They were the last entry in the form of the early *sapiens* breaking into a continent of *erectus*.

The modern location of the Bushmen in a desert has prompted many anthropologists to say they were pushed into that harsh environment by more powerful people. This presupposes that the earlier Bushmen knew there was a desert somewhere to go to. It also presumes the Bushmen chose to move under pressure rather than fight to the death as hunters usually do. It is not explained how they foraged for food in unfamiliar territory while traveling. We are not told the response of the people whose areas they must have moved through (or did they all shift one space at a time?). It is also hard to see how the Bushmen prevailed upon the residents of the Kalahari Desert to let them in, then to conveniently disappear themselves.

Actually the Bushmen are well adapted to their environment, both physically and culturally, and the archeological record indicates they have been there for a long time. The Bushman type once did occupy much larger areas which have recently been taken over by black and white farmers and ranchers. Local histories record some of the conflicts where the Bushmen failed mainly for lack of numbers and organization, and who mostly died on the spot.

The same thinking that has Bushmen being pushed into the Kalahari would also have prehistoric man making classic migrations in response to climatic changes. Peoples and other groups of animals do not move in response to climate changes any more than trees do. Individuals and families move, but wholesale population shifts are not possible.

As a climate deteriorates with an advancing glaciation the areas facing it will suffer, food supplies may dwindle, and some people will starve or freeze. You do not panic over a few bad years, rather you tough it out hoping for good times to return. When it is evident that good times are not returning the population has already been decimated and strength is at its lowest. At this time you will certainly not conquer your neighbors who are better off, as well as being on home ground. They are not likely to admit many stragglers either, as their conditions may be getting difficult too. Quite simply, people do not move out from the climatic disaster, they are consumed by it just as surely as the rooted trees. People do not move very far, only frontiers do.

If climatic conditions are going the other way, expansion will occur along the frontier, as already described, for the occupying of uninhabited territories. Hunting areas will expand and divide, leaving half behind and half to repeat the process. People move little as the frontier advances.

You might try to visualize the alternative process. The desert is advancing on one side and a thousand kilometers away the glaciers are melting and opening up new land. Now everyone over this whole length is told to move ten km north this year in order to keep pace with the environmental shift. Those on the poor end would welcome such a command, those on the good end will do it anyway, while the great mass in between will simply refuse. Why move when things are fine and that would mean having to get used to some unfamiliar territory and giving up some that is known? How and by whom would such a shift be organized? Looked at in this light it appears rather silly.

Modern technology and social organization can move large bodies of people, but hunters and simple farmers must move themselves, and only under some very strict limitations.

With the advent of the Neolithic revolution, farmers were able to support many more people on a given piece of land than they previously could as hunters. This kind of population explosion set in motion advancing frontiers of farmers over hunters in many parts of the world. The advance is almost irresistable and will progress wherever crops can be grown. Sheer weight of numbers will prevail in any conflict situations. Where the advance is peaceful it is by infiltration of enough farmers to upset the ecology. This will ruin things for the hunter who will fight, join the farmers, starve, or flee if there is somewhere to go.

The widespread language families, such as Indo-European, Sinitic, Afro-Asiatic (Semitic), Austronesian, etc. could have been spread so fast over such areas only by agriculturalists advancing over hunters.

In describing the distribution of climatic races in the natural condition of 10,000 years ago one must keep in mind the ability, or lack of it, of hunting peoples to expand their areas. Two major expansions occurred prior to 10,000 years ago, the sapienization process which triggered two movements in the far south, and the successful invasion of lands north of the fifty-third parallel. This last movement involved occupation of new territories and ultimately led to the great expansion of the Mongoloids into America. Aside from these, there is no reason to think any population made significant inroads into new territories. Certainly none possessed any kind of advantage that would permit them to take over territory occupied by other people.

Reference will be made to certain climatic races expanding or spreading, but this is a spread of genes, not of bodies. A superior adaptation will transfer by gene flow between tribes, then be selected into increased frequency, and then be spread again. In this manner a set of classical traits can pass into a population which still maintains its major descent lines little touched by the intrusion. The possibility was entertained that Bushmen existed in northern Africa at an early date, having spread from the south of that continent. This does not require a physical movement of Bushmanoid people over any great distance, no more than occasional contacts across tribal lines. Such contacts would spread genes as well as cultural items. Those in each category that proved more useful would be differentially perpetuated in later generations and into more distant places. Likewise the spread of the Negrito to uncertain distances into Asia was one of traits, not a physical movement of many people. Not until the agricultural revolution occurred was this situation drastically changed. Until then constellations of classical traits could develop and spread over a stable base of mostly nonmoving genetic populations.

EARLIER RACES.

Some comment should be made about the probable distributions of classical traits prior to the *sapiens* revolution. In other words, we might examine the climatic races of *Homo erectus*. Some of the traits are evident in the skeletal material, such as body size and build, and the nose form. Their distributions can be plotted from the recovered fossils combined with analogies to recent distributions. Given the assumption of reduced hair cover we can predict skin colors for all areas with some confidence. Cranial hair form can also be predicted for each temperature region, but there is also some uncertainty as to the dates of development of each type. Body fat, eye-folds, and light eyes can be little more than guessed at. As to lip eversion we pretty much draw a blank.

Prior to sapienization two of the climatic races in the western world, Caucasoid and Saharan, were most likely just as they were later. The Pygmy race didn't exist at all, and southern Africa should have been inhabited by people with classical traits just like the Saharans with their north-south clines reversed. It would be tempting to add that all Caucasoids, at least those to the north of the Mediterranean, were also light-eyed and blond-haired. Logic would seem to force this conclusion, but it seems so extreme that emotion pulls away from it. This would picture Neandertals in "Nordic" skins as perhaps the only pure representatives of that coloration pattern.

In the east, the Mongoloids would not exist except as an incipient development on the greater-Ainu fringes. These Ainus would resemble their descriptions of somewhat later times. The Australoids, assuming they were there then, would look as they do today but on *erectus* skeletons and very much like those in northern and southern Africa. The Negrito region and the Veddoid region of India would have people of normal stature presumably, but quite lineal in build and of medium to dark color depending on local cover. At some time some of them developed the peppercorn hair but we don't know when.

The amount of differentiation of classical traits was probably much less 100,000 years ago than it is now. Only in terms of pigmentation would *erectus* populations show about the same diversity as today. The other traits were progressive developments not found in our ape ancestors and are not critical for survival, as is skin color, just highly convenient. Hence they did not appear immediately but developed over time. The Arctic adaptations of Mongoloid hair and epicanthic eye-folds may have been the last to evolve, only after man invaded the far north.

The major variation would have been in pigmentation. Size and body shape would vary some. Nose projection would vary, but the large teeth would keep breadth variation to a minimum. Hair form would have been uniform at first and its variations developed gradually over time, but how fast we don't know. All in all, *erectus* classical races would have been much more toned down from the extremes of today, but easily recognizable, as with any other geographically widespread species.

The question will be asked, to what degree have *erectus* races continued directly into the *sapiens* grade of evolution? In terms of classical traits, the climatic races continue straight through with some disruption, some exaggeration, and some very new developments that were not there before. As to the actual named races I see reasonably direct continuity only for Caucasoids, Saharans, Ainus, and Australoids. The entire equatorial forest area was either mostly uninhabited, as in Africa, or sparsely inhabited by something like Australoids in India and southeastern Asia. In terms of classical traits the Pygmies and Negritos are new developments and the Veddoids are at least somewhat new. Mongoloids are a fully new race in spite of their genetic descent from Peking man. Bushmen are equally original with our species. If one wants to know how old each of these climatic races is, it depends on which one, and on what degree of continuity one means.

6.
GENETIC TRAITS

SUMMARY.

To begin with, a distinction was made between classical traits which are quantitative and governed by many factors, and genetic traits which are qualitative and whose inheritance is known. Going beyond this it becomes evident that many of the classical traits are environmentally adaptive and are selected to suit various climatic regions. In contrast, the genetic traits are mainly nonadaptive and their tendency toward continental distributions is governed largely by chance factors—founders effect, mutation, and drift. This last set of contrasts is here considered to be the most meaningful. Accordingly, many traits are included in this chapter which are polygenic or quantitative (often both), but their distributions and the apparent factors governing them are more similar to those for the usual genetic traits.

The more familiar blood types of the ABO series, Rh factors, MN series, and some lesser known ones, all show random effects to be their primary geographical determinants. This comes in two levels, the first being local, short-term drift which introduces many irregularities that must be overlooked as so much "noise" in the system. More basic are the tendencies toward continental regularities which can be seen, but which have also been largely overridden by human movements and gene flow.

Other genetic traits that support this picture are PTC tasting, earwax distinctions, light vs. dark eye color, and fingerprint patterns. The more unconventional traits which are placed in this category are cephalic index and a number of detailed dental and cranial peculiarities which seem to have no adaptive value.

GENETIC TRAITS.

For the most part, the traits described in this chapter are those for which we can predict the pattern of inheritance. We commonly refer to this as knowing the genetics of the trait. We are equally certain that the classical traits, described in the preceding chapters, are also genetically inherited. The major difference lies in that each genetic trait can be pinned down to a single gene whose effect can be determined on an all or nothing basis. Each classical trait is inherited by many genes and we cannot single out the effect of just a single one.

The measurement of genetic traits is different from classical ones. In most cases it is sufficient to note simply that the trait occurs in one individual and not in another. After this, one counts how many occurrences there are in a sample and gives this as a percentage. Genetic traits, being qualitative, cannot be averaged, but must be expressed as a percentage or frequency of occurrence in a given population. These frequencies are then compared between populations instead of averages as for classical traits.

Since many alleles are dominant over others, we can also calculate the actual gene frequencies which will differ from the trait frequencies. I'm not convinced this is a good practice, but I will follow it here when the available data is in terms of these gene frequencies. It is true that it is the genotypes that determine the phenotypes, but on the other hand it is only the phenotype upon which natural selection can work. In the case of genetic traits, drift is the major factor influencing change and this can be said to work on the genes just as directly as on the resultant phenes.

A number of traits will be included in this chapter which are not genetically known. This is because they are qualitative and must be given in frequencies, as fingerprint patterns; or else they seem to be affected in their distributions more by drift than by selection, as some cranial characteristics. The proper assignment of some traits between classical vs. genetic is still very uncertain.

The guiding principle that has been followed in the distinction made here is how the traits came to be distributed as they are. If selection for climatic adaptation is primary, then they are treated as classical; if founders effect, mutation, and drift are primary they are considered to be genetic. Often even this cannot be determined by any direct means. In such cases it is ultimately the kind of geographical distribution the trait shows that decides its categorization. If we then argue significance from how genetic traits are distributed, there is a certain amount of circular reasoning involved. But since a number of such distributions were legitimately arrived at, the reasoning should still be secure.

Many genetically known traits will not be included here because they are specifically disease related. These occupy many pages in any other book on human races, but their pertinence is dubious. Disease distributions are often geographical, but they are independent of any other factors that affect humans in a racial sense. Any genetic defense against such diseases will tend to parallel the distribution of the disease and not any racial category established on other criteria. The famous sickle-cell anemia is not a Negroid genetic trait, it is a tropical trait that is concentrated in the western region. It largely coincides with racial traits that are called Negroid, but it is not found in all of these people and it is also found among some non-Negroid peoples as well. There are many other such traits that will not be included here.

The distributions for the genetic traits will again be given in the ethnographic present, 1500 A.D., or as soon thereafter as the people were discovered by western Europeans. All the genetic data is, of course, determined from very modern populations. It was all gathered in the present century, and most of it since World War II. The data is plotted on the maps where the tested people lived some 500 years ago. For the Americas, southern Africa, Australia, most of Oceania, and a strip across Siberia, this has meant that much of the data is not available and never will be. What is available is often plotted on the maps at some distance from where it was obtained. These are the same rules as were applied to plotting the classical trait distributions in the ethnographic present.

ABO BLOOD TYPES.

The first variations in human blood types were discovered around the turn of the century, when it was found that while some blood transfusions worked, others did not. The antigen and antibody clinical situation does not concern us here because ancient man did not make blood transfusions. What does concern us is that four alleles at one locus are responsible for these variations, and that they are very unequally distributed around the world.

The alleles are commonly referred to as A, B, and O. Since A and B are dominant over O, but not over each other, we get the four blood types of A, B, AB, and O. The A and B types may or may not be carrying a recessive O allele, but the AB and O are genotypically known. An additional complication is the more recently discovered distinction between A_1 and A_2. Considering the number of possible phenotypic combinations it seems simplest to give the distributions of the three major alleles of this gene and to note the fairly simple contrast between A_1 and A_2 locations. The frequencies of these genes around the world are the best known and the maps are reasonably accurate.

A single individual in almost any population could have any one or two of these possible alleles. A family or other small social unit could, by chance of inheritance, have all just one or another of them, or some unusual combination. To minimize the chance of sampling error a large number of people, preferably one hundred or more, should be selected at random from an area to determine the local gene frequencies.

The frequencies in a local population may have been subject to random drift in recent generations, and they may still be at variance with neighboring local populations. To even out this kind of background "noise" many local samples are pooled into larger regional units. The larger the unit, the more even the distribution. If this is carried too far it will average out the variations that one is looking for. In fact, pooling at any level may serve to conceal clues about the significance of the differences.

Fortunately, blood-type data have been collected by a general system that has made it useful for racial studies. It has been pooled into geographical units of ever increasing size without regard for other preconceived pooling units. This gives a world-wide distribution for these alleles, which we may then compare with the distributions of other genetic traits to see whether they correspond or not. We may also compare these with the distributions of classical traits, again looking for correspondences or the lack of them.

The alternative procedure would have been to pool all Negroid blood samples to find the "Negroid" frequencies, the Caucasoid blood for the "Caucasoid" frequencies, and so on. Such a procedure would have assumed before the fact that blood type differences will divide up according to categories established on other criteria. There is a strong tendency for researchers to do just this kind of thing. Every racial study that begins by taking a sample of blacks and a sample of whites fails right there. The act of sampling has already assumed the answer, that the data will divide themselves into these two categories and not cross-cut in some other way. For classical traits the same problem continually plagues us, as when broad noses are found among many blacks it is assumed to be characteristic of all blacks, without checking to be sure if this is indeed the case.

It has become a standard practice with blood typing to make racial separations where modern life has brought ethnic groups together, and whose origins are far apart. Within each ethnic breeding population the data is pooled and is reported at that level without any pooling of higher units. Even peoples like the Basques or the Lapps are reported in smaller units, then pooled or not, depending on the point being made. Given this approach, the maps illustrate the distributions of these gene frequencies totally independent of, and unprejudiced by, any other trait distributions.

The distribution of the frequencies of gene A is given in Fig. 31, without regard to the distinction between A_1 and A_2, which will be discussed shortly. The range in frequency is great, from essentially zero in South America to over half in Lappland, and it is very uneven around the rest of the world. There must be some describable reason, or reasons, for this. There are two major areas of High A, Europe in general, with a focus among the Lapps, and Australia with an emphasis in the southern half. Two other high spots are in the Canadian plains, and in southern Greenland. Further variations in terms of intensity are all of a lesser magnitude, but not necessarily of lesser importance. The apparent absence of A from Mexico through South America may be as important as its high frequency is elsewhere.

It is tempting to say that genetic drift is responsible for all the various highs and lows, and that if a map were made 500 years earlier the pattern would have been randomly different. On the other hand, disease selections for or against type A may have affected it. Maybe many of the responsible diseases are not now noticed or have long ago disappeared. There are a number of possible disease relationships with this and other blood types, but nothing that would seem to cause this kind of distribution.

Another way of looking at all this is to see a tendency toward continental distributions. Europe and Australia have much A. If at some past date they had been entirely type A and some population shifting took place, maybe the present distribution would be the automatic result. If these continents were once infiltrated by large numbers of people with lower frequencies of A, then one might look for the highest A to be found in those areas that would have been last or least affected. This fits rather well on first examination but gets a bit problematical as we look more closely. For one thing, on the westernmost fringe of Europe A drops slightly in frequency where one would think it should be especially high. For the moment little more can be said, but I will return to this problem.

The frequency distribution of gene B, given in Fig. 32, shows little or no relationship to that of A. Its range is not so great and it rarely excedes 25%. The high point is in northern India, Pakistan, and Afganistan, and it is generally high throughout most of Asia. Some lesser highs and lows in Siberia may represent no more than recent, local drifting among small populations, but it is difficult to be sure. In general, there is no tendency for the distribution of the B gene to coincide with that of any other recognizable phenomenon. The high concentration in Asia and a lesser one in western Africa, combined with its virtual absence from Australia and both of the Americas, illustrate a tendency toward continental distributions. Applying the same thinking as with the A gene, one could visualize continental concen-

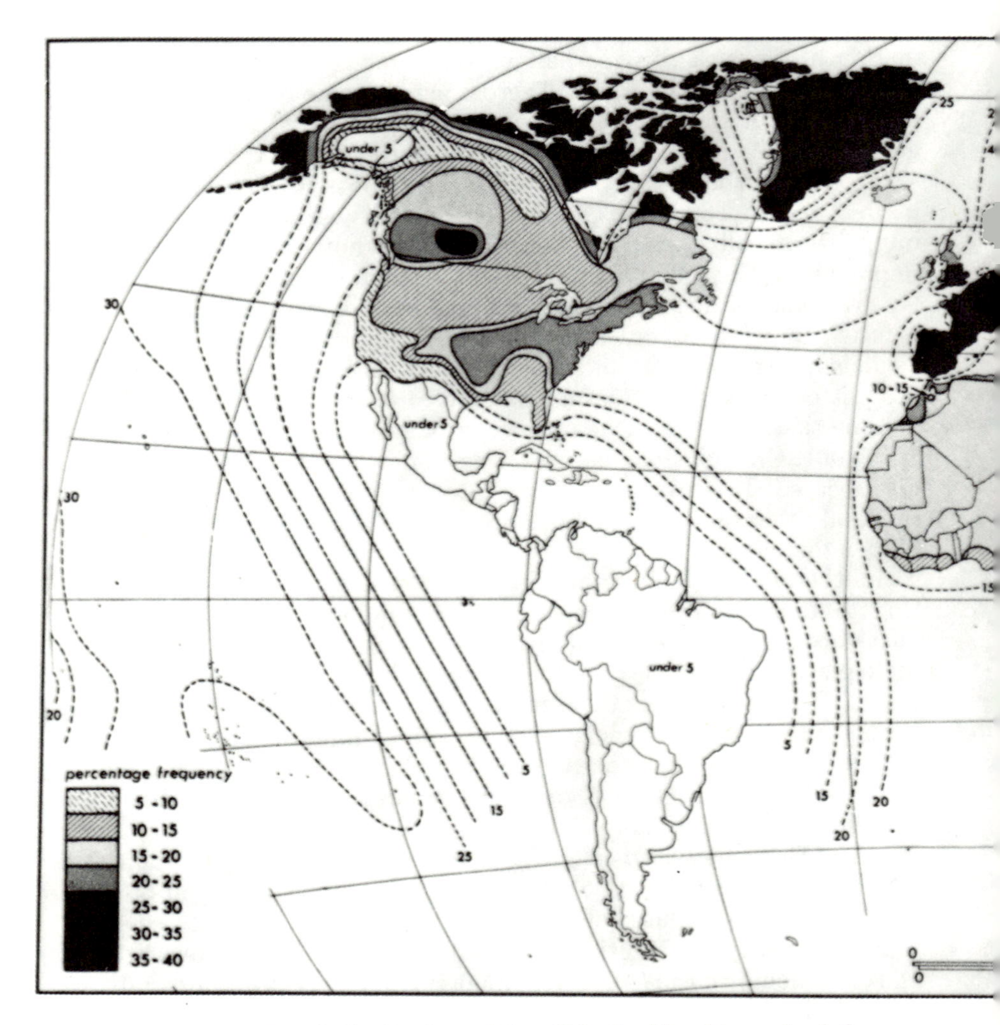

FIGURE 31. World distribution of the allele for blood type A of the ABO series. Frequencies have been rather recently determined but their locations are all given as of the ethnographic present. (Reproduced with permission from *The Distribution of the Human Blood Groups and Other Polymorphisms* by A. E. Mourant, A. C. Kopec, and K. Domaniewska-Sobsczak, Oxford University Press, Publisher.)

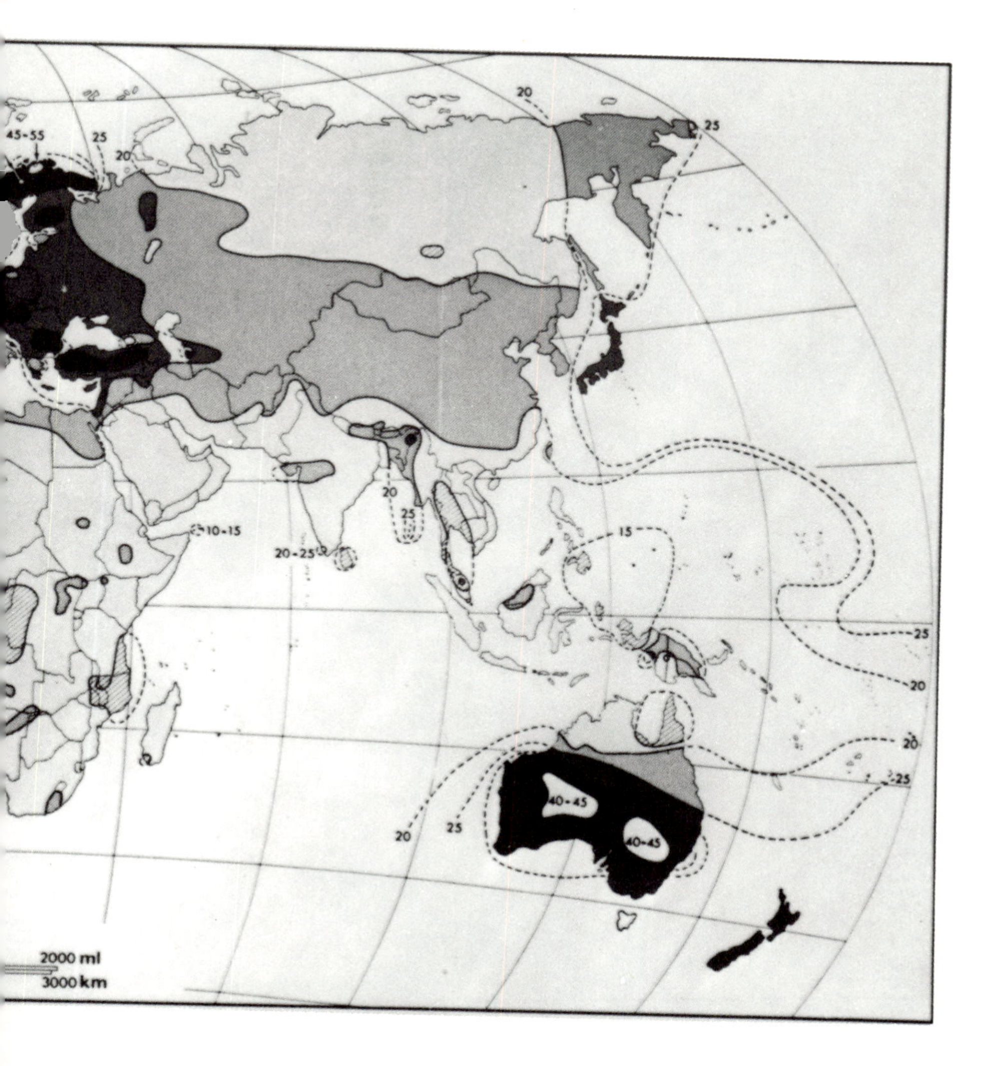
45-55
25
20
20
25
20
25
10-15
20-25
15
25
20
20
25
20
25
40-45
40-45
2000 mi
3000 km

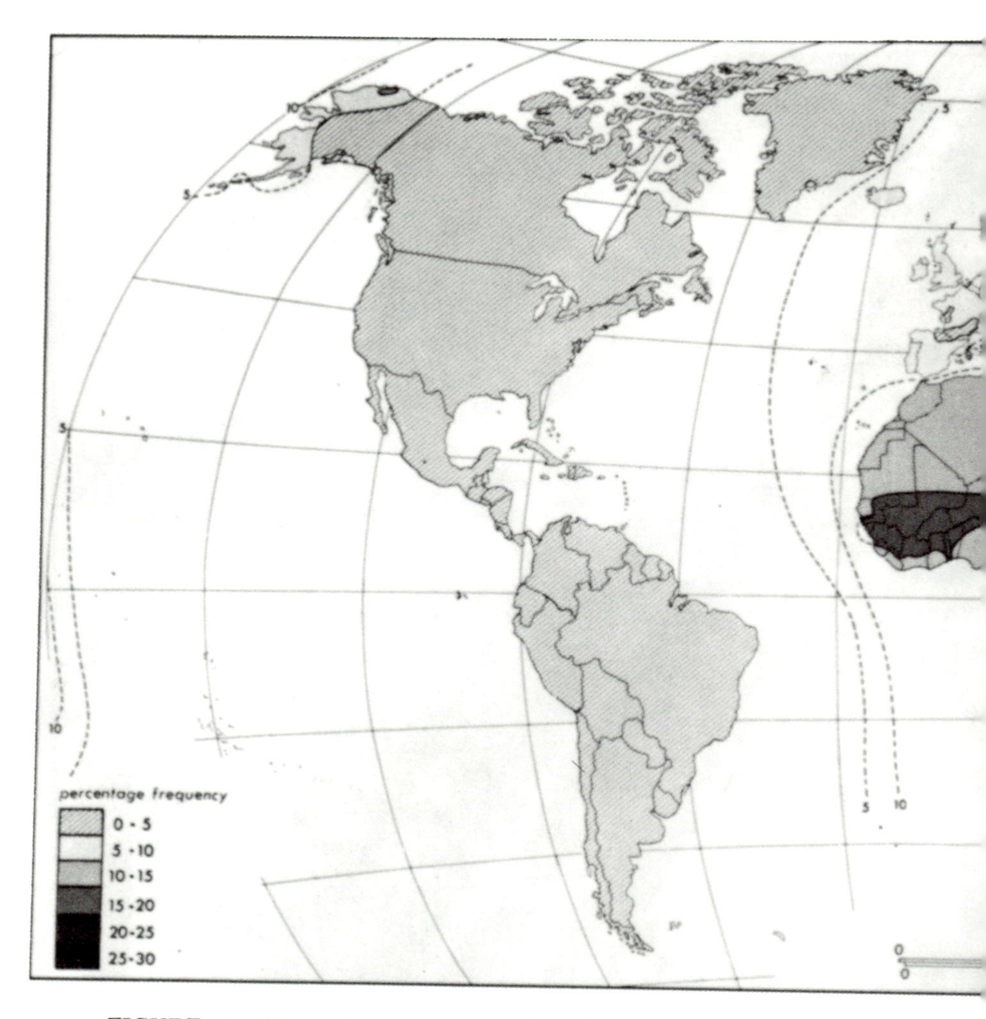

FIGURE 32. World distribution in the ethnographic present of the allele for blood type B of the ABO series. (Courtesy of A. E. Mourant and Oxford University Press.)

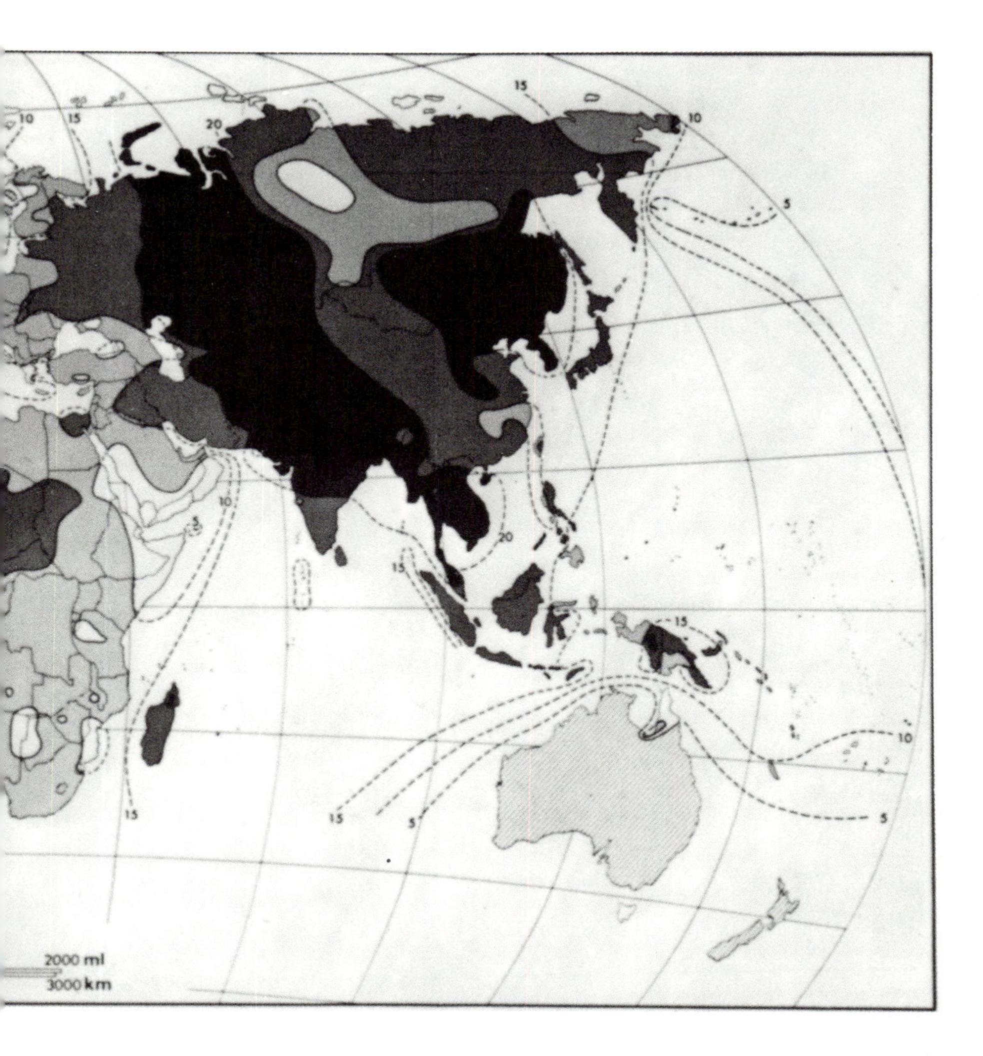
10
15
20
15
10
5
10
20
15
5
15
15
5
10
15
5
2000 mi
3000 km

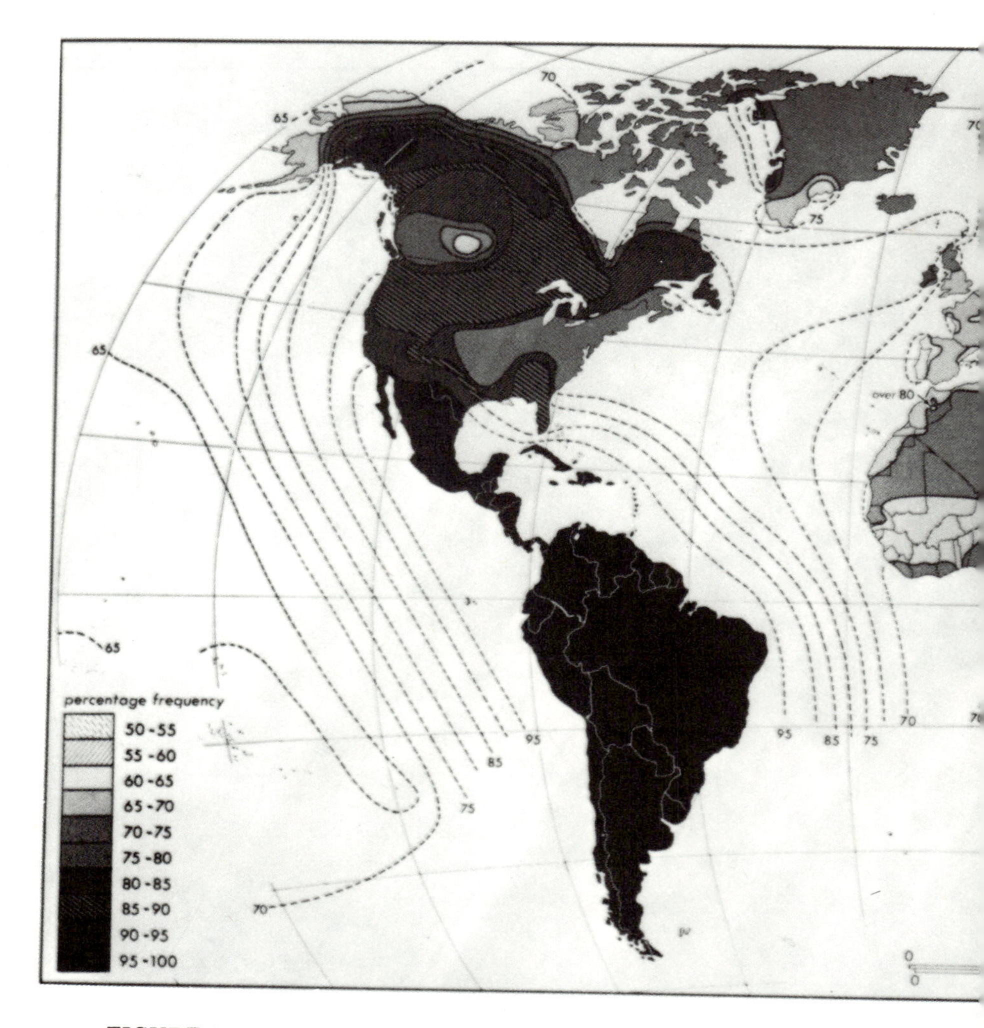

FIGURE 33. World distribution in the ethnographic present of the allele for blood type O of the ABO series. (Courtesy of A.E. Mourant and Oxford University Press.)

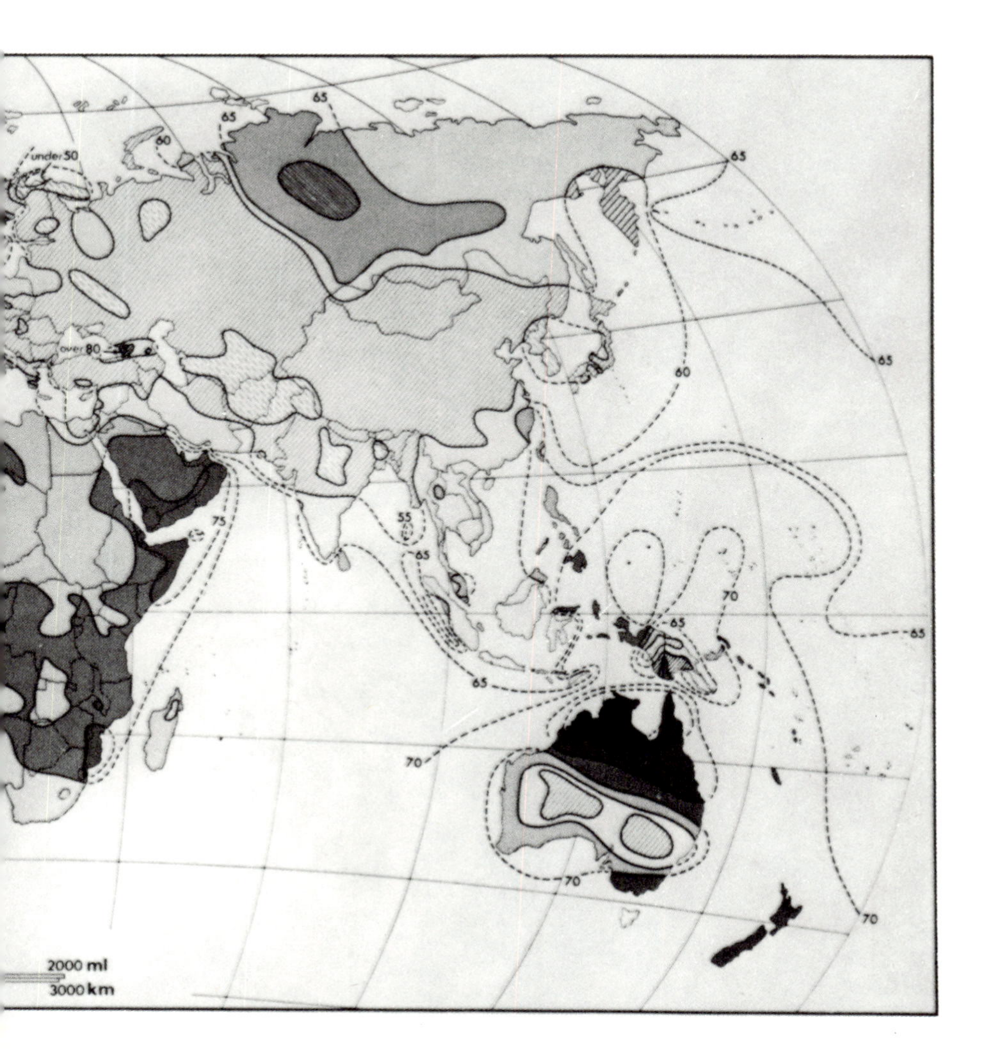
65
65
60
under 50
65
over 80
60
65
75
55
65
70
65
65
65
70
70
70
2000 ml
3000 km

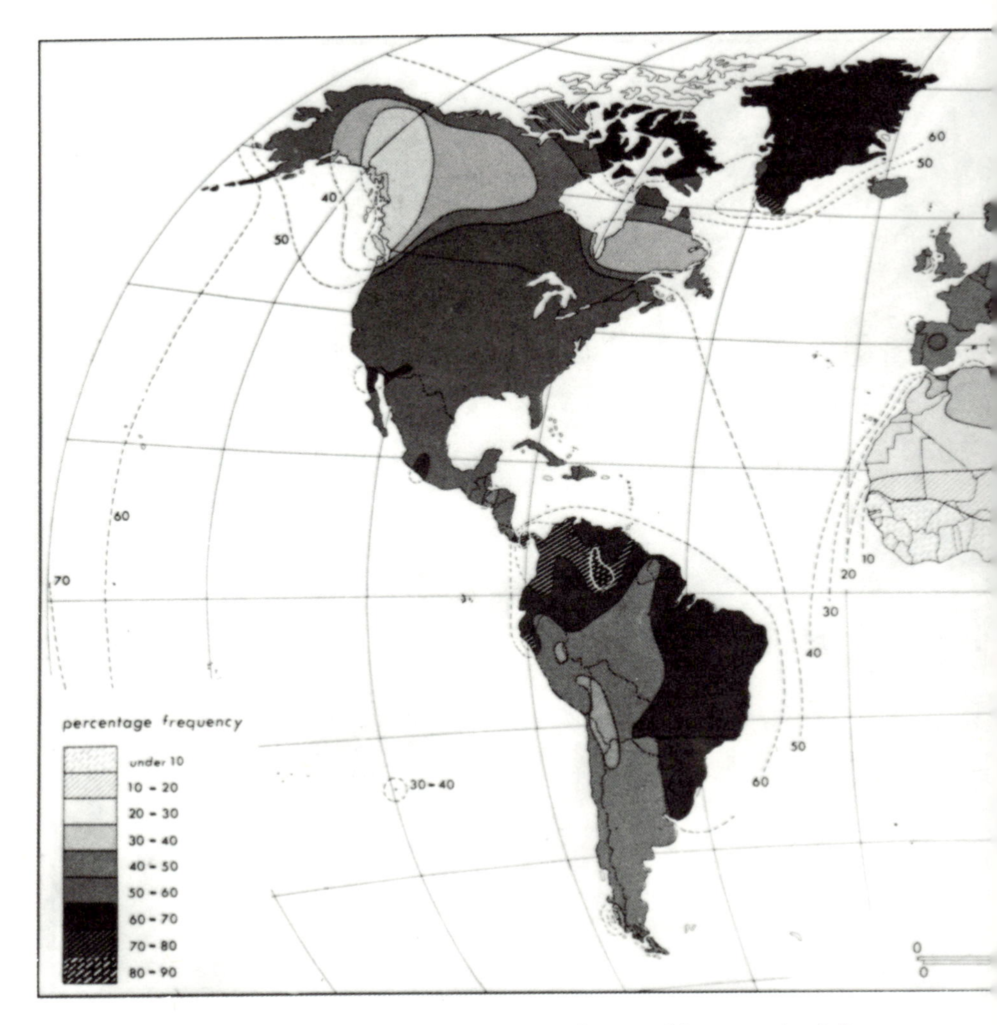

FIGURE 34. World distribution in the ethnographic present of the allele C of the CDE or Rhesus series. (Courtesy of A. E. Mourant and Oxford University Press.)

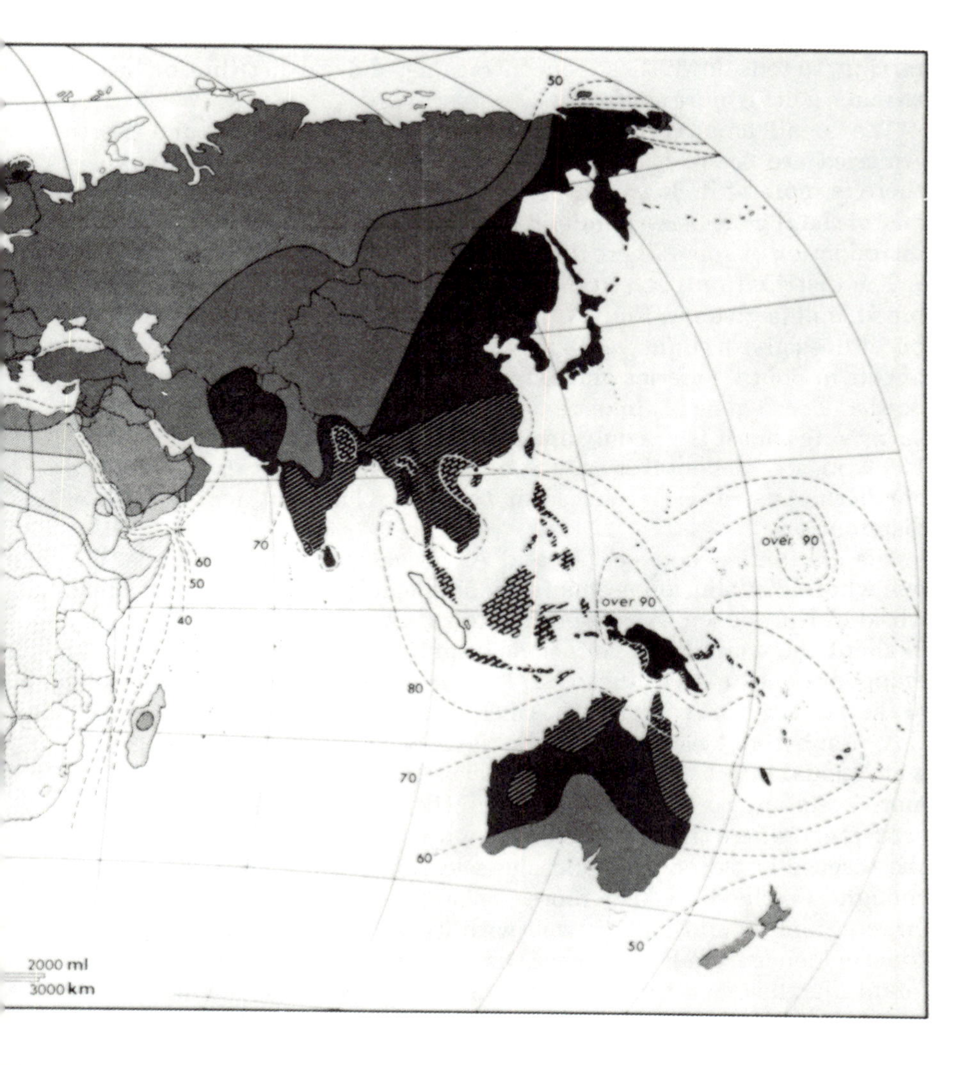
50
70
60
50
40
over 90
over 90
80
70
60
50
2000 ml
3000 km

trations in the past which divided along physical barriers to gene flow. Then follow this with some increase in gene flow, or other source of mixing, to tone down these concentrations, and the distribution begins to make a little more sense.

The small amounts of B that do occur in Australia and North America are both located near to adjacent continental areas where there is more of it. It would be desirable to know whether this is the last of the B gene being eliminated from a continent, or more likely, the introduction of some where it had been totally absent before.

The distribution pattern of gene O is the inverse of A and B combined, and is given in Fig. 33. This does not show anything really new but it does give a slightly different perspective. The concentration area of O is in South America and extends up to the present United States' border. The O gene is almost everywhere the most common so it is not surprising that it is the only one that reaches a frequency approaching 100% in a continental area. Its other concentrations in Alaska and northern Australia do not seem to show this continental type of distribution.

The distinction between A_1 and A_2 introduces a new variable, but one whose distribution seems fairly simple at present. In the western world of Europe and Africa both kinds of the A gene exist, reportedly in about equal numbers. Variations from this 50–50 split are too poorly mapped to mean anything so far. In sharp contrast to this the A blood of the eastern world and North America is all of the A_1 variety.

A number of selective factors have been observed or suspected which could affect the ABO frequencies. It seems that blood type O is more resistant to syphilis than the others, and its nearly universal occurrence where that disease began may be more than a coincidence if the disease is old enough and the selection pressure has been great enough. O blood is also more resistant to bronchopneumonia in infants, but this doesn't fit well with its world distribution. There is some evidence from Europe that the B gene confers some resistance to infant diarrhea, and this may be a significant selective agent. Both B and A_1 seem to be more resistant to plague than are O and A_2. This might account for some of the distributions of these genes and would imply that prior to 1300 A.D. Europe may have been entirely O and A_2 blood. The geography of A and B bloods might be indicative of their resistance to smallpox, but this is only speculation. Still other disease correlations have been suggested, but so far little geographical sense can be made of it all. There are too many variables of space, time, and disease, and too little hard data on many of them.

Another effect that may ultimately be more important than disease is the incompatibility between the bloods of mother and fetus. The major problem is when the mother is type O and the child is either B or A_1. When such a child is lost it carries with it an O allele and one of the other two. Since O is generally in the majority, such equal losses would tend to remove the minority allele from the gene pool and eventually leaving it all O. If A_1 is in the majority for some reason, then O would tend to drop out.

Not all blood genes work this way with each other, but many do and still more of them might. This provides a selection pressure which works to make the majority allele become the universal one within any breeding population. Local breeding units will often select at cross purposes with one another, but given interbreeding and enough time, the continental areas ought to move gradually toward genetic uniformity in these traits. (Given still more time even the whole species might become uniform.) We have here an actual selective mechanism which tends to produce the continental tendencies seen or postulated in the ABO genes. Genetic drift by itself also tends to work in this same direction of uniformity by the chance dropping out of rare alleles. Thus drift and incompatibility selection will both work toward continental distinctions. The interplay between these two pairs of forces over great spans of time may be the major solution to the blood-type distributions.

Blood types can be determined only on living or recently deceased individuals. A few years ago there was some excitement over reading the ABO blood types from bones. This proved to be mostly futile as one ended up "typing" the dirt as much as the human remains.

Rh BLOOD TYPES.

The best known of the mother-fetus incompatibility problems is the Rh factor, named after the rhesus monkey on which early studies were made. Many people know themselves to be either Rh positive or Rh negative. These constitute only one of a number of possible contrasts in this system. There are two theories as to the genetics involved. One theory would have a single locus with many alleles, while the other theory would have three closely placed loci with two alleles for each. The latter system, using the letters CDE for the dominant alleles, will be used here. The major contrast is between the dominant D for positive and its recessive d for negative.

The most commonly encountered of the Rh types are CDe, Cde, cDE, cDe, and cde. The other three possible combinations are everywhere extremely rare. Rather than map the occurrence of the five major combinations, it will be simpler just to show the incidence of one allele from each pair beginning with C in Fig. 34. In the Old World, C is quite rare in Africa and is very common in eastern Asia, reaching its peak of over 90% in New Guinea. Europe and western Asia have frequencies near 50%, and in Australia it declines from north to south. Something of a continental tendency is again evident, with both Africa and Australia seeming to be receiving input of C from the outside. Australia's higher level represents the far higher frequency in its soruce area as compared with Africa's. It may also represent two waves of input, the first being with the original *sapiens* invaders and the second by gene flow from later contacts. In Africa, C would have come in from an area of modest concentration with the advent of agriculture.

In the New World, C has high concentrations in Venezuela and Greenland and other irregularities that fit no obvious pattern, not even one of continentality. A tempting conclusion would be that New World polymorphisms entered with considerable variation and have not had time to drift and/or select into uniform blocks of large size.

The incidence of D vs. d is easiest shown as the frequency of the recessive allele, as it is virtually confined to the western half of the Old World (See Fig. 35). Europe is clearly the heartland of d, or Rh negative, with the Basque area being its high point with over 50% of this allele. This becomes rarer in both the far north and in the south of Europe. Another center of over 50% in the southern Sinai is so isolated as to look suspicious. Still one more high point in the Sahara is shown in some maps and not in others. Gene d also extends into Africa with declining frequency to the south until it virtually disappears among the Bushmen. It maintains a frequency of 20% most of the way through India and then is negligible beyond there.

Rh negative is as characteristic of Europe as is A blood. Its concentration approaches continentality and there is the obvious suggestion that it once was universal there. Indeed, such a high concentration does not otherwise make sense. Mother-fetus incompatibility should select heavily against the minority allele so the European average of 40% can only be temporary and it is now on its way out. The only way it could be so high now is that it once had somehow reached 100% and then Europe was invaded by great numbers of people with lower frequencies of that gene. If the same people who brought some of the dominant allele D into Europe also invaded Africa, then they are the source of the recessive d allele in that continent. This then calls for a population explosion of a group which had a fair proportion of both D and d, who then invaded Europe which was all d, and Africa which was all D, and diluted them both. The only reasonable source where such a mixed population could exist would be on the genetic interface between the two extreme continents, at the eastern end of the Mediterranean Sea. The implications of this will be returned to later.

The distribution of allele E of this series is given in Fig. 36. In the

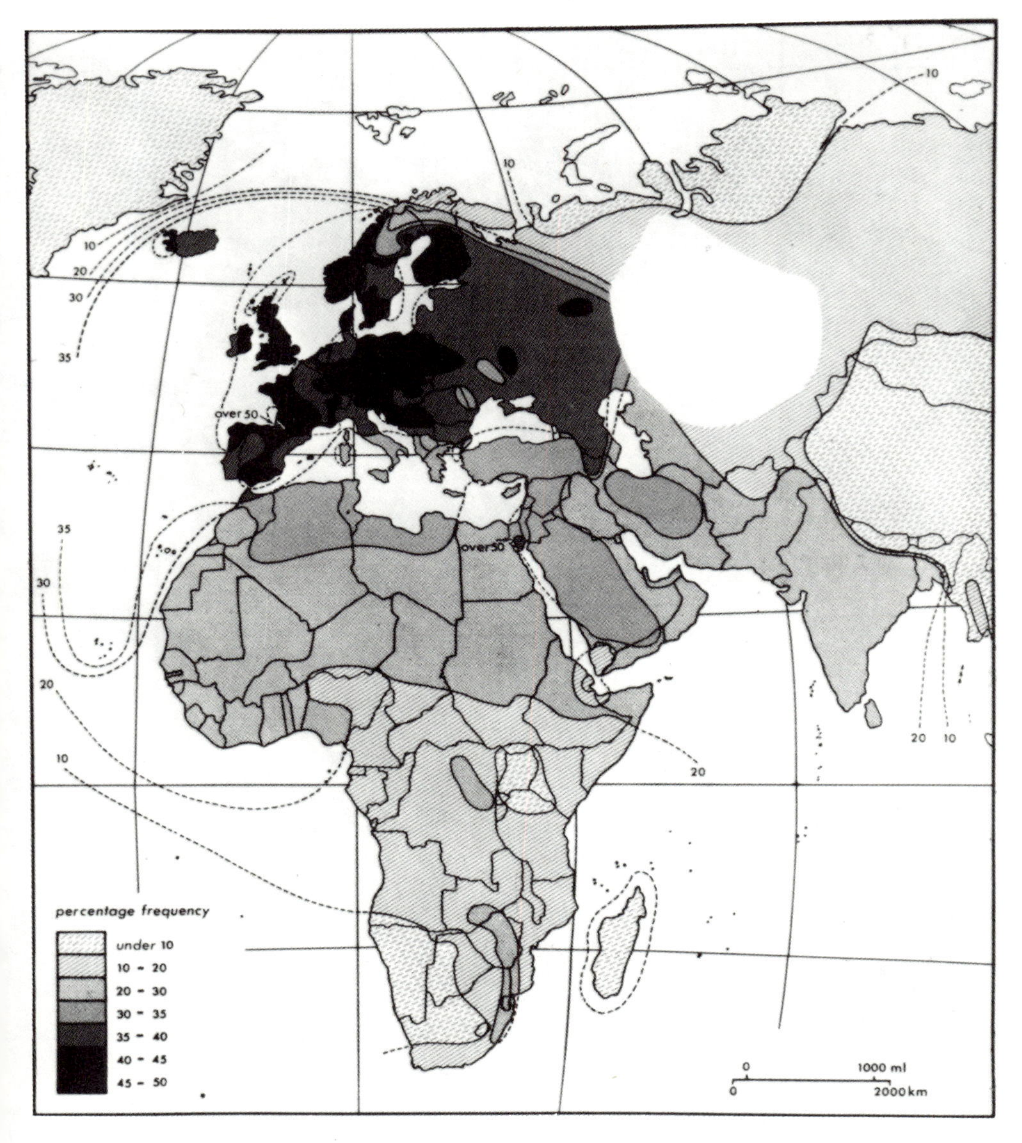

FIGURE 35. Distribution of the d allele of the CDE series in the western part of the Old World in the ethnographic present. In the rest of the world the dominant allele D is virtually universal. (Courtesy of A. E. Mourant and Oxford University Press.)

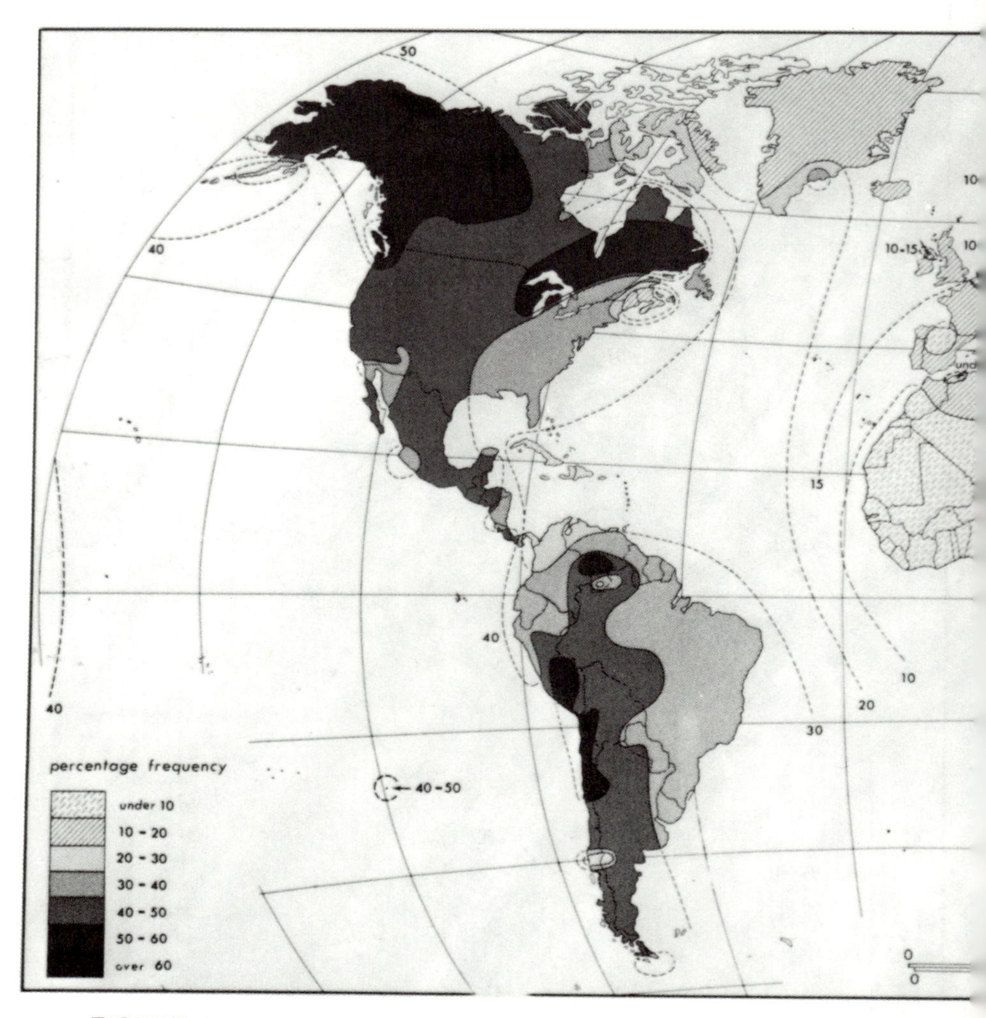

FIGURE 36. World distribution in the ethnographic present of the allele E of the CDE or Rhesus series. (Courtesy of A. E. Mourant and Oxford University Press.)

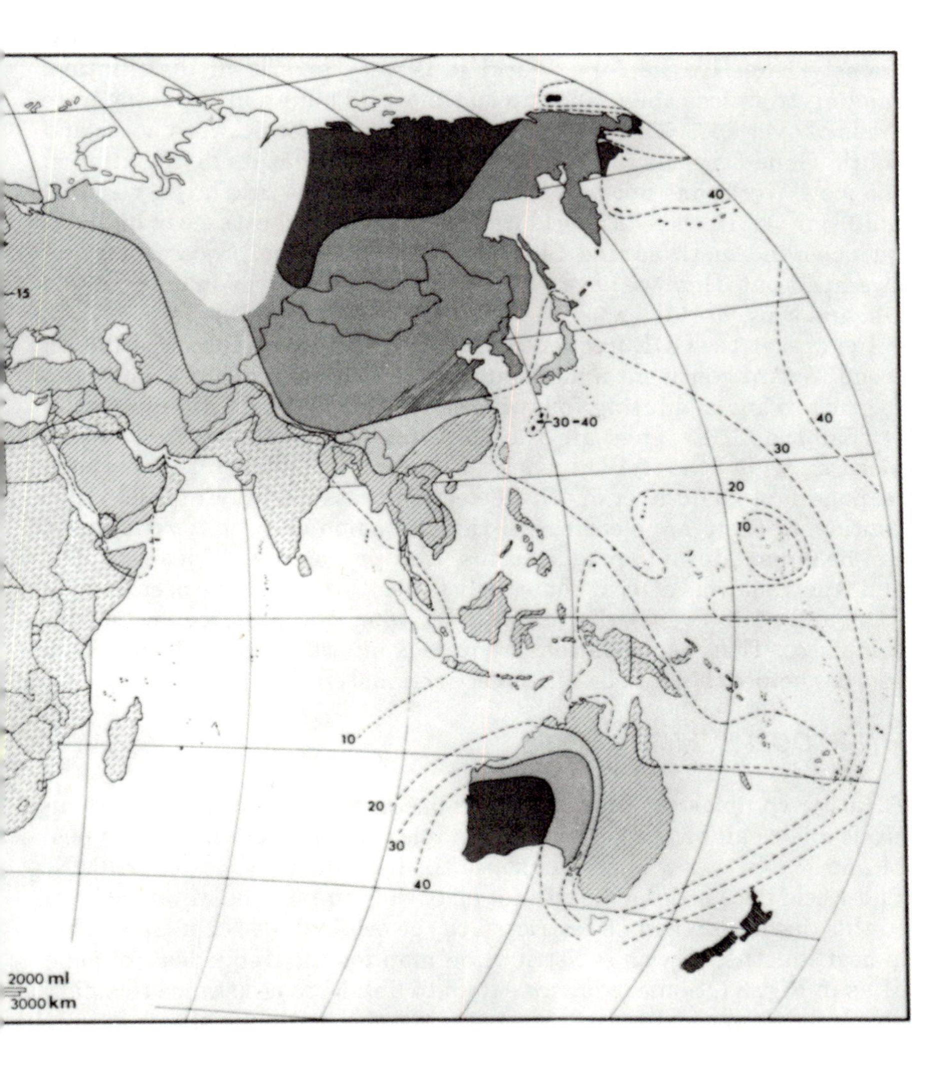
15
40
30-40
40
30
20
10
10
20
30
40
2000 ml
3000 km

Old World its only high areas of over 40% are in southwestern Australia and in north central Siberia. Elsewhere it is low, but not extremely rare. In the New World it is very erratic in distribution, ranging from less than 10%, up to the world's high in three separate areas of over 60%. There is no tendency to separate between north and south. Gene E seems to illustrate well the idea that its distribution in the New World has not had the time to settle out into large, regional uniformities. In the Old World its distribution suggests early high frequencies in Australia and Siberia which are in the process of being swamped out. Here we have a case of an incipient division between the Old and New Worlds.

In general, the CDE frequencies suggest what the ABO series did—a trend toward continental distributions with some indications of more recent mixing or diluting following a definite pattern. My impression is that the CDE genes are the more reliable indicators of this big picture, while the ABO genes are more locally erratic, perhaps responding to a number of other selection pressures. For at least three continents there are clear suggestions of some early uniformity that can be pinned down in precise terms. Europe was cde, Africa was cDe, and Australia was cDE at some early time. Asia may have been mostly CDe, and at an even earlier date, CDE, when the Americas were first colonized. These speculations require supporting data from other sources before they can be taken very seriously.

MN BLOOD TYPES.

A rather complex set of blood types based on adjacent loci and numerous alleles all began with a very simple contrast between two types, M and N. Neither was dominant, so the heterozygote was called MN. Full world data is not available for all of the complicated ramifications, so this discussion will be restricted to the original M–N contrast. This is best illustrated with a distribution map for the frequencies of gene M as in Fig. 37. Some evidence exists to link M to resistance to smallpox and rheumatic diseases. M women are also less often sterile than N women. These would lead to a world of M except for the fact that MN men somehow produce sperm carying more than half N alleles.

The most conspicuous concentration in the Old World is in Australia and New Guinea where N is high and M is at world lows of 10% or less in some areas. In terms of ancient continentality this means that it was not Australia alone that had run a trait to one extreme, but this time New Guinea was included and the dividing line was somewhere well to the west. The subsequent influx of gene M into Australia was not from the more usual source in the north, but from the northwest, and only by occasional contact. Curiously, New Guinea retains an even lower level of M which suggests only that area had previously reduced it completely to zero.

The next major low spot of M would be in western and central Africa where it is mostly under 50%. This contrasts with eastern and southern Africa where about 60% is the central tendency. Eastern Africa would appear to be an extension or flow-over from the high area of Arabia where there is over 70% M. In southern Africa the 60% or more M is an isolated Bushman phenomenon.

The far northern fringe of Europe and western Siberia also has M well under 50%. These range from Lapps to Samoyeds who are linguistically related, but show no similarity in this trait to their other supposed relatives—Finns and Hungarians.

Asia, in general, is high in M, everywhere over 50% except for the Ainu who are just under that figure. Some not-so-high areas are Korea and eastern China, and the eastern end of Siberia. Western Europe is also down almost to 50% which suggests an earlier condition of a great deal lower frequency, perhaps 40% or less. This would imply a continuity of western Europe either with the Lapps or with western Africa, but not likely with both. The continental trend shows only moderately in the Old World at the present level of analysis.

In the New World there are five areas where gene M excedes 80%, which it nowhere does in the Old World, and in two of these it passes 90%. About 60% is as low as it gets anywhere in this hemisphere. There is no suggestion of continentality in this distribution.

The distribution of M is reminiscent of CDE in that the New World is erratic and the Old World tends toward continental regions. These continental distributions do not always coincide, but sometimes they do tend to divide along similar lines. By contrast, the ABO system is most erratic only in North America and has a continental tendency elsewhere, the clearest being in Australia and South America.

OTHER BLOOD TYPES.

Many more genetic variations are known in human blood, most of them being named after the first patient in whom they were discovered, and then labeled positive or negative. None of these can be well mapped on a world-wide basis, but a little can be said about the distribution of some of them.

Duffy positive is 100% among Australian natives and decreases counter-clockwise around the Indian Ocean to reach near zero in Africa. It is not well reported in those places where the major breaks might be looked for. Lewis positive is zero in Australia. It is around

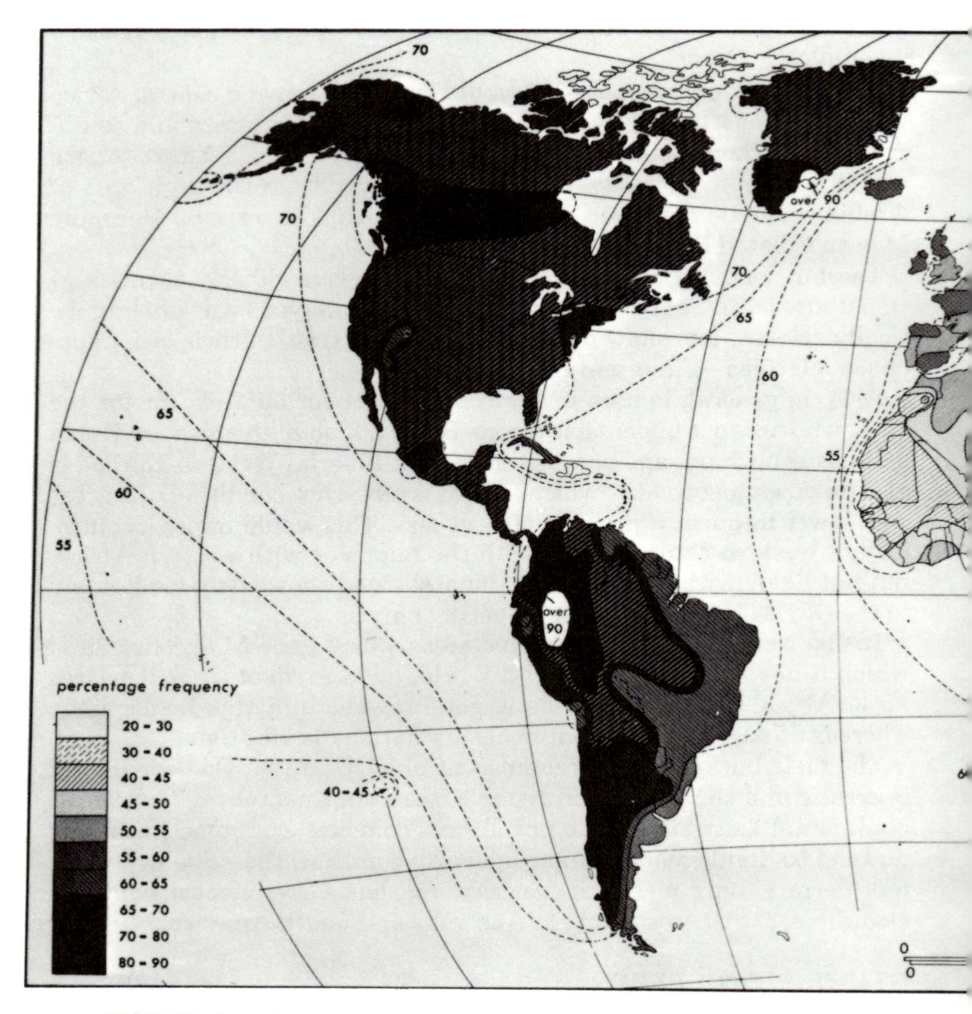

FIGURE 37. World distribution in the ethnographic present of the allele M of the MN series. (Courtesy of A. E. Mourant and Oxford University Press.)

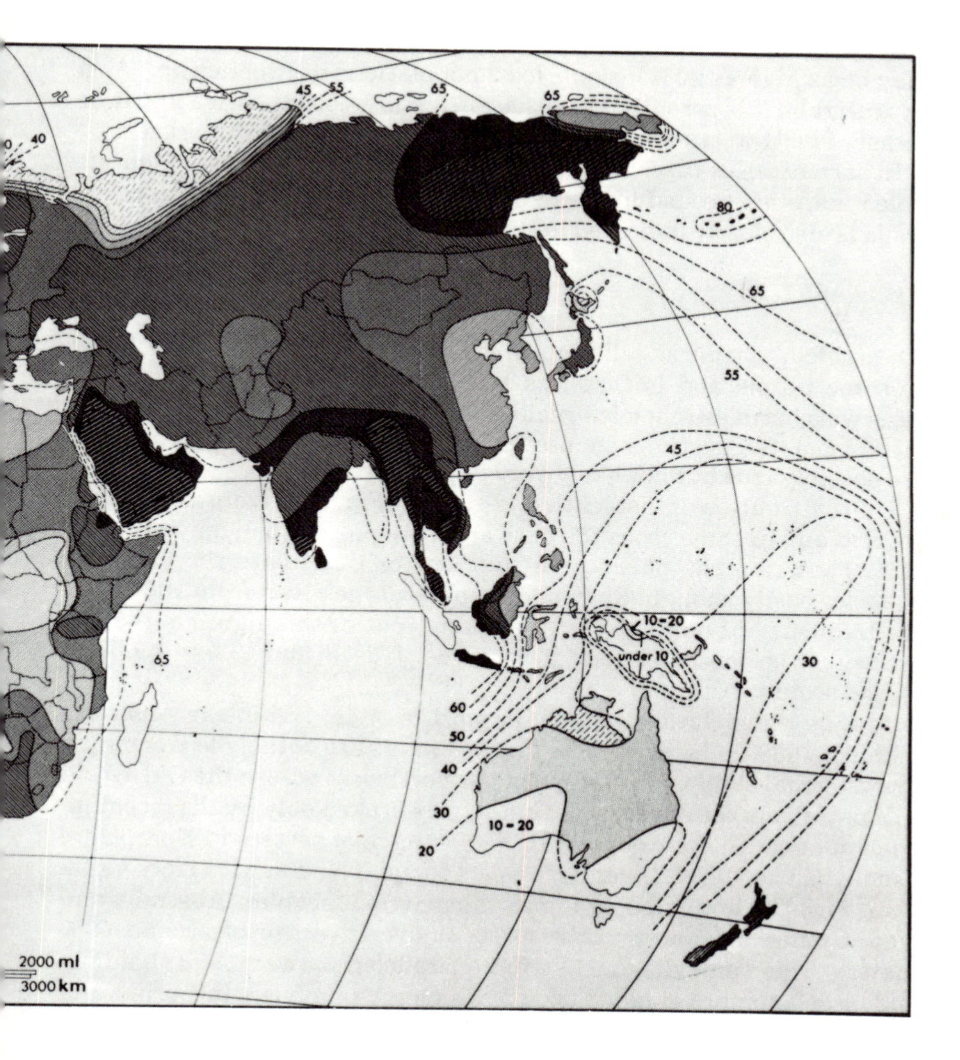
40
45
55
65
65
80
65
55
45
65
10-20
under 10
30
60
50
40
30
10-20
20
2000 mi
3000 km

40% for most of the world, more like 50% in southeastern Asia and Polynesia, and 20% in America. Diego positive is rare anywhere, but it may be as high as 20% in some local populations in America and Asia. In Australia it is zero. Kell positive is 70% in western Africa and it decreases in all directions away from there to reach zero in America.

In each of these cases a sense of continentality is suggested, but detailed maps are needed for us to be sure. The extreme position of Australia is also clearly indicated in three of these four cases.

PTC TASTING.

An artificial chemical called phenylthiocarbamide tastes quite bitter to some people and is tasteless to others. The ability to taste this otherwise harmless chemical, called PTC, is inherited as a simple dominant gene. Suggestions connecting nontasters with various diseases are possibly true but not likely very important.

The distribution of tasters that is given in Fig. 38 is from a variety of sources and in some cases the data are more pooled than may be desirable. These are the phenotypes, but one can calculate the gene frequencies easily enough. Subtract the percentage given from 100 to get the frequency of nontasters. The square root of this figure is the frequency of the nontaster gene. (64% = .64, $\sqrt{\ }$ is .8; and 49% = .49, $\sqrt{\ }$ = .7; and so on.)

Tasters are highest in Africa, in most of Asia, and in the Americas with 90–100% in most of these areas. Tasters are notably less common in a diagonal strip from Europe in the northwest across the Old World to Australia in the southeast. This strip is broken only by the recent intrusion of southern Mongoloids. Percentages of tasters in Europe are usually in the 70's. Similar figures are found in India, with more variation, with the lowest being found among tribal peoples. Australia and New Guinea are lower yet with an all-over average of around 60% tasters. This same diagonal strip is paralleled by wavy hair, balding, and large amounts of blood type A which is commonest in Europe and Australia. Before any excitement is generated on this last item it must be pointed out that Europe is different in having A_2 as half of its A blood, and also the greatest A concentration is among the Lapps who are Asiatic in their level of tasting.

Eskimos have a curiously low level of tasters, near 60% in the east and over 70% in the west. This adds another genetic line separating them from the Americans. More detailed distribution data from Siberia would be illuminating. It might also be noted that Ainus are typically eastern Asian in their 95% of tasters. Considering the Eskimos, Ainus, and Lapps, it is

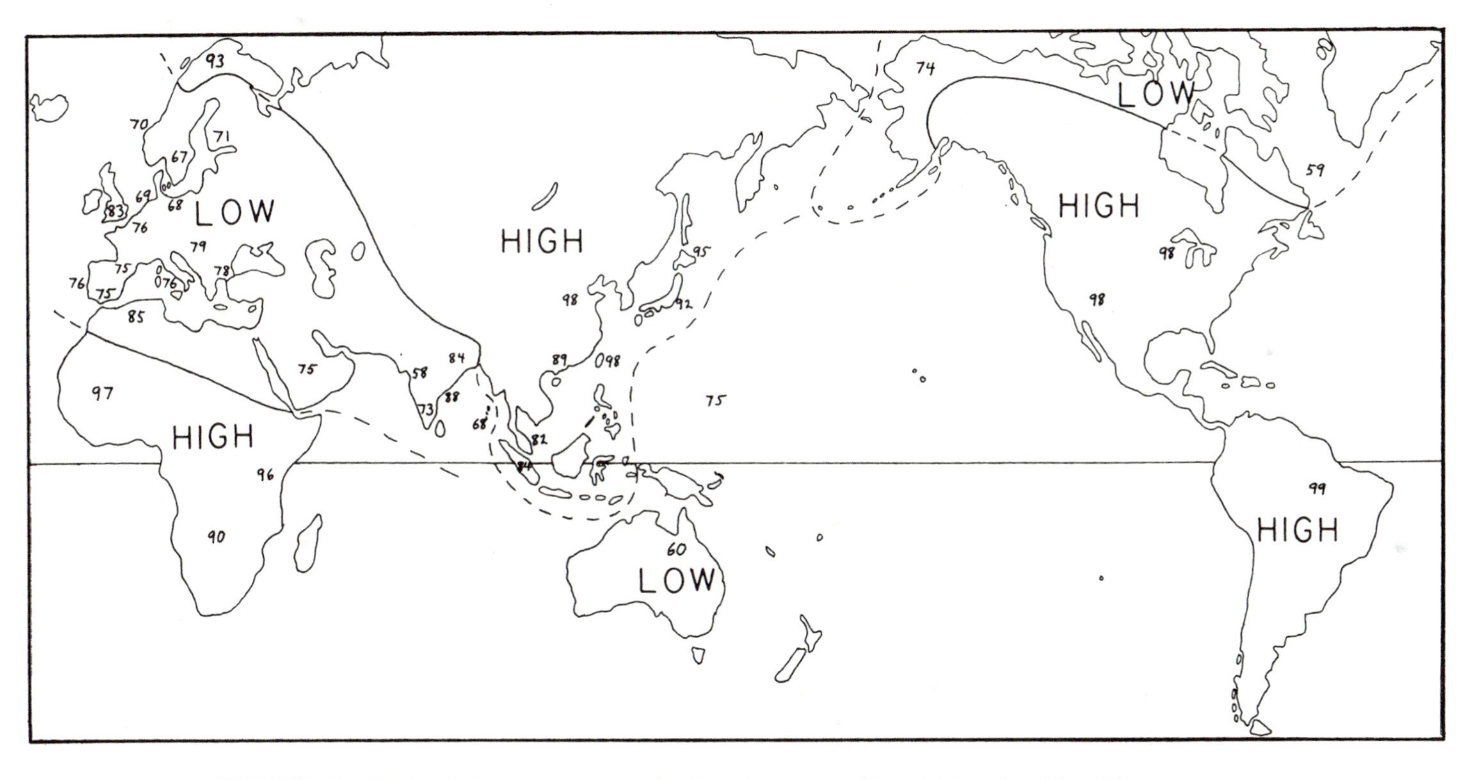

FIGURE 38. World distribution of the T allele for tasting Phenylthiocarbamide. The nontasters are everywhere in the minority, but are commonest in a diagonal strip across the Old World from Europe to Australia. This distribution of nontasters roughly parallels that of A blood, male balding, wavy hair, and blondism, but no connection can be shown.

evident that a Caucasoid-Mongoloid contrast in tasters is not a simple matter.

The distribution of tasters could best be described as continental, but the data are not detailed enough to sense whether there are any disruptions from agricultural migrations as in the blood types.

EARWAX.

The waxy substance found in human ear canals is properly called cerumen. It may be either wet and sticky, or else dry and crumbly. This is determined by a single gene, and the allele for wet earwax is the dominant one. There is some indication that dry earwax is more resistant to bacterial infections than is the wet variation.

The distribution of dry earwax is commonly reported as a Mongoloid trait as opposed to Caucasoid and Negroid where it is virtually absent. A closer look at its world distribution shows the above statement to be one of the classic oversimplifications that has plagued race studies. Indeed, if one pooled all samples that are labeled Mongoloid on other criteria, then the dry earwax is predominant in that category. But this pooling already presupposes the limits of distribution which we are looking for in the first place.

The center of dry earwax concentration is in northern China and it declines in frequency in every direction from there. Some representative gene frequencies can be given in declining intensity with an added breakdown into degrees of Mongoloid "affiliation."

Classical Mongoloid:	
North Chinese	.98
Koreans	.96
Tungus	.95
Mongols	.94
Japanese	.92
Southern Chinese	.86
Ryukyu Islanders	.79
Mongoloid Affiliated or Mixed:	
Li of Hainan	.67
Navajo Amerindians	.65
Micronesians	.61
Taiwan Aborigines	.53
Melanesians (not Papuans)	.53
Plains Indians	.50
Uncertain Affiliation:	
Ainus	.37

Non-Mongoloids:	
Germans	.18
American whites	.16
American blacks	.07

This distribution is reminiscent of many blood types in having a clear geographic focus, but without a good correlation with other traits or with climate. It could be taken as a Mongoloid trait that is somewhat selected against in less cold environments, but the north American Indian figures should be much higher if that were the case. It could be taken as an advantageous mutation that just happened to appear in northern China and is now spreading out from that source. The high frequencies in Micronesia and Melanesia may be taken to indicate a high Mongoloid contribution (about half) to their genetic make-up. It could also simply reflect their geographical proximity and availability for gene flow and thus selection for this new trait. It may also be looked at as a neutral trait which was once fixed by drift at 100% in central Asia, and which has since been shuffled around by human movements. A combination of these factors may also be the case.

The intermediate value for Ainus would be taken as indicating Mongoloid mixture (gene flow) if one considers them as Caucasoids. The Ainu may also be classed with Amerindians as a more early "Mongoloid" type before the dry earwax became prevalent. In any event, the trait does not have good climatic correlations and seems to behave much like other genetic traits.

EYE COLOR.

This variation was fully discussed among the classical traits, but in some respects it belongs here among the genetic ones. The major contrast between light and dark iris coloration follows simple Mendelian inheritance rules with the light color being recessive. The low pigment level which permits light eyes is climate related, but how that pigment is distributed is almost arbitrary. One could easily assume the trait made little difference in Europe during the last glaciation and it became fixed at 100% of light eyes by drift. The visual impact of looking at another person's eye color may have added to this by putting selection pressure on the minority just because they looked so different in this small but very noticeable place. The subsequent influx of new peoples, possibly with the process of sapienization, and certainly with agriculture, brought back a mixture of colors which has not yet settled out. There is something of a parallel here with blood type

A and Rh negative, at least in the way all these traits behave geographically.

FINGERPRINTS.

On the interface between the dermis and epidermis there are irregularities called papillary ridges that occur over the palms and soles. These are sets of parallel ridges that are also represented by similar ridges on the surface of the epidermis. Sweat glands are lined up along these ridges and together this forms a sort of friction surface to aid in grasping smooth surfaces. They are found on the hands and feet of all primates and also on the tips of those tails which are prehensile. In small primates these friction surfaces are very useful in climbing, but in larger animals their utility in this function drastically declines. In animals the size of apes the effect of this adhesive surface becomes negligible compared to the weight of the body. In man especially, a secondary function appears when the hand mainly supports objects being picked up with it, instead of the weight of the body itself.

Variations occur in all areas of these ridge patterns but the ones that interest us here are those which have long been of use in individual identification. These are the fingertip patterns, and their study is called dermatoglyphics. There are three main types of prints that are distinguished in the first sorting and they constitute the only variation that will concern us here. A triradius is a point where three sets of ridges meet in a triangular pattern. A fingerprint will have none, one, or two such triradii, and the resultant patterns are called arches, loops, and whorls, respectively (See Fig. 39).

Most people's prints can be classified in one or the other of these three categories, they are all-or-nothing qualitative traits. A population is then described as having various percentages of each of these three types, all adding up to 100%. So far this sounds much like mapping the frequencies of the ABO genes, but there is a difference here that makes things simpler. These three types do not vary independently of each other. The rule for this is simple: as arches decline in frequency, whorls increase relative to loops. This can be shown on a simple graph with arches decreasing from left to right, loops also decreasing in the same direction, but with whorls increasing from left to right (See Fig. 40). This graph can also be read as showing the "average" number of triradii, ranging from 1.05 on the left edge up to 1.65 on the right.

Most human populations occupy a particular position on this scale. Bushmen are on the left edge at 1.05 triradii, Europeans and Africans are generally between 1.20 and 1.25, most Asians and Amerindians are

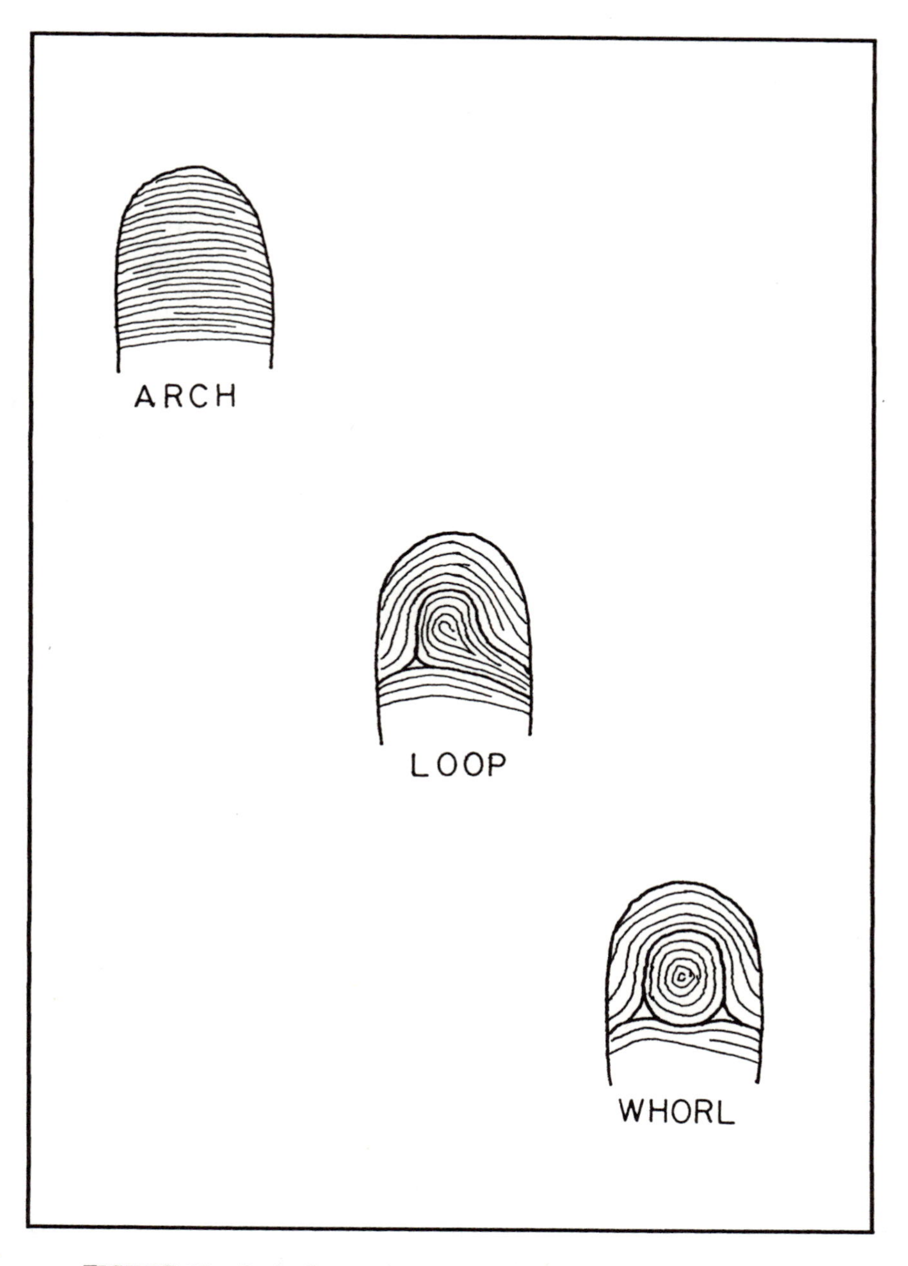

FIGURE 39. Basic fingerprint types. Arches are the simplest and rarest type, and have no triradii—the meeting point of three converging groups of lines. Loops have one triradius and whorls have two of them. Extensive population data are available on the frequencies of these types, but not for other differences in fingertip patterns.

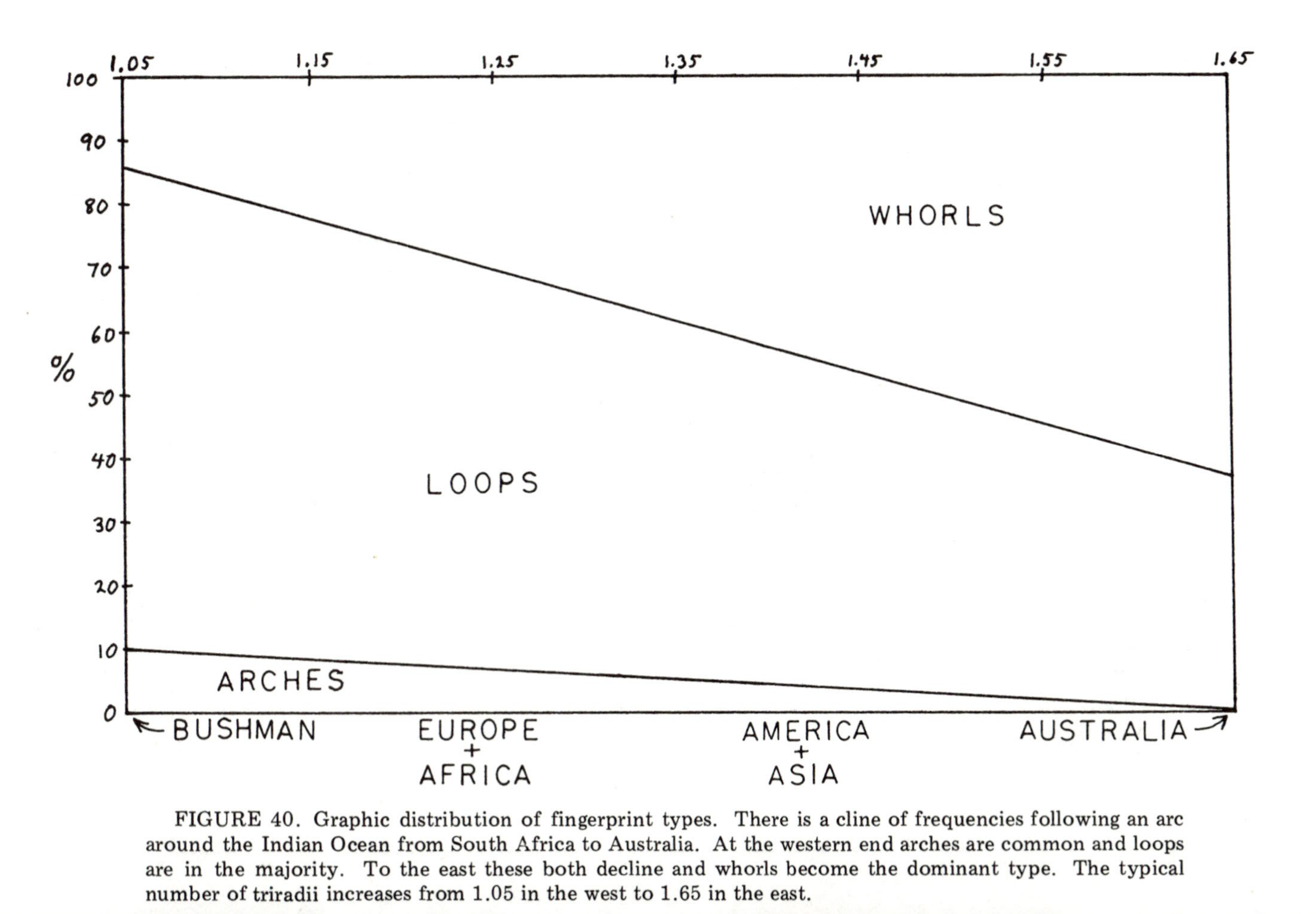

FIGURE 40. Graphic distribution of fingerprint types. There is a cline of frequencies following an arc around the Indian Ocean from South Africa to Australia. At the western end arches are common and loops are in the majority. To the east these both decline and whorls become the dominant type. The typical number of triradii increases from 1.05 in the west to 1.65 in the east.

around 1.45, and Australian Aborigines and Negritos are on the right edge at 1.65 triradii. It is interesting to note how this scale curves rather neatly around the Indian Ocean from one extreme in southern Africa to the other extreme in Australia. Available data on Ainus do not fit the pattern. They are western in their loop-to-whorl ratio, but eastern in their percentage of arches. It may never be possible now to get enough data to resolve this particular issue.

The impression might be gained that the small hands of Bushmen and Pygmies should lead to fewer triradii, thus more arches. This is contradicted by the similarly small Negritos who have no arches. The largest fingerprint ever reported appears to be of the arch type. This is from a handprint in very fine mud of what is purported to be a Sasquatch, or Bigfoot, the legendary wild and gigantic hominid of western North America. The authenticity of this print cannot be verified.

The geographical pattern of fingerprints is again reminiscent of other genetic trait distributions, even though we cannot pin down the particular genes involved here. They appear to distribute as a continuum between two polar extremes, but this may be somewhat illusory. One can imagine early man in the west having the Bushman average, but deviating locally to a fair degree. A small hunting band that is the first to enter India from the west just happens by chance to have no arches and far more whorls than loops. They expand to occupy all of the Eastern world and their descendants maintain this new all-over average. This example of founders effect will have divided the Old World into two fingerprint areas at the bottleneck west of India. Later human movements of contact in central Asia, of sapienization, and from agriculture will all tend to cause some blending towards the center where the two areas gain larger contacts. At the same time the two southern extremes would be essentially unaffected. The continuum is thus automatically built up from what was once a neat, two part division that in turn resulted from a chance event one million years ago. This might not be the explanation, or may be only part of it, but its simplicity is at least attractive.

DENTAL TRAITS.

There are some characteristics of human teeth which vary in a genetic sort of way even though the details of their mode of inheritance are not known. These are traits which have no obvious selective advantages and which seem to have continental types of distributions. I say "seem to" because they have generally been classed as racial by most investigators and their actual distributions are not given in detail.

The Carabelli cusp is an extra projection on the inside edge of the upper molars near the forward corner. It is often called functionless because it does not rise high enough to reach the occlusal surface of the unworn teeth. Obviously it provides an additional cusp for chewing after the molars have worn down somewhat. This might be advantageous for people with otherwise small teeth. It is found in 40 to 60% of various samples of European dentitions, in less than 20% of Amerindians, and in 10% or less from any other populations. It is not clear whether this should be regarded as a genetic trait with a continental distribution centered in Europe, or if it is positively selected for there.

Enamel extensions beyond the crown of the tooth and onto the root are common among Mongoloids and Ainus. Isolated spots of such enamel, called enamel pearls, are also found among them. No function seems possible, so they are probably genetic anomalies that cause no harm and which tend to be concentrated in a geographical area—in this case eastern Asia.

The number and arrangement of cusps, especially on the lower molars, includes a few variations that have been noted (See Fig. 41). At one extreme is the *Dryopithecus* or Y5 pattern with four cusps arranged in a rough square and with a fifth added on behind. The outer, rear cusp of the square extends to make a large contact with the cusp diagonal to it, and the resulting fissures resemble the letter Y. This may be simplified to a true square and it is then called +5, and if the fifth cusp is missing it is a +4 design. Large-toothed people usually have Y5 lower molars while those with smaller teeth are usually +4. There seems to be little of what could be called racial variation here except as an adjunct of tooth size itself. Australians have the largest teeth and the most Y5 patterns, while Europeans have the most of the +4 pattern of the major races.

Crowding of the teeth causes twisting of the incisors and impacted wisdom teeth because of lack of room for them to erupt into. Civilized people suffer most from crowding and it is commonly blamed on the jaws being too much reduced to accommodate the teeth. This is not exactly correct in that tooth and jaw sizes usually match if the teeth are worn properly. In normal (not civilized) usage there will be strains placed on individual teeth, causing them to move slightly in relation to their neighbors in the same jaw. Eventually this develops a wear facet on each tooth where it rests against another. By the time the last molars are due to erupt, the accumulated wear on the thirteen contact surfaces of each tooth row ahead of it is enough to move the second molar three or four mm ahead to make room for the third to come in. Civilized diets usually do not include enough hard chewing to cause this amount of interproximal wear and the teeth are longer, from front to back,

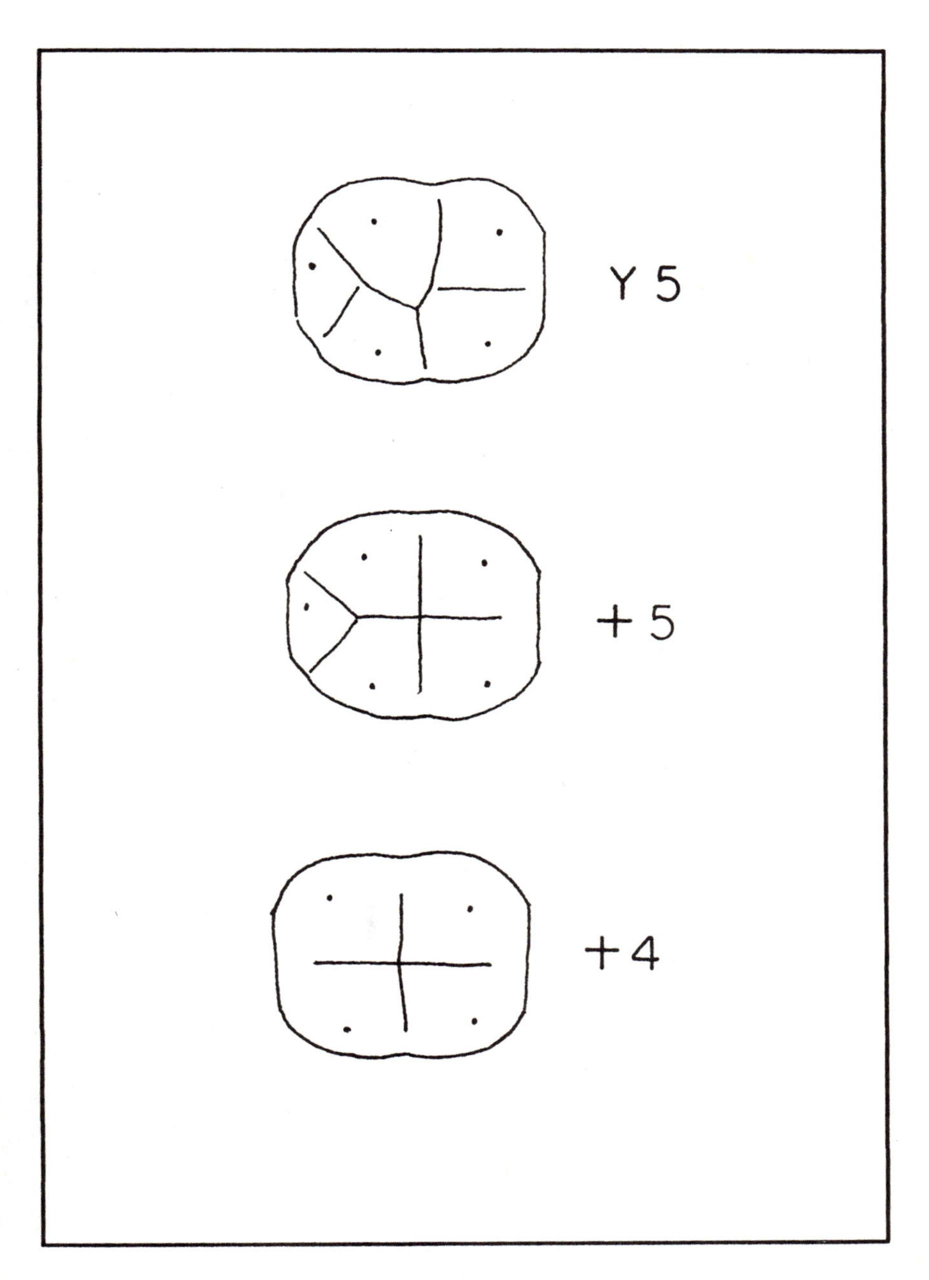

FIGURE 41. Lower molar patterns. The *Dryopithecus* Y5 pattern is commonest in populations with large teeth. The +4 pattern is more common where teeth are smaller, and +5 is an intermediate type. Increasing frequencies of +5 and +4 also tend to go along with civilization.

than they should have been. Technically it is not that the jaws became too small, but that the teeth have become too big. Crowding of the teeth is not a racial trait; it is a consequence of civilization.

CEPHALIC INDEX.

Human braincases come in a variety of shapes, some of which can be measured in terms of a length to breadth ratio. The cephalic index is simply the breadth (taken just above and behind the ears) expressed as a percentage of the length (from between the eyebrows to the farthest back). This index was devised by the Swedish Anthropologist Retzius in 1842 and has become one of the best known, and at the same time most puzzling, of human variations.

Cephalic index is known to be inherited because round-headed people have round-headed children, and likewise for long heads. It is easy to measure with a simple tool. It has a great range of variation—from heads which are half as broad as they are long (index 50) to fully round ones (index 100). It can also be measured on a skull, where it is properly called cranial index. Head shape has no known function, and because most people scarcely notice it, there would be no sexual selection or racial bias involved in its perpetuation. There are considerable geographical areas of concentrations of one head shape rather than another. For all these reasons it was early thought to be one of the most significant of racial traits. It is currently in considerable disfavor.

Cephalic indices are grouped into three categories:

Brachycephalic — index over 80
Mesocephalic — index between 75 and 80
Dolichocephalic — index under 75

In addition to these, some workers use extreme categories for those over 85 and for those under 70. For skulls the same scale should be set about two points lower, but this is rarely bothered with. The reason is not because of the temporal muscle on the side of the head, as is usually stated, which supposedly adds more to the living breadth than to the length. The difference in tissue thickness is not that great and is only a small part of the reason, the rest being simple geometry. If a constant amount is removed from both diameters of an elongated shape, the result is automatically even more elongated.

There are various ways of mapping cephalic index distributions, most of which are confusing to look at. The simplest way is to outline the several areas of the world where almost all of the group means are about the same (See Fig. 42).

There is a great belt of brachycephaly which runs across the Old World from Germany to Manchuria with total disregard for all other variations which distinguish its two ends. Indexes within this belt hang very closely around 85. Cephalic indexes drop rather abruptly on the border of this belt to become 80 on the west, north, and southeast. Only in the west is there a significant cline where the indexes taper off to 78 in the far west.

There is also an equatorial belt of dolichocephaly in Africa, southern Asia, Australia, and Melanesia where indexes all cluster around 75. Some odd areas which may be noted are the Lapps at 85, Ainus at 76, Andaman Negritos at 83, India deviating a bit to 78, and a region in central Africa at 80. Madagasgar's 80 is the expected value for an Indonesian extension.

In the Americas there is an all-over trend toward a cephalic index of 80, with their own belt of brachycephaly from California to Panama. The southeastern strip of South America takes a drop to 75, as do the eastern Eskimo. There are many more minor variations but this fairly represents the big picture.

It is immediately evident that this kind of distribution makes about as much sense as do most of the blood types. A feeling of continental centrality is about the only way to describe it.

There are two other variables that seriously affect cephalic index, deformation in growing individuals and changes over time. Cranial deformation begins in early childhood by restricting the growth of the head in one plane, thus forcing its growth to occur in other directions. Such deformations are usually easy to spot by their shape and usual asymmetry, and are simply not considered for this index. It is possible, as some have suggested, that cradling practices are still sometimes causing a slight deformation which has not been detected. This may be true, but it would have only a slight effect on the index.

Changes in cephalic index over time have stirred considerable interest because they have almost always been in one direction, toward brachycephaly. Early *sapiens* were rather consistently long headed and most of the round heads of today developed this trait within the last thousand years or so. In a classic study, Weidenreich (1945) documented this progressive brachycephalization and tried futilely to relate it to improving head balance.

Several correlations have been noted between brachycephaly and other phenomena but there are problems with all of them. When heads become round the loss of length is mainly behind the ears (postauricular) which means there is little shortening of the nasal chamber. This

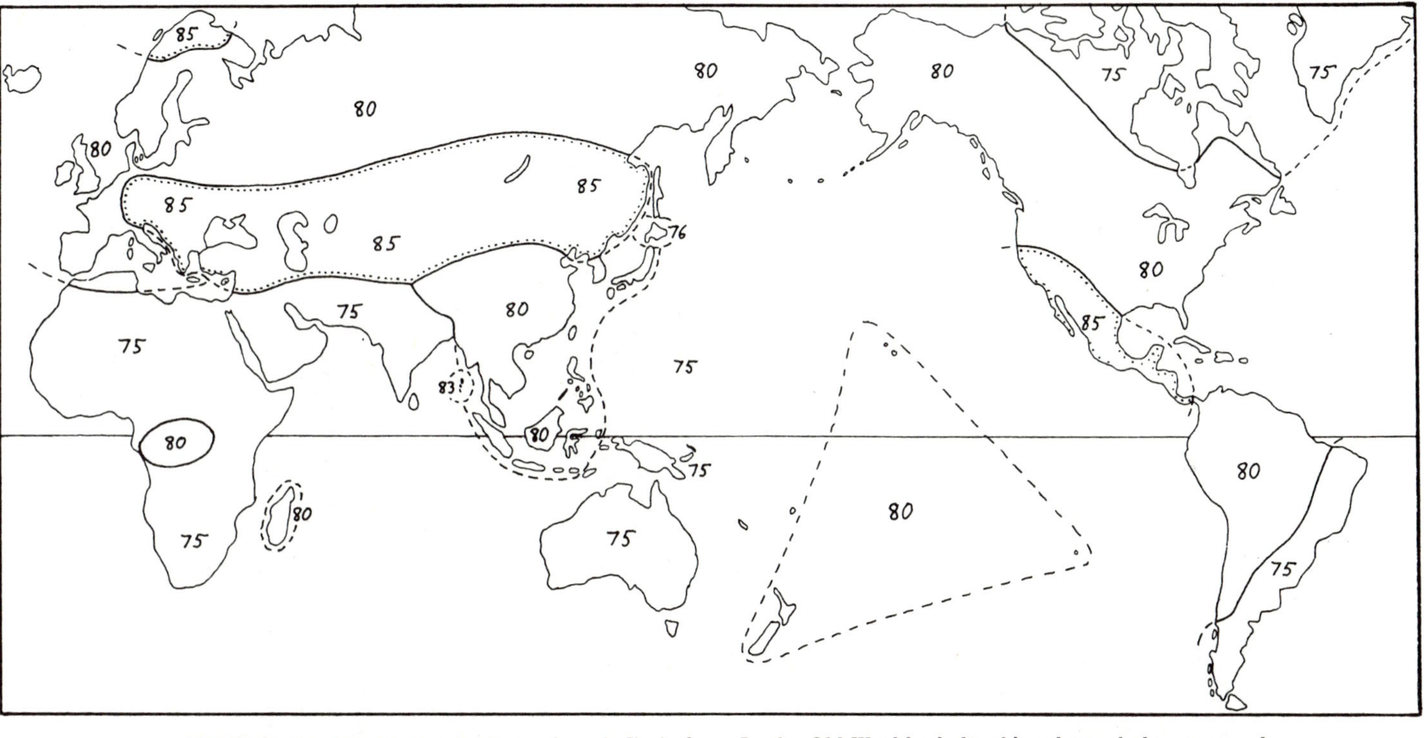

FIGURE 42. World distribution of cephalic index. In the Old World a belt of brachycephaly, or round headedness, runs from Germany to Manchuria with indexes usually around 85. From there, indexes decline towards dolichocephaly in all directions. A similar belt of brachycephaly is centrally located in the Americas. Dolichocephaly everywhere tends to be peripheral.

could be turned around to say an elongation of the nasal chamber toward the rear is forcing the broadening of the head, but the mechanics of this don't seem to work out. There is some correlation between round heads and cold temperatures, but this fails badly in the Americas and doesn't account for the lower indexes to the north of the great belt of brachycephaly in Eurasia. Heavy alcohol consumption has some correlation with round heads, as does horse riding vs. walking, but there are too many exceptions to make much of either of these.

A more promising approach might be to turn the problem around and try to account for dolichocephaly. There may be some neurological reason for the brain to tend toward a more rounded shape if all else is equal. An index of about 85 seems to be where brachycephalization stops. Roundish heads are also common among the apes and australopithecines. *Homo erectus* shifted to a more elongated braincase though the cranial index figures exaggerate this by including too many ridges. *Homo sapiens* dropped the index still more by narrowing the cranial base substantially. Only in recent times has it begun a return to what may be a more normal shape with the removal of some selective force that caused the elongation. That force may have been the pull of the temporal muscle against the side of the head, in particular the pressure of its outer layers on the inner ones and against the bone. The area occupied by the temporal muscle is prominently convexed or bulging in round heads and is almost flat in long heads. In the latter case the temporal muscle has an almost straight line of action without one layer pressing very hard on another. The change to a partly meat diet in *erectus* correlates in time with this flattening of the temporal fossa. The narrower cranial base of *sapiens* requires still more narrowing of the braincase to maintain the flat temporal fossa. Just what has happened to relax this proposed selection remains to be shown. Carnivorous mammals tend to emphasize the temporal muscles whereas herbivores tend to emphasize the masseters for chewing. There is no good evidence of a diet change from meat to vegetables among recent round heads.

At present, the variations in cephalic index remain unexplained and will be treated like the genetic traits which distribute themselves by chance factors and human breeding patterns. If a functional significance can someday be shown and the selective pressures identified for sure, then the cephalic index will have to be considered in a different light.

OTHER CRANIAL TRAITS.

Several other variations in cranial design have distributions that may be more like those of genetic traits than like classical ones. Sometimes this is difficult to determine since their occurrences are reported on the assumption that they correlate with the more usual race designations. Often a good clue is simply to note the apparent lack of any functional significance to the variations.

The Mongoloid emphasis on the anterior part of the chewing apparatus has already been mentioned in connection with some cold-climate adaptations. The large anterior teeth and high frequency of the failure to develop third molars may also be a genetic trait of eastern Asia in general that goes back to *erectus* times. The significance of this to cold weather is not evident and the *erectus* Lantian jaw was lacking a third molar.

There is a consistant difference in brow ridge design in all the eastern *erectus* skulls as opposed to the western ones which is largely carried on into *sapiens* in each half of the Old World. Seen from above, the eastern brows run almost straight across the front of the skull while the western ones are notably pulled back at the outside corners (See Fig. 43). The Peking skulls did not seem to have anteriorly set cheeks, to judge from Weidenreich's reconstruction, but this would be a simple adjustment where the brow-ridge corners are already well forward. To make the same change in the western skull with its more laterally oriented orbits would take much more remodeling. The brow-ridge orientation in the east can be treated as a genetic trait whose distribution began as a chance event very much like that of fingerprint patterns. Given this difference, there was a pre-adaptation for a cold weather design that did not exist in the western skulls.

The Inca bone is a separate ossification on the back of the head resulting from an extra suture running across the occipital bone (See Fig. 44). This condition can hardly confer any selective advantage or disadvantage and none has been suggested. It therefore may be expected to behave like a genetic trait. Inca bones are reported as common among Mongoloids in general, and reaching their highest frequency of 30% in Peru. Just how consistent this distribution is has yet to be demonstrated. Indications of an Inca bone appear in three out of four Peking skulls. This again tells us something about genetic traits over time in eastern Asia that cannot easily be ignored.

There is a notable depression at the root of the nose, called the nasion notch, in most Australians and Melanesians which is rarely noticed elsewhere to this degree. This gives to the side view the antithesis of the "Grecian profile" where the forehead and nose form a straight line. It is exaggerated by the frequently over-hanging brows, but it exists in its own right. Until a function can be shown for it we may treat this trait's distribution as a genetic one. The late *erectus*

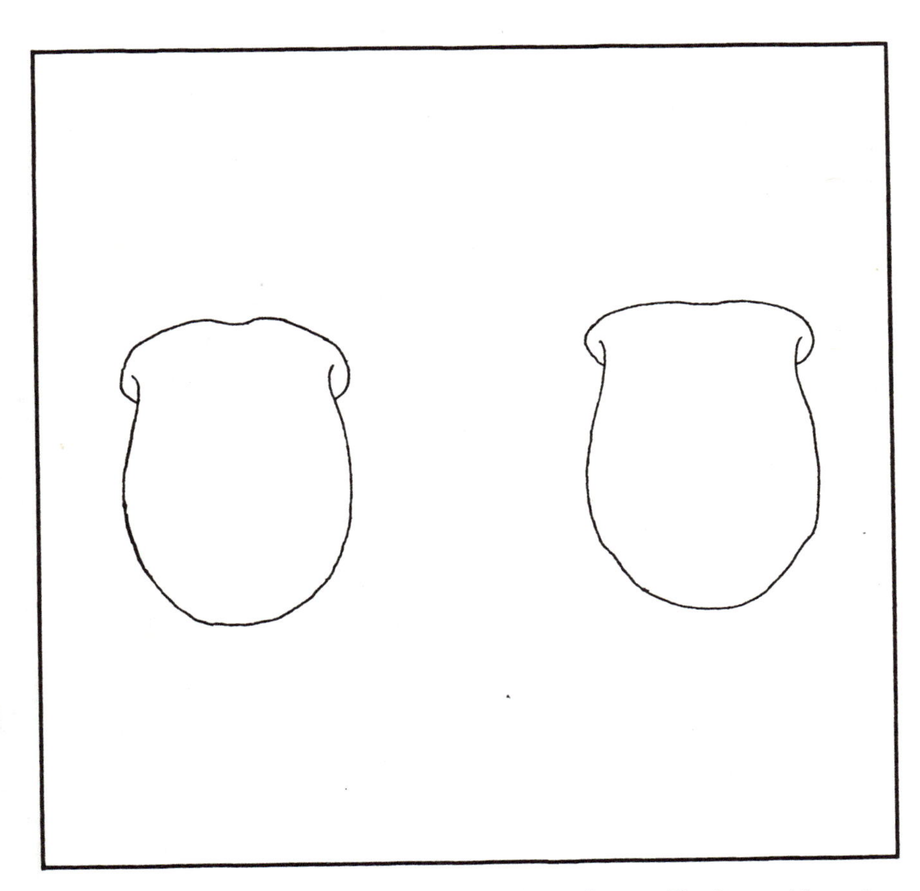

FIGURE 43. *Erectus* skull outlines from above. The brow ridges at the top of each drawing are of two types. In western *erectus* (left) the outside corners are drawn back, while in eastern specimens (right) they run more nearly straight across. This is one of the many line traits that characterize particular geographic regions over long periods of time, unaffected by evolutionary advances in grade.

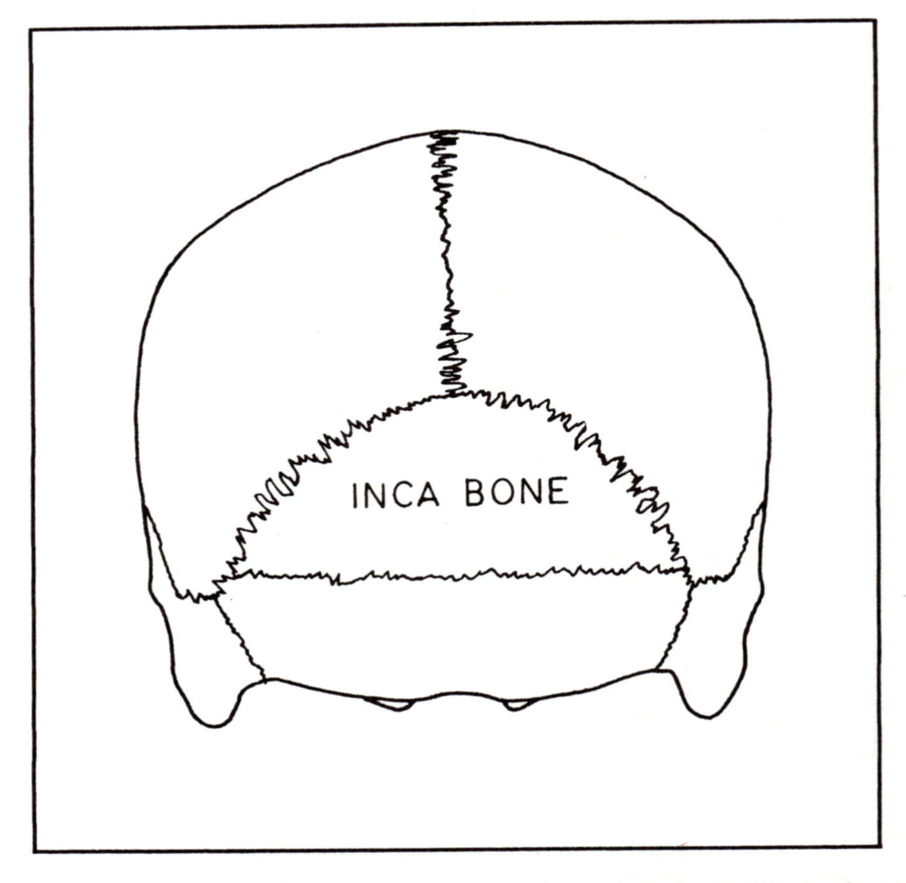

FIGURE 44. The Inca bone. This extra bone on the back of the head is formed by a horizontal suture which separates the top part of the occipital bone. It is a line trait that occurs in varying frequencies from Peking *erectus* through recent Mongoloid populations.

skulls from the Solo River in Java do not show this nasion notch, even with their very prominent brow ridges. This fact is ignored by those who propose a genetic continuity from Solo man to the aboriginal Australians. The facial withdrawal in the process of sapienization may have produced this notch, when for some reason, the brows could not withdraw as far.

Total size of the braincase, along with the enclosed brain, shows variations around the world that mainly correlate with body size. Direct data for the brain itself is surprisingly meager, but the skulls can be measured to find their capacities. Population averages range from just under 1300 cc to well over 1500 cc, and apparently normal individuals go a little smaller and a lot larger than these figures. Males have larger brains than females, on the average, in every human population simply because they are larger in body size. As bodies get bigger, brains do too, but at a slower rate. Female brains are larger than males in proportion to body size.

Judging from their body sizes, Australian natives should have about average-sized brains, but measurements of skull capacities put them at the low end of the human range. While there may be some significance to this in terms of evolutionary grade, there is another factor which may have influenced the reported measurements. Aborigine skulls are picked up in a variety of places where occasional English skulls can also be found. Ordinarily these can be distinguished by associated cultural remains or tooth wear, but not always. Half-breeds might also be included among Abos of purely native culture. To select out the pure and partial English skulls from a collection may also involve the experienced eye who "knows" the natives have smaller braincases. We do not know how many large braincases have been rejected from Aborigine series simply on that assumption alone.

Braincase sizes form a continuum from small to large, and correlate with body size. In these terms such sizes should be viewed as classical traits. If some populations have braincase sizes that do not match their bodies (Australians too small and Mongolians too large) then something like a genetic distribution may be involved as well.

The functional significance of brain size variations, which correlate closely with braincase sizes, has been the basis of much literature. Most of this can be characterized as nonsense that was written to support a view based on some other source of information. My own observation, after measuring the heads of hundreds of people, is that a personality difference can usually be seen between large and small-brained people. For what it's worth, large-brained people react slowly, ponder things longer, are slow to anger and slow to calm down. Small-brained people usually react faster in all respects. The trouble is that this cannot be separated from body size variations which possibly are the real source of this difference.

When viewed from behind, some skulls are nearly round while others have straight sides and gabled tops (See Fig. 45). There is a continuum of shapes between these two extremes, so it is technically a quantitative trait. Brachycephalic skulls tend to be round and dolichocephalic ones gabled, but not always. Powerful development of the masticatory apparatus tends to go with gabled skulls also. Exceptions to these two rules have not been well mapped, but could prove interesting if they were. Neandertals are notable for having rounded vaults while the rest of the late *erectus* skulls are all gabled. There may be a genetic type of braincase variation involved in modern man as well.

Further variations will be found in virtually every book on human races. This should suffice here, as I have already pushed some of these traits farther than their known distributions should allow.

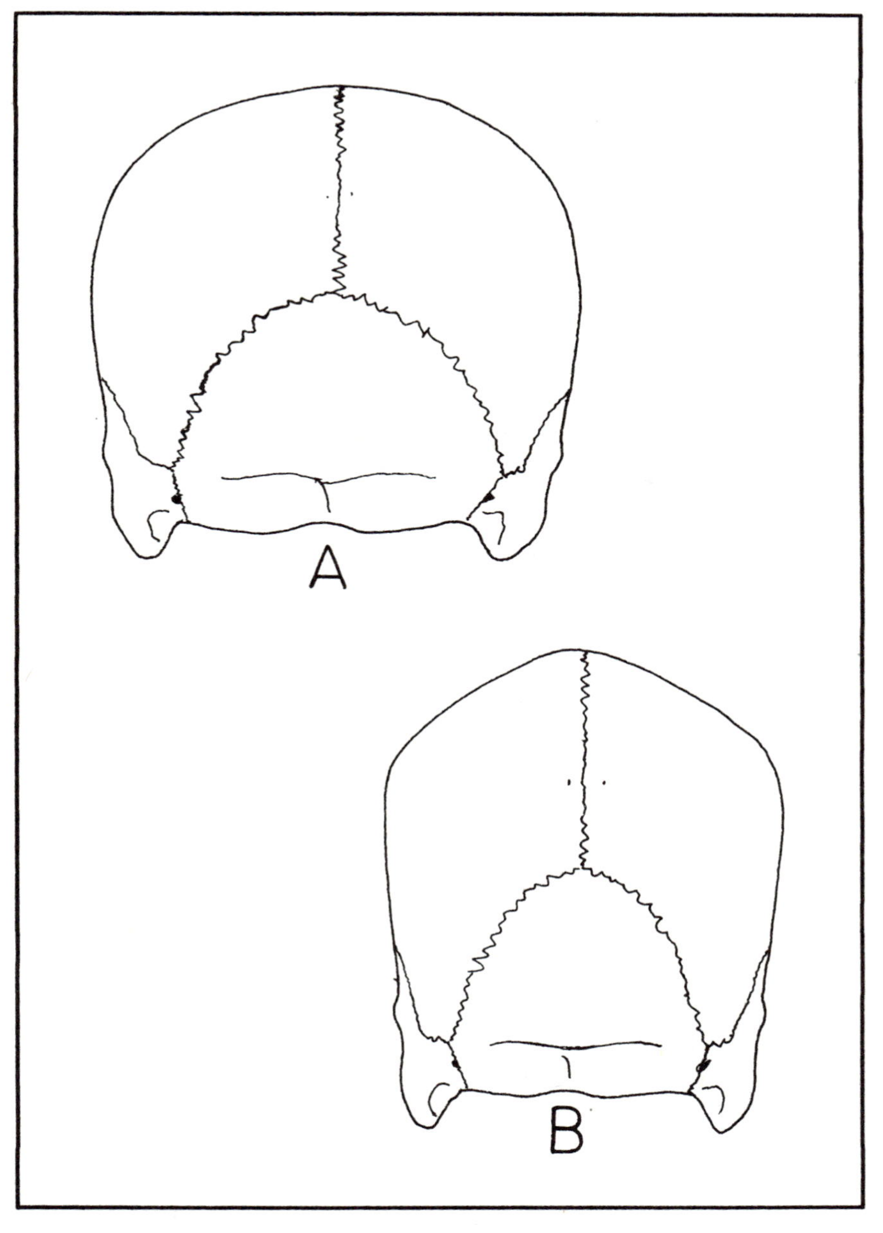

FIGURE 45. Rounded vs gabled braincases. As seen from behind, the braincase may be nearly rounded in outline (left), or may range to the other extreme of somewhat angulated with sagittal and parasagittal ridges along the top (right). The more angulated specimens are usually those with powerful jaw muscles, are often elongated, and sometimes are small.

7.
DESCENT GROUPS

SUMMARY.

The distribution pattern of genetic traits around the world might be described by some as being based only on chance. Each trait can be given in terms of locations of highs and lows scattered randomly over the world, and the magnitudes of these highs and lows are also random. Then if one allows some gene flow to even out the worst of the irregularities we supposedly have the kind of map that each genetic trait presents us with. On a superficial level this picture is about as accurate a description as can be given, but this is just the background "noise" below which another pattern can be sensed.

The underlying pattern is basically one of continental regularities between the barriers to gene flow. These have been seriously disrupted, shifted, and diluted within the last 10,000 years by agriculturally based peoples. At least three authors in recent years have tried to describe these genetic areas in their attempts at racial classifications. Stanley Garn's highest level of classification (his nine geographical races) is based mainly on genetic barriers, while his next level (of local races) stresses climatic adaptation more. William Boyd made a six-fold classification of genetic races without even pretending to use classical traits. Carleton Coon's five subspecies are based on both classical and genetic traits, but the latter were highly influential in his setting of boundaries.

My own scheme of seven descent groups does not differ greatly from any of the other three. It is based on a combination of genetic barriers to hunting man before agriculture with some evident genetic distributions that can be reconstructed as of 10,000 years ago. The method of reconstruction for this time depth is much the same as that which was used for classical traits. Migrations are withdrawn and relict genetic types are expanded. Blanks are filled in by assuming genetic continuity between barriers and not by any kind of adaptation.

A reconstruction of 100,000 years ago can be outlined roughly as an extension of more recent distributions still farther back into the past. From *erectus* to *sapiens* there were some major changes that extended the territories of certain descent groups. The North African group apparently expanded into southern Africa in a wave of total replacement. The Papuan group based in New Guinea similarly overran part of Australia. The European and Asian groups expanded northwards to include the rest of the habitable world. The Asian group not only was the most successful in Eurasia but was also situated so as to provide the whole human input into the Americas.

The ultimate origin of these descent groups lies in the evolutionary explosion of the first *Homo erectus*, tool-using, big-game hunters. Relaxed selection provided unusual amounts of raw material of variation and founders effect distributed it unevenly in the various habitable areas. Later mutation, drift, and some selection served to accentuate some differences and to introduce still more.

An early meeting of *erectus* populations coming from Europe and eastern Asia may have occurred in central Asia. A third interglacial contact of this kind would have mixed both cultural and physical adaptations to cold climates and neutral genes would have flowed too. This would have been the first bypassing of the narrow passage between the western and eastern gene pools.

GENETIC AREAS.

It has been described how genetic traits show a tendency to be distributed in geographical areas which do not necessarily correspond to the climatic regions of classical traits. The next step is to define these genetic areas as closely as possible and to give them names. This may be approached from two different directions and may be studied at various time levels.

The actual distributions of genetic traits in the ethnographic present give clear indication of geographical variation but they are very unclear about where boundaries might be drawn, except in a very general sense. The other approach is to consider where the barriers to gene flow might have been most pronounced in 1500 A.D. Such barriers ought to coincide with the postulated boundaries between the genetic areas.

Because of the human movements since agriculture we might also attempt to define the genetic areas as of 10,000 years ago. This means pulling back genetic traits to their sources in a manner analogous to what was done to reconstruct climatic races. Relict populations may then be expanded in terms of genetic traits as far as seems feasible.

Filling in the blank areas would be done on the assumption that there was a high degree of genetic uniformity in each area between the major barriers to gene flow.

A still earlier reconstruction can be made to try to approximate distributions during *erectus* times. Again movements are pulled even farther back to their sources and some guesses are made for filling in the spaces. Where movements are not indicated, a high degree of continuity is postulated. This can be checked against the fossil record in terms of a few traits that are here considered to behave like genetic ones.

The effects of human movements on genetic and classical traits must be clearly distinguished. When people expand into a new territory, they carry with them both the genetic and the classical traits they began with. This makes their frontier a common boundary for both kinds of traits. Given enough time for them to settle in, the differences will begin to appear. Classical traits will be selected according to climate, and, barring cultural restraints, will eventually return to whatever adaptations the climate called for before the migration occurred. The genetic traits will blend at random with whatever populations are now in breeding contact and the genetic areas will tend to level off their frequencies. Eventually many of these will reach zero or 100%, especially if they were near these figures with the first blending.

Both processes take time, more time than has passed since each of the major shufflings that are described here. Sapienization triggered some movements which were far from being settled out when the agricultural explosions began. The ethnographic present catches the distributions of traits in two different stages of recovery from the two disruptions, and just prior to the third one of modern times. Trying to disentangle all this from maps of present gene frequencies may seem all but impossible, but I think a good start can be made. It all depends on whether the processes involved have been correctly identified.

GARN'S GEOGRAPHICAL RACES.

Our first step is to review some attempts to map out the genetic areas in the ethnographic present. Stanley Garn (1961) did not explicitly set out to do just this, but it is roughly what he ended up with anyway. Garn's system for classifying human races was to begin at a high level which he called (macro) geographical, and then move down to subdivisions of these which he called local races. A still lower level of micro (geographical) races includes all of the actual breeding populations, and are distinguished by a few gene frequencies only. The criteria given for the divisions at each of the two higher levels are broadly the same, but at the geographical level he emphasized genetic traits and their barriers, while at the local race level he emphasized climatic adaptations. This distinction can be pushed all the way, an action which Dr. Garn may or may not approve of, but which serves a useful purpose. Here we will look at his geographical races as an attempt at defining genetic areas alone.

There are nine such geographical races as shown in Fig. 46. The barriers dividing them are primarily oceans, and secondarily they include prominent mountain ranges and deserts. The recent expansion of the Eskimo leaves one barrier of social noninteraction only. In general, these presumed barriers pass through areas of very low population density, if not areas of no population at all.

Low population may be a barrier to gene flow in terms of quantity, but in terms of quality it can be the fastest route of travel. Where population density is low, social units maintain a constant number of individuals by covering larger areas. The normal human face-to-face contacts in deserts are over far greater distances than in more fruitful terrain. Advantageous mutations can there be spread over greater distances in a given length of time. Since most of the genetic polymorphisms that divide mankind have no special selective advantage, desert areas do function as efficient barriers.

Garn's Micronesian and Polynesian geographical races are so recent in origin that most other workers do not bother to classify them as significant units and just treat them as offshoots of some other, better established groups. Yet they do show some genetic distinctions and qualify under his term of geographical races to at least some degree. It is only this degree that may be questioned.

Within any such geographical race the inhabitants will tend to be related to one another in terms of common descent, but this has two meanings which are often confused. Common descent may mean that all members of the group can (theoretically) trace their origins back to some common ancestor from which all their racial traits derive. This seems to imply a strong unity among the people involved. Actual tracings of genealogy, even with the aid of linguistic approximations of genealogy, can go back only a few thousand years. In terms of classical traits, at least, many apparently unified groups may not owe their similar traits to a common ancestor but to similar selective agents in the environment. The strong sense of identity among a group of people is not so much the result of common ancestry in this sense, but rather it is the cause of their believing in it.

The other sense of common ancestry is that one's ancestors are concentrated in one geographical area as opposed to being spread evenly over the world. This follows from the law of limited ancestors which in

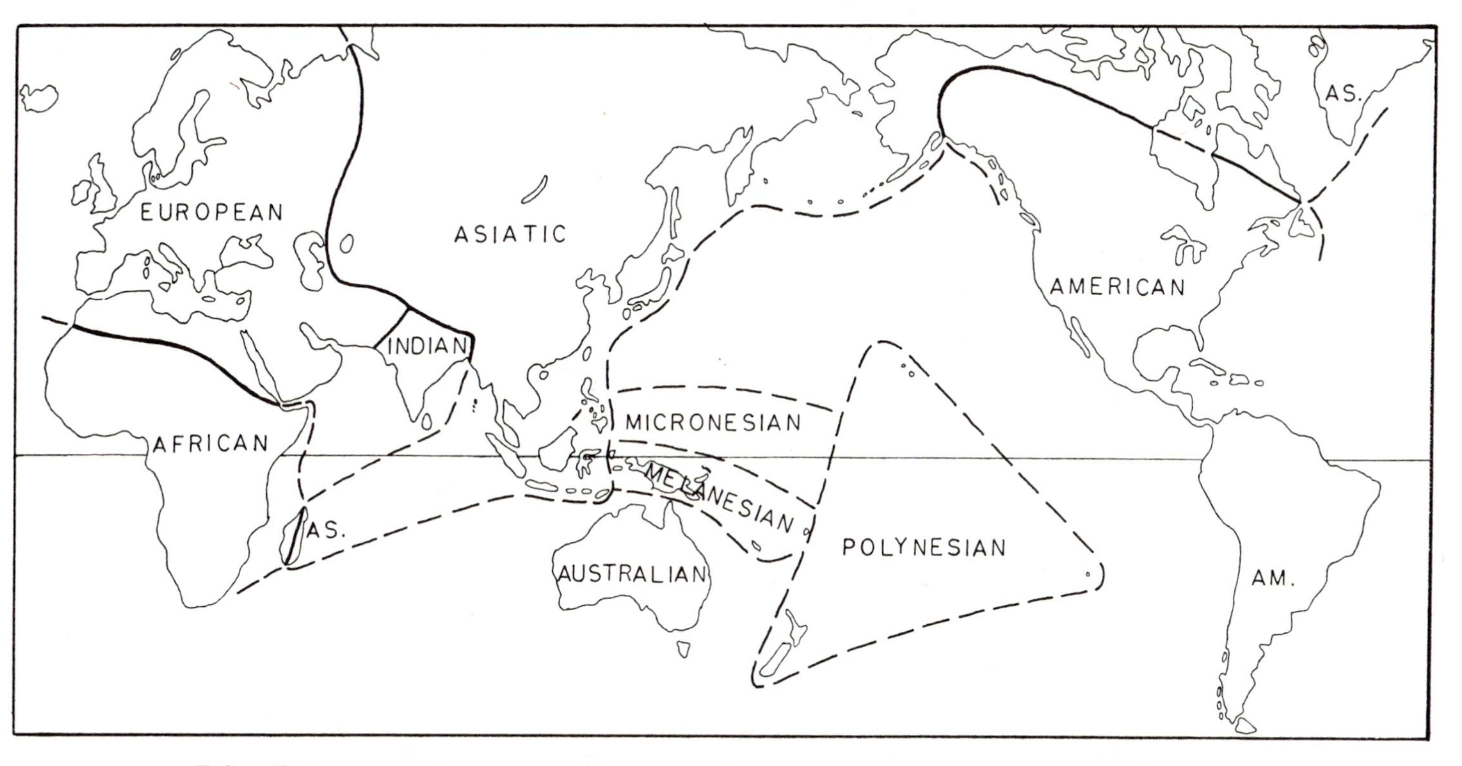

FIGURE 46. Stanley Garn's geographical races. These are the nine major races at the highest level of classification with their distributions shown in the ethnographic present. The areas shown here are based mainly on geographical breeding patterns over many generations; the dividing lines are barriers to gene flow. At the next lower level in this classification, local races, climatic adaptations become the major differentiating factor. (Redrawn from Garn, 1961.)

turn follows from the simple observation that each person has two parents, four grandparents, eight great-grandparents, and so on, doubling with each generation back into the past. A bit of simple arithmetic will show that a young adult today will have had over two billion ancestors in the year 1200, allowing 25 years per generation, and that is far more than the world's total population at that time. Obviously there are many people in the past who occupy a number of different positions in the family tree of an individual living today, and this is true for each of us. There simply weren't enough ancestors to go around, and a certain degree of combining of roles had to occur. This clumping of ancestors would also be concentrated within the genetic areas that we are looking at now. People usually mate at convenient distances. In a single generation matings are mostly among people born only a few kilometers apart; over many generations one's ancestors would fan out from one point, but this ancestral fan would tend to fold back on itself between geographical barriers to breeding. All people within such a breeding area will have their ancestral fans tending to coincide in that space and sharing personnel. Sharing ancestors in this sense may be called common ancestry but it does not necessarily imply any single original group of founders.

Within such a long-term breeding pool, or genetic area, natural selection can maintain differences in classical traits between two parts of that area. Similarly, in an adjacent genetic area with which gene flow is minimal, the same climatic factors can select for the same classical traits on both sides of that barrier. In this way areas of classical unity and areas of genetic unity can exist that are independent of each other and not coinciding in their boundaries.

Garn's geographical races are basically genetic areas of long-term inbreeding between barriers to gene flow. They are determined by world geography in relation to man's ability to live and move in its various locations. The distribution of classical traits is quite independent and follows from climate alone. The boundaries of these genetic areas are the limitations of human movements which will then limit the free spread of any and all genes. The boundaries of climatic races are the limitations of classical adaptations which may permit human movement but which will filter out the phenotypes of climate-adaptation genes.

BOYD'S GENETIC RACES.

The most straightforward attempt to divide the world into areas of genetic similarity was done by William Boyd in 1950. Boyd specifically ruled out any consideration of the classical traits on the grounds that he was trying for a classification that was meaningful in terms of common descent. The genetic data available at that time were not very complete as compared with the present, but even then some fairly clear divisions could be seen. His map of the "genetic races" is given in Fig. 47. The unaccounted-for-areas are where intermixture is presumed, or sufficient data are lacking.

A careful examination of the blood group data which Boyd used showed there was little to distinguish most of his races from each other because the ranges of the frequencies were so high and overlapping in many cases. The most consistent feature that did emerge was a very clear distinction between West and East in five out of the eight genetic traits he used. His Western "races" of European, Early European, and African showed significant differences from each other in only two or three traits. His Eastern "races" of Asiatic, American, and Australian were no better differentiated. Still, this was the first attempt to see through the random noise of genetic distributions and it did reveal something of a pattern underneath.

For the most part Boyd drew his dividing lines, or zones, along what we would call the traditionally recognized genetic barriers. One major exception was his distinction of Early European from the rest of the continent. This consists of the Basques today and he considered them to be the major remnant of a pattern that was once common to all of Europe. These had since been diluted for the most part by outside sources of genes and leaving this major island. If one applies the same reasoning that distinguished the Early Europeans, an Early African type can be seen in the Bushman that stands out in the same manner from the rest of Africa. The reasoning is simply to take the traits that characterize a continent generally from the rest of the world and look for the group within it that carries these differences to an extreme. Having found such an "Early" population one has two ways to account for the continental frequency of a trait which will be somewhere between that of the world in general and the high point. There may be some unknown reason that concentrated the genetic trait in a small area and it has since flowed out to the rest of the continent. The alternative is to assume the whole continent once had the high concentration and an influx of people with more neutral gene frequencies have diluted it in all but the refuge area. If we knew of a good mechanism that would cause very high local concentrations of a number of different traits at the same spot we could favor the first explanation. There are known mechanisms that will cause extreme levels of gene frequencies on a continental scale so we may favor the second explanation. The spread of agricultural populations provides the source of the influx of people with more neutral gene frequencies to dilute the continent.

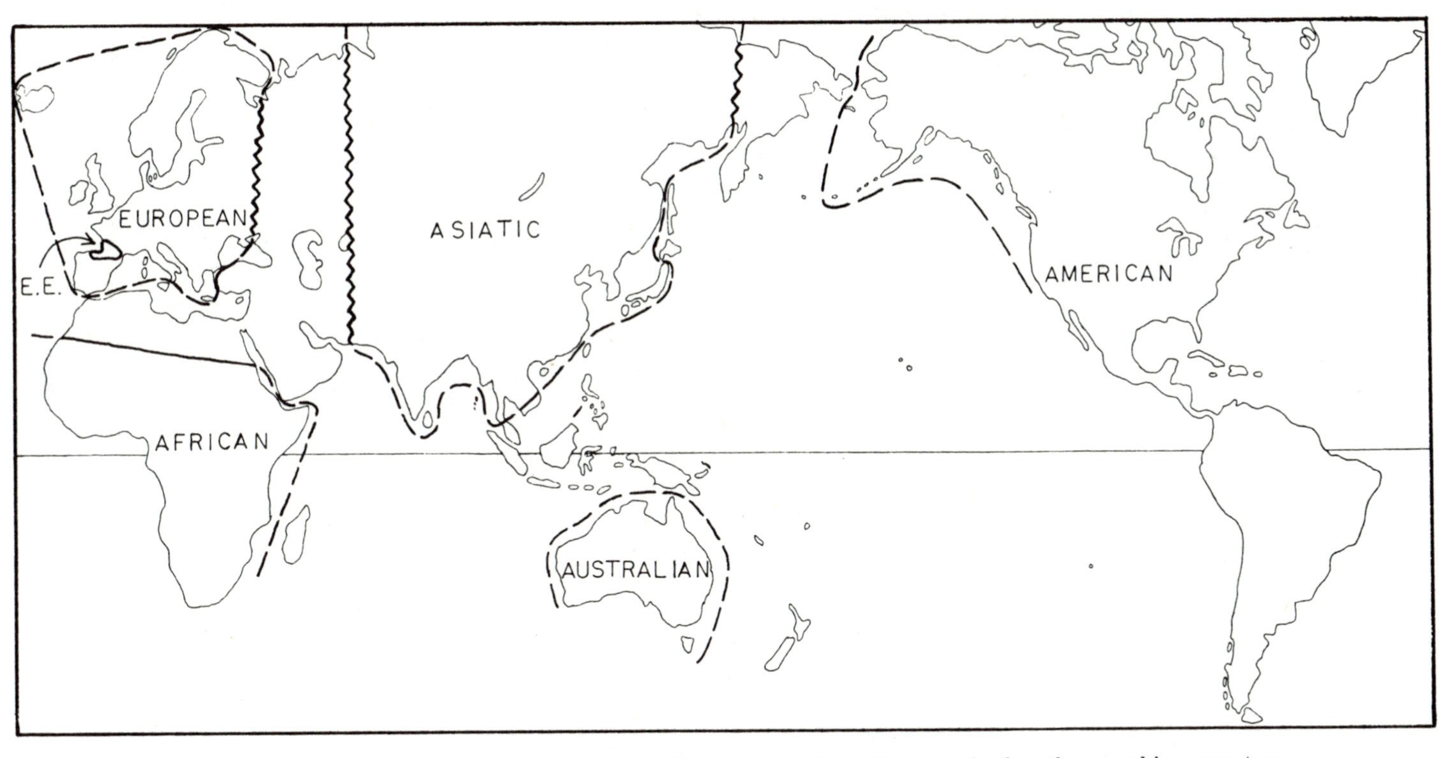

FIGURE 47. William Boyd's genetic races. These are the six major races in the ethnographic present as defined by differences in genetic trait frequencies. The divisions fall largely along lines of barriers to gene flow. Early European was the first postulated relict race based on blood-group contrasts (Redrawn from Boyd, 1950.)

A direct comparison of Boyd's genetic races with Garn's geographical races shows only a few differences, none of them very significant. They would each recognize the divisions the other makes but differ only on which to use as major categories and which to consider as only secondary.

Garn, 1961	*Boyd, 1950*
European	European / Early European
Indian / Asiatic	Asiatic
American	American
Micronesian	X
Polynesian	X
Melanesian	X
Australian	Australian
African	African

Garn did not recognize the distinction of the Early European, while Boyd did not distinguish Asiatic from Indian. Garn included three Oceanic races which Boyd did not bother with. Garn gave to his Europeans all the border zones which Boyd left unassigned, and also put Eskimos with Asiatics rather than with Americans. Otherwise the two systems are pretty much in agreement.

COON'S SUBSPECIES.

In 1962 Carleton Coon published his detailed classification of human races and their origins. His views upset many people, especially on the antiquity of the five subspecies. Coon dealt with the contradictory distributions of classical and genetic traits by forcing them together anyway. Whatever discrepancies could not be handled by some direct means were few enough to be ignored. It is not my intention here to deal lightly with Coon's treatment of classical vs. genetic traits because almost everybody equates them and only he came directly to grips with this and tried to merge them. Because genetic unity was taken as one of the bases of this classification it may fairly be compared with the other two which were just discussed. Coon gives three different time-level reconstructions of his five races in terms of geographical distributions, that of the ethnographic present is given in Fig. 48. The terminology is somewhat different here, but some of the groupings are still directly comparable to those of Garn and Boyd. Again, the further contrasts are mainly a question of judgment as to which should be split and which should be merged. A comparison of categories can be made of Coon's system with those of both Garn and Boyd simultaneously.

Garn, 1961	*Coon, 1962*	*Boyd, 1950*
European Indian	Caucasoid	Early European European Indian part of } Asiatic
Asiatic American Micronesian Polynesian	Mongoloid	Major part of } Asiatic American X X
Melanesian Australian	Australoid	X Australian
African	Congoid Capoid	African

Because Coon used only five categories he lumps many of those from both the other systems. This is reversed only for Africa where Coon sees the Bushman (Capoid) contrast from the Negroid (Congoid) as being great enough to distinguish them at the highest level. Coon sees the Micronesians and Polynesians as mixed, but primarily Mongoloid, and sees too little distinction in the Americans to separate them either. One of the biggest bones of contention among the three is what to do with India. Boyd puts it in his Asiatics, Coon puts it with his Caucasoids, and Garn gives it a race of its own. All other differences are relatively minor.

If asked which of these most correctly represents the real descent groups of man in the ethnographic present I would be forced to pick Garn's map. The greater number of categories expresses the divisions better than either of the other two. Boyd's suffers, unavoidably, from the fact that the data are old, incomplete, and sometimes inaccurate. Coon's suffers from the fact that he was combining genetic with classical traits instead of depending on the genetic ones alone.

DESCENT GROUPS.

If one is to understand the distribution of genetic traits in the ethnographic present it is necessary to reconstruct their distributions as of 10,000 years ago. The agricultural revolution disrupted genetic distributions probably even more than it did those of classical traits. This is because climatic adaptations tend to return to their original distribu-

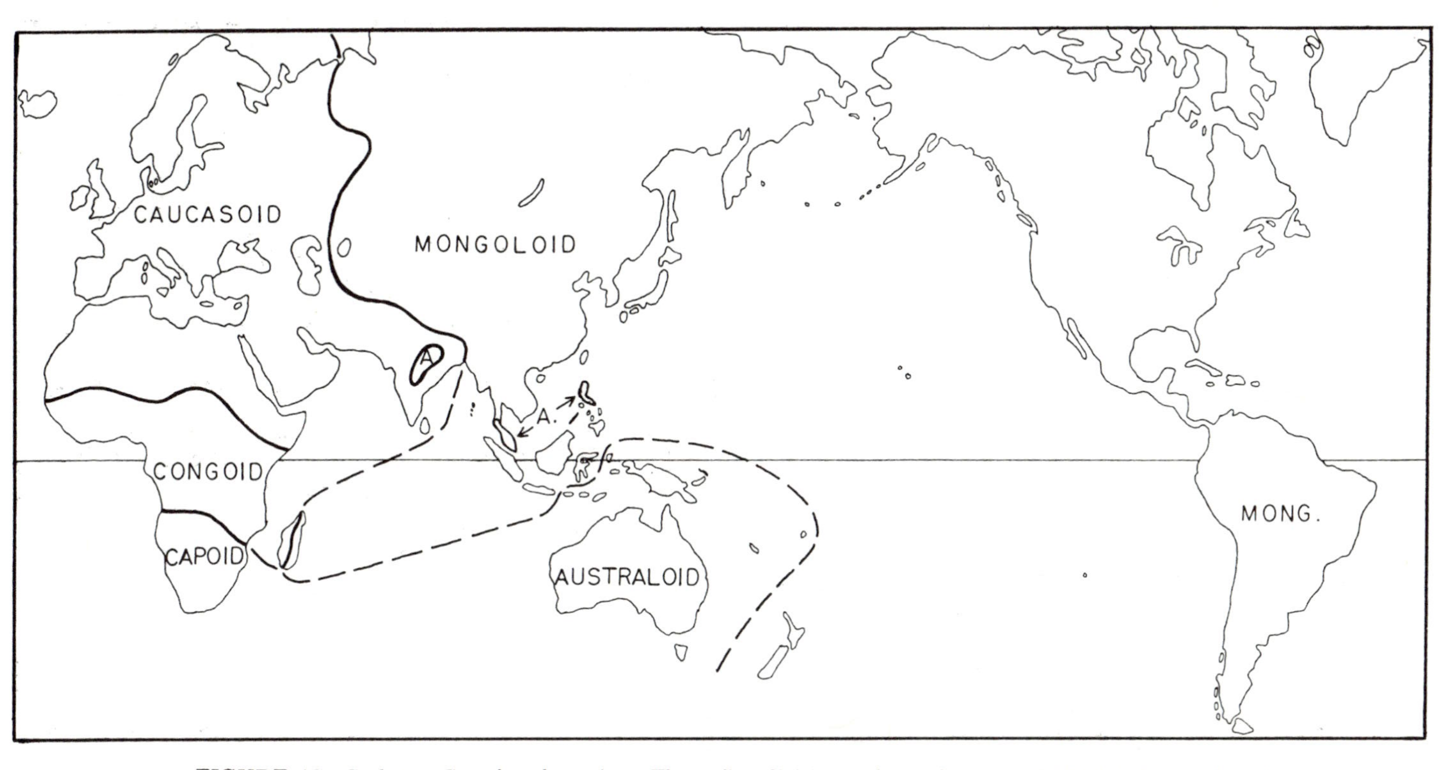

FIGURE 48. Carleton Coon's subspecies. These five divisions, shown here as of 1500 A.D., are based on both classical and genetic traits. The genetic aspect of their delineation is large enough and the number of races is small, so they can be compared directly with the classifications of Garn and Boyd. (Redrawn from Coon, 1962.)

tions while genetic traits take up new patterns and hold them.

The process of reconstructing descent groups is a difficult one and will only be partly done here. Untangling the pattern will also involve some considerations of the *sapiens* revolution which preceded the agricultural one and the effects of which can still be seen. This reconstruction will begin with the most obvious case and move toward the more difficult ones and finally will bog down in a certain amount of uncertainty when the job is just over half done. A map of these groups is given in Fig. 49.

Australia has what might be called the clearest blood group distributions where one can see through the random noise to a rather clear-cut continentality. The gene frequencies to pay attention to are those in which Australia is rather distinct from other, nearby land masses. These important ones are genes C, E, A, B, and N, whose world distributions were discussed in the last chapter. Other genes are not useful; D is essentially constant throughout Australia, genes O and M are the inverse of some to be discussed, and for other genes there is not sufficient detailed data available.

Gene C has a low concentration and it is lowest across the south of Australia, Gene E is high, and highest in the southwestern corner. Gene A is high, and is highest mainly in the south. Gene B is almost absent, being found mainly in the north. Gene N is high, especially in the south. All these give the same picture of having the continental extremes in roughly the same areas of the south or southwest. They all cline away to the north toward the most likely source of dilution by gene flow or immigration. In all but one case the un-Australian extreme is in the Cape York peninsula which is nearest to New Guinea. The exception is for gene N in which New Guinea is just as high as Australia. The source of the allele M is clearly from Indonesia and its entry into Australia is accordingly from the northwest.

Random gene frequencies could not have set up a continent as neatly as this, with all the extremes not only coinciding, but also being located most distant from the sources of dilution. Even the one which came from another direction is distributed accordingly. Some rough calculations show that if the original Australian condition for all of these was like the present southern extremes, then an influx of genes or people in the north would have had to outnumber the residents there by over two to one. The ratio of immigrant genes would decline to the south with the changing frequencies. If one assumes the original Australian condition was more extreme, perhaps 100% of some of these genes, then immigration has been much more. A ratio of two immigrants to one resident for the whole continent, not just the entry area, would be required in that case.

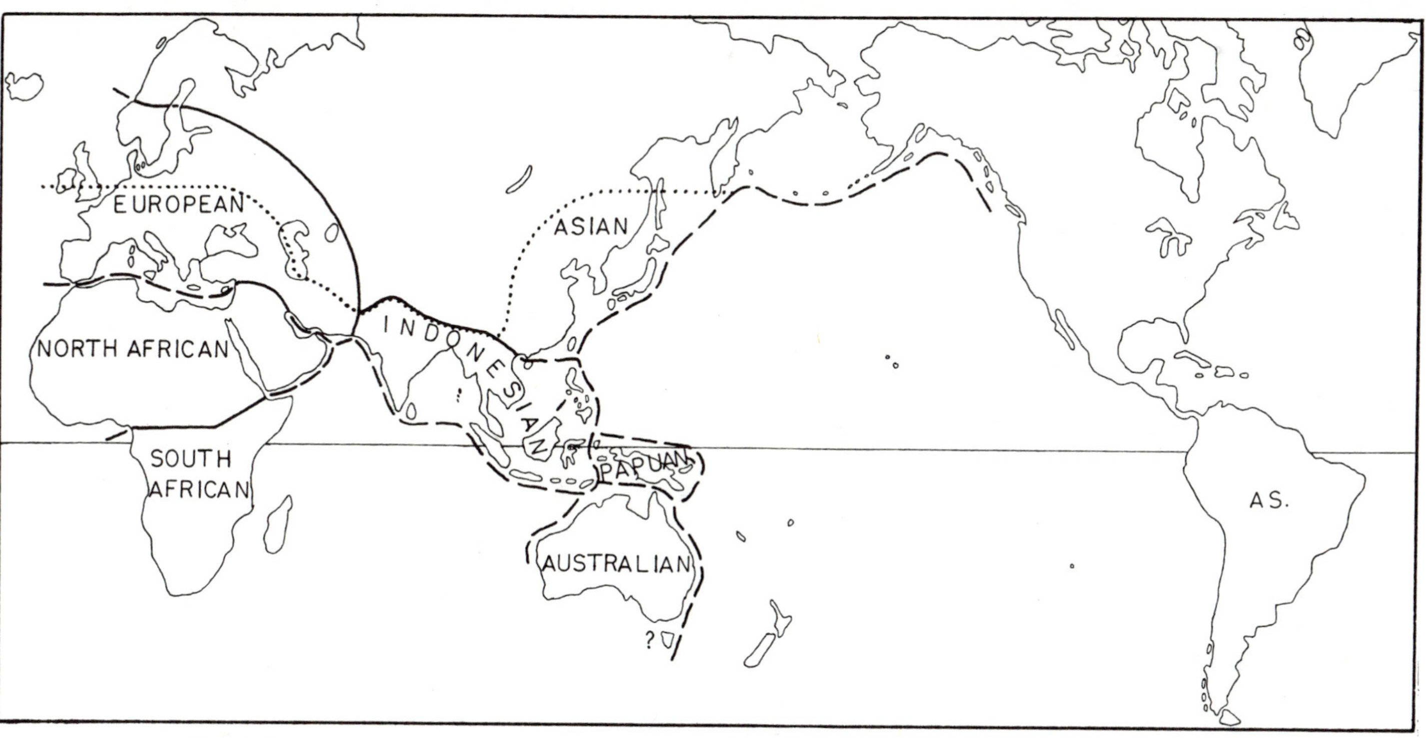

FIGURE 49. Natural distribution of the descent groups. These seven areas are mapped as of 10,000 years ago, or before agriculturally based expansions caused some major disruptions. The descent groups are deduced from genetic-trait distributions of the ethnographic present projected back to hunting and gathering times. They are also correlated with probable major barriers to gene flow at that time. The dotted lines in Europe and eastern Asia show the limits of human occupation early in the Pleistocene. These descent groups may be compared directly with the races postulated by Garn, Boyd, and Coon in their content, but not in their distributions because of the different time line used here. The time of natural man may be equated with Coon's "early post-Pleistocene" for which he also gives a map of his races.

There were no agriculturalists in Australia in the ethnographic present so such people would contribute genes only by occasional contacts along the more accessible coasts. It does not seem likely that this would have provided the quantity of gene flow indicated by the clines within Australia. What is indicated is rather an actual immigration of large numbers of people in the north from New Guinea, who then spread over much of Australia before merging with the local population. Such a spread should have been largely west along the northern coast and also down the entire eastern coast before expanding greatly inland. Since this invasion was not by farmers, and hunters have no obvious means of massive migration, the only answer would be that these were early *sapiens* entering a continent populated by *erectus*. This is exactly the same conclusion arrived at quite independently by studying their classical-trait distributions. If we had data for the Tasmanian blood it ought to settle this for sure, as they should have frequencies most similar to those in the north. It is not yet possible to date this immigration but it may not be as old as the *sapiens* transition elsewhere. Australia thus preserves good indications of a very ancient blood type distribution as well as the pre-agricultural one as of its discovery. In general, the Australian descent group of 10,000 years ago should be described as having about 60% C, 30% E, 30% A, no B, 70% O, and 35% M. These are all just the averages of their recent frequencies in the south.

New Guinea and the Solomon Islands to the east should constitute another descent group because of their geographical near-isolation before the development of significant water craft. The recent impact of true Melanesians along most of the coastal areas has greatly influenced the Solomons, but probably has had little effect on most of New Guinea. The indigenous Papuan horticulturalists there show blood-type frequencies mostly at variance with not only Australia but also with the farmers to the west. There does not appear to be a source for the Papuan frequencies other than local development. There was no major influx of farmers who replaced a native hunting population. Some immigration was indeed likely, but it could not have been much more than 10% of the local numbers. This is seen in gene M which is less than 10% today and quite high to the west. If it had been zero originally and the farming source had 70% of it, a one in ten immigrant ratio would account for the present frequency. Gene C at over 90% gives a similar conclusion if it had originally been 100%. Immigrants from a lower frequency area would have lowered it still more if they had been numerous. Other genes are too irregularly distributed to help in this matter.

The recent Melanesians proper have also had some genetic influence, but evidently none of significance in the interior of New Guinea. Clearly the indigenous Papuans had horticulture and considerable numbers before the Melanesian speakers arrived. Prior to this development of water travel, New Guinea and the Solomons would have constituted a rather isolated genetic area. Considering who the more ancient inhabitants were, it would be preferable to name this the Papuan descent group as of 10,000 years ago.

The Papuan blood-type frequencies differ from the Australian ones in some cases: gene C at over 90% was no doubt originally 100%, and gene E at 10% was once zero. One was the same as the Australian, gene M being 10% now and was no doubt zero before. Of the ABO series, A is low among Papuans and maybe was absent; B is also low, but since its highest frequency tends to be centrally located, it was probably at 15 or 20% before agriculture as well.

The next area worth reconstruction is Europe where three gene frequencies tend to set it apart from the rest of the world quite clearly. There is a notably high frequency of Rh negative which translates into a low frequency of the gene D of the CDE series. Gene D approaches 100% in most of the world but drops to under 80% in northern Africa and India, then still further to about 60% in most of Europe. Among the Basques it is less than 50%. The Lapps do not participate in this and have around 90% of the D gene. This has been interpreted as indicating Europe once approached zero in this gene and was all Rh negative except for gene flow around the edges.

If the source of dilution was from the eastern Mediterranean and it moved out in all directions, a D frequency there of 70% (which is about what it is) would work out rather nicely. One then might assume for the moment an original European frequency of 40%, the rest of the world at 100%, and the source of dilution on the border of the continents with an understandable 70% which is just half way between. Then we can assume an outflowing of farming peoples who mix with the hunters in all directions at the ratio of one farmer to two hunters. This would give the 60% of D in Europe and the 80% found in northern Africa and India. Such numbers are not impressive for farmers, but any way the figures are juggled it comes out about the same. At the very most, gene D would permit farmers to intrude in numbers equal to the resident hunters who are incorporated. And that works only if we assume an original European D frequency of 50% and elsewhere of 90%. In either case the Lapps are not part of Europe in this sense as they show the typical world frequency of 90% or more.

The A gene is also a European trait with a frequency of close to 30% in general, more like 20% in neighboring regions, and a major Asian and African level which is still lower. By applying the same reasoning we get a near eastern source at 25% A diluting a European original of 35% by equal numbers of immigrants as of residents which were incorporated. That same source mixing in equal numbers with hunters at 15% would give the 20% of A which is found surrouding Europe. In this gene the Lapps give contradictory results as their 50% frequency of A genes is the highest in Europe. All these A genes also show the western trend of a high proportion of A_2. It may be that A_2 is a Lapp phenomenon primarily, and is independent of A_1 which has diffused to the north only in modest numbers. Turkey is also anomalous in having a fully European A frequency and being much less European in terms of D.

The European low frequency of the B gene is roughly the inverse of gene A. It thus indicates a similar picture of an original very low frequency which has more recently been diluted with higher numbers from an outside source, which in this case can only be said to be somewhere to the east. In terms of B the Lapps are low like their European neighbors. But the Lapps' linguistic relatives to the east are among the world's highest in B genes. Since these northernmost Uralic speakers are united in most other genetic traits it makes one a bit suspicious of the ABO reliability.

Gene E seems to support the general picture given here, but in frequencies that vary so little it is difficult to read proportions. The other genes do not distinguish themselves enough in this area for us to conclude anything about them.

The European descent group of 10,000 years ago had some strong distinctions from its neighboring areas and the divisions followed the Mediterranean Sea and the interior of Russia where distance was more of a barrier than low population. It is interesting that the boundaries of this descent group do not entirely coincide with those of the Caucasoid climatic race. The climatic race appears to have extended considerably farther to the south.

The last of the clear-cut descent groups is the South African which consists of the Bushmen and Hottentot in the ethnographic present. There are a number of so-called genetic markers of Africa which are here found in extreme frequencies. The gene combination of cDe is the most outstanding of these which is around 60% in Africa generally and reaches 90% in the Bushmen. A similar pattern is found with gene M which is only around 50% in most of Negro Africa but which rises to over 60% in the Bushmen. Other genes make similar distinctions to lesser degrees.

The position of the Bushman in relation to Negro Africa is in some ways analogous to the Early Europeans in Europe. Here we also know of an agricultural sweep that has left a remnant of its predecessors. In this case the intrusion is only 2,000 years old in half the continent and the remnant can still be identified by their hunting economy. Bushmanoid peoples once occupied much more of southern Africa than they did in the ethnographic present. Archeological evidence does not delimit descent groups except for showing rapid, massive human expansions, and by noting the absence of human occupation in places. From the evidence of blood types in modern Africa and the probable location of genetic barriers, it seems reasonable to put the boundary of the pre-agricultural descent group of South Africa well into the Congo rain forest and to include eastern Africa in it as well. There is no presently obvious way to estimate numbers of intruding farmers compared with hunters incorporated into their population, but archeological data suggests the intruders were relatively numerous. The South African blood types can be described as originally 100% cDe, quite high in the M gene, and perhaps a bit low in O.

One reason why the South African descent group is somewhat difficult to reconstruct is that we know even less about the North African one which was its only neighbor. This North African descent group would cover all of Africa not already included in the South African group, and the Arabian peninsula as well. Pygmy territory is here divided between the two. The western African rain-forest strip was narrow, and gene flow should have affiliated it with the north. The central African forests are here included with the south for no very good geographical reason, but the extant Pygmy genetic traits are mostly rather like those of the Bushmen.

In general, North Africa could be characterized by fairly high B (over 15%), slightly lower A, very low values for C and E, and less than 50% M. Arabia sometimes deviates from the African part, especially in its unusually high frequency of M at 70%.

Most of southern Asia can be distinguished as another descent group which might be called the Indonesian. This extends from India, through all of southeastern Asia, and into the offshore islands as far as Celebes. This group is somewhat marked off from the North African group at the Afghan gap, the lowlands between the mountains of Afghanistan and the Arabian Sea, which form the major dividing line between the West and East in terms of genetic traits. The boundary with the Papuan group is fairly clear, with only a few islands between Celebes and New Guinea being unassignable. The Himalaya Mountains form much of the border to the north, but otherwise it is arbitrary.

Root-crop horticulture was developed within this area but this did not seem to have involved any very large-scale population dispersions. The technology did apparently spread as far as India, Japan, New Guinea, and later throughout Oceania.

The Indonesian descent group has, however, been badly overrun by cereal-grain agriculturalists from the west into India, and from the north into its entire eastern half. This makes it almost impossible to determine which frequencies represent 10,000 years ago, and which are introduced. Gene B was probably fairly high, gene A originally absent, C was probably high but is confused with the area to the north, E was likely absent, and M was high. These are all rather uncertain and there is no point in trying to assign actual values to these, other than the ones presumed to have been absent.

The last descent group might best be called Asian. Its geographical extent has already been delimited by the others. The Asian group is not only the largest of the Old World, but it can also be extended to include the Americas as of 10,000 years ago. Accordingly it is the most diverse in terms of frequencies which vary from place to place. Subdivisions would have been desirable, but there are no obvious places to put them, either in terms of gene frequencies or in terms of breeding barriers. A separation at or near the Bering Straits is rather obvious today, but it was probably not valid at the time-line being used here.

Considerable human movements have occurred in the Asian area, but their record in terms of gene distributions is not nearly so clear as in the other areas discussed. The broad band of moderate A blood across the center may be in part from cereal-grain agriculture originating in the near east. It could also be from the later military expansions out of the Ukraine with their horse-based technology. The B gene is generally high, but has a few notable low spots that make its value questionable. The C gene was high, especially in the east, and it may have been lowered by some early invasions from the west. Gene E looks as though it were anciently rather high, and this is shown in its still high frequencies in the Americas. The M gene was originally low for most of the Asian group, but somehow a high area developed in eastern Siberia and continues into America. While these generalities are difficult to deal with here, a couple of specifics can be handled with some certainty, the Lapps and the Ainus.

The Lapps and Samoyeds may be treated somewhat as a unit. They are distantly related linguistically, although both may have adopted so much of their languages from the Uralics to the south of them that a different genealogical connection may have become obscured. Their reindeer herding, hunting, and fishing economies are broadly similar. The obvious classical traits show a contrast, with the Lapps looking very Caucasoid and the Samoyeds looking more Mongoloid.

Into this contradictory picture the genetic traits can be added. In one trait they contrast strongly, with the Lapps showing high A frequencies and the Samoyeds showing high B. This is overwhelmed by their strong similarities to each other in gene M, gene D, and in PTC tasting. There is also some similarity in gene E. Of these, M connects them only remotely with the Asian group, but the rest of them show strong connections to Asia and not at all to Europe. Gene C also ties the Lapps to the Asian group but is nondistinctive for the Samoyeds. If one is to accept the weight of genetic evidence, first the Lapps and Samoyeds must be connected with each other, and second they must both be made part of the Asian descent group. This does no great violence to the generally presumed Samoyed ancestry, but it will raise questions about the Lapps. Only A blood ties the Lapps to Europe, and it has already been noted that the high proportion of A_2 makes this association a bit less clear. It is also true that the ABO series is more erratic than the others and may have been more often affected by disease selection. What remains to be accounted for is the clearly Caucasoid classical traits of the Lapps. The obvious answer is gene flow from neighboring Scandinavians and some reason for selection favoring these traits while leaving the genetic ones less affected. This presupposes a long and close social contact between the Lapps and the Europeans with the latter always having the greater social prestige. I am not at all comfortable with this kind of explanation, but it will have to suffice.

The most interesting thing about this assignment of the Lapps is their contradictory classification. They are at the same time members of the Caucasoid climatic race and also part of the Asian descent group. Other examples of such contrasts occur as well, but this is perhaps the most unexpected case.

The Ainu present a similar picture in terms of Asian affiliation in their genetic traits. In most respects they are very similar to or identical with their neighbors. One exception is their rather low frequency of gene M but this probably is an old Asian condition and would ally them more with Australians than with Europeans anyway. The other partial exception is in fingerprints where their high loop to whorl ratio is western, while their arch percentage is eastern.

Ainu classical traits are superficially rather Caucasoid, but also not too unlike those of southern Australia. These can all be put down to parallel climatic adaptations. Ainus are not classed here with the Caucasoid climatic race because it was an independent development with no flow of these adaptations from one population to the other. Logically, by the rules given here, it would be permissible to combine such parallel developments. They are kept separate also partly because of some differences in their classical traits and partly to emphasize their independent origin. So the Ainu are members of the Asian descent group, but have Caucasoid features even though they are not formally classified in that climatic race.

There are other examples of how race and group are independent of each other. Negroes and Melanesians could easily have been put in the same climatic race, just as Caucasoids and Ainus, and they are kept separate here for the same modest reasons. Yet these two climatic races are almost poles apart in terms of their genetic traits. The Pgymies and the Negritos present the same contrast. The northern fringe of Africa, especially before agriculture, was tied to Europe in terms of classical traits but more to the rest of Africa in terms of genetic ones. India leans toward Europe in its classical traits, especially today, and towards the rest of southeastern Asia in its genetics. The east horn of Africa 10,000 years ago was almost certainly with the South African descent group, but the correct affiliation of its classical traits is uncertain. The horn was here assigned to the Bushman climatic race but it might almost as easily have been part of the Saharan race.

In certain other cases climatic-race boundaries coincide with those of descent groups, but that's just what it is—coincidence. The Himalayas form a good genetic barrier and they also draw a line between two very different environments. Central Asia divides races and groups in roughly the same area. New Guinea and Australia are separated by a water gap which lies close to the dividing line between tropical rain forest and desert environments.

The basic arrangement of climatic races and descent groups 10,000 years ago is that of two fully independent sets of data by which people can be classified. With agriculture causing extensive human movements the two sets of traits would advance together on each frontier. In this sense migrations tended to simplify things by bringing race and group boundaries together. With modern methods even more populations have been brought into contact, with race and group categories coinciding exactly. I have in mind here the white colonies in various parts of the world and the descendants of Negro slaves. Given another hundred thousand years or more these will all settle into new climatic races and descent groups. The races can be predicted on the basis of ideal climatic adaptations, especially when civilization breaks down. The groups will depend on the actual distribution of genetic traits within the breeding boundaries when they again become effective, and drift will gradually exaggerate the contrasts between them. Of course, if civilization ends abruptly there may be some drastic reductions in numbers that would select against certain categories of people, and so alter some gene frequencies for future generations.

ERECTUS DESCENT GROUPS.

It is possible to speculate on the distributions of genetic traits prior to the *sapiens* revolution. The boundaries of each group are fairly easy to determine, but specifying the exact contents in terms of genetic differences is much more difficult.

For the most part there is no reason not to simply extend the descent groups of 10,000 years ago back to ten times that figure. Old World archeology gives us a few guidelines regarding where man's ancestors did not live. The European group is drawn back to south of the 53rd parallel and probably out of central Asia. The Asian group likewise must be withdrawn to the south, and in this case also to the east, away from the colder winters and lack of vitamin D. The significance of the Afghan gap now becomes obvious, as this is the narrow funnel through which all gene flow must have passed between the western and eastern halves of the Old World. It is not surprising that genetic differences between west and east are usually greater than between any other groups.

The North African group should be withdrawn from the rain forest which seems to have been uninhabited at this early time. The entire South African area, minus the rain forest, must now be left as a blank because whatever it contained then was eliminated later when the first *sapiens* got through the forest and replaced the *erectus* population. There is little hope of deducing their blood types except as extensions of trends existing at that time near eastern Africa.

The Indonesian group should be essentially unchanged except for the periodic splitting and merging in the island area as sea levels rose and dropped with glacial fluctuations. Incidentally, the lowering of sea levels may not have coincided with glacial advances as is usually assumed. It is possible that in an equatorial belt, the sea levels were shifting in just the opposite directions from what they were doing nearer the poles. This follows from the fact that water drawn from the seas in general is shifted closer to the earth's axis of rotation when it is frozen in polar ice caps. For the earth to maintain the same angular momentum a compensation must be made. Part of this comes from an increased speed of rotation and part comes from a change in the surface shape of the remaining hydrosphere into a more flattened spheroid. In an equatorial band this flatter spheroid should more than make up for the loss of water into the ice caps and the sea level would have been higher than at present. In full interglacial conditions the process reverses, and while most sea levels rise, in the equatorial belt they would drop. This simply means, if the theory is correct, that the timing of connections between the Asian off-shore islands would be with interglacials rather than with glacials.

The Papuan group should have been a constant one over time, with its gene frequencies going back as far as it was inhabited. Australia was also essentially unchanged in its boundaries, although Tasmania might not have been included at first. The contents of the Australian descent group were apparently drastically affected by the incursion of *sapiens* from the Papuan group sometime since 40,000 years ago. Because of the evidently incomplete population replacement it is possible to reconstruct its *erectus* genetic types from the extremes found today in the southern part.

The names of the various descent groups given for later dates apply just as well to 100,000 years ago or even ten times that figure if *erectus* goes back that far in time. The continuity of the various descent groups that is indicated here is the same sort of continuity which Coon postulated for the human races as he defined them. The difference here is that only one set of traits, the genetic ones, are postulated to have that kind of antiquity and degree of unity through so much of the past. Coon combined these with classical traits on the asumption that they all went together in a package. I find that package can be divided into two parts, the histories of which have to be traced separately from one another. Over the short term, race and group tend to go together, but over the long haul of prehistory they are quite independent.

DESCENT GROUP ORIGINS.

It has long been a puzzle just how so many polymorphisms came to exist in the first place in our species, especially when most known selective factors as well as drift should have operated to reduce their number and to simplify things. At least some thoughts can be offered here that go back to the time of the origin of *Homo erectus.*

The first hominids of our genus probably originated in Africa, although for present purposes it could almost as easily have been in Java. Their new adaptation was serious tool-making and big-game hunting. These innovations were followed by their spread over the inhabitable world in a relatively short period of time. When natural selection takes its usual course, all variations that are unsuitable, or even neutral, tend to be weeded out. When a population is rapidly expanding, natural selection is not taking its usual toll and an abnormally high proportion of these moderately deviant types will survive simply because there is room for them. A rapidly expanding frontier of *erectus* into uninhabited territory would be just such a case of relaxed selection. This would provide a variety of raw material for chance alone to distribute in odd combinations. On passing through the various bottlenecks to reach each new area, the genetic frequencies could drastically alter from one instance to the next from founders effect. Each genetic area would be dealt a new hand from the highly varied gene combinations in the last one.

If the original area of genus *Homo* is placed in southern Africa the first bottleneck would be in their passing from the east horn area into northern Africa and Arabia. Gene frequencies would probably alter in at least a few cases with this passage. The move from Africa proper into Arabia may also have led to changes but there is little indication of it in this case except perhaps for the still existing high frequency of gene M. The passage into Europe would be around the eastern end of the Mediterranean into Anatolia, then between the Agean and Black Seas into Europe proper. There are here two chances for significant variations to be introduced. This leaves the western part of the Old World in three major divisions in which later drift would tend to exaggerate the initial distinctions that occurred between them. New mutations could also become fixed in one or another of these genetic areas because interbreeding between them was at a minimum.

From the easternmost part of the western world, human habitation would almost pinch out between the mountains of Afghanistan and the Arabian Sea. Beyond this, there would be a great expansion into the Indian subcontinent. This Afghan gap proved to be the biggest source of genetic deviation between west and east. The continuing narrow corridor through here for hundreds of thousands of years would also act as a barrier against any leveling of gene frequencies between the two sides. It would permit new deviations to become fixed by drift on one side without materially affecting frequencies on the other side.

From India throughout southeastern Asia there are no very great barriers to gene flow except those which intermittently closed and opened the connections among the offshore islands such as Sumatra, Borneo, and the Philippines. The permanent water gaps beyond there were a barrier to be crossed before reaching the Papuan genetic area. From Papua to Australia is another major barrier which may have been crossed on dry land at times. The genetic distinctions between Papua and Australia suggest this has long been a major barrier, perhaps always water covered or otherwise difficult of passage. From southeastern Asia to the north there is no very conspicuous barrier, but there exists a series of minor ones in the form of rivers and mountain ranges, and some constriction between the major inland mountain masses and the sea. These in combination led to enough of a restriction to gene flow for the Asian genetic area to become somewhat distinguished from that of Indonesia in the sense it is used here. In *erectus* times this Asian area was not very large because climatic limitations restricted human occupation. In later times it proved to be the most expansive as new adaptations permitted human habitation in colder climates. The four major genetic areas in the eastern part of the Old World would have been differentiated from each other by founders effect at first. Later mutation and drift would then exaggerate their collective differences from the west and in other differences from each other.

There would be no necessary trend for all genetic traits to become differentiated at each boundary. By initial chance alone, the founder population into a new area may carry a major change of proportion in some traits and a normal distribution in terms of others. At the next barrier the dice are rolled again; some that changed at the last crossing will change again, while others will not; some traits that remained the same over the previous barrier will change at this one, and some will still continue. At the next genetic barrier the whole process begins again. The initial habitation of the various genetic areas will then automatically introduce certain differences between the populations of each of them. Each area then has its long-term inbreeding pattern as the ancestral fans begin to fold in on themselves after many generations. Local drift and temporary selection relating to various diseases will introduce a great deal of "noise" into this system, but continental tendencies should still tend to level out.

During the hundreds of thousands of years after the initial spread, some further processes will add to the continental distinctions. Many allele contrasts confer some measure of incompatability between the maternal and fetal blood, and the less frequent allele will tend to be selected out. I suspect this is much more common than has so far been demonstrated. Drift and short-term selection will work against this long-term selection in various times and places. In the long run, however, those with incompatabilities will tend to become uniform in each descent group while the mixtures would continue to occur at the bottlenecks between them.

There are some traits, most notably sickle-cell anemia, where the heterozygote has the selective advantage and genetic uniformity will never be achieved. This kind of phenomenon, called heterosis, is suspected by many workers to be much more common than has been demonstrated so far. This opinion is sometimes offered as an explanation for the continuing genetic diversity in man that seemed otherwise difficult to account for. This kind of explanation may not be necessary in view of the above considerations resulting from rapid expansion, low selection pressure, and founders effect as *erectus* first populated the world. A comparable genetic diversity in many other animals should not be expected unless they too had a rapid initial expansion over such a great part of the world and with so many bottlenecks dividing up their resultant areas of occupation.

Genetic drift will only continue the trend toward uniformity within each area by eliminating rare alleles. It can also serve to fix rare alleles as well. The likelihood of drift's fixing an allele at 100% is inversely proportional to the population involved and it is usually assumed that continental areas are too large for drift to have significant effects. This may not be the case. Small populations can drift by chance to great extremes for a given gene, but they are normally bordered by other populations which are not drifting in the same direction. Intergroup mixtures will eventually catch up with most such extremes and level them off again. For the continental areas of descent groups there is a minimum of adjacent population to effect this leveling by gene flow. While it may be less likely that the genetics of a large area such as Europe or Australia may drift far in one direction, it is also less likely that such a drift will ever be pulled back or toned down to the species' average condition.

It is also true that with larger populations there are more mutations. For any given genetic innovation, the number of individuals showing it will be in direct proportion to the population numbers. When we consider the likelihood of a new mutation appearing and fixing, we must consider the numbers of the raw material as well as the drift-limiting effect of total population. It becomes quite possible that in something like a million years some significant new frequencies and new traits can have appeared in each descent group by chance alone.

The various descent groups do not appear to have changed much in their outlines during most of the Pleistocene Epoch with the possible exception of central Asia. It looks as if the European and Asian descent groups made direct contact during the last interglacial period, thus by-passing the Afghan gap well to the north. While both ends of the Old World were limited in their northward expansion by the vitamin D line of about 53° north latitude, their penetration towards the center of Asia was limited by winter temperature extremes. Both physical and cultural adaptations were accumulating over time to cope with cold weather. During each interglacial the European frontier would push eastward and the Asian frontier would advance westward. During each glaciation the severe winter conditions probably removed much of these penetrations and added to the selection pressure for cold-survival adaptations. With each succeeding interglacial the gap between west and east would narrow, and it would appear that they contacted during the last interglacial. This meeting would lead to interchange of both cultural and physical adaptations to cold-winter survival, and the best developments along each line would be passed rapidly back to the other source population. Not surprisingly it was in this last interglacial that classic Neandertal anatomy appears in Europe with the Ehringsdorf and Saccopastore skulls. The Neandertals may owe some of their cold-weather adaptations to the descendants of Peking man by means of direct contact across central Asia.

It is not clear whether there was a significant influx of genetic traits into Europe from eastern Asia at this time, but it is doubtful. The degree of difference between these two areas is so high today as to make a postulated still-greater contrast in the distant past seem unlikely. It is a safe presumption that little gene flow went to the far east either. The distinctive European genetic traits do not appear there to any greater degree than can be easily accounted for by some later movements in this direction. A dilution of traits certainly would have resulted from this central Asian contact, and a great cline of them runs across the double continent. Unfortunately one cannot distinguish the gene flow of such an early contact from the effects of more recent meetings and mergings.

One other area of Pleistocene change in descent groups would be the extension of the Indonesian group into Papua, and from there into Australia. There is no direct evidence to date any such movements, but that they occurred during *erectus* times is indicated by at least two lines of evidence as noted earlier.

8.
THE SAPIENS REVOLUTION

SUMMARY.

There were three major events in the development of human racial diversity, the original differentiation, the *sapiens* revolution, and the agricultural explosion. These have all been discussed in some detail, but the *sapiens* revolution merits a separate chapter because its influence is the most critical from a theoretical point of view. The process described here will not meet with total agreement and much of this material appears in print for the first time here.

The antiquity of human racial variation, both in terms of climatic adaptations and in genetic distributions, is much older than *Homo sapiens.* The time available since the transition to our species is not long enough for racial differentiation, and many of the distributions of traits can already be seen in *erectus* times. Sapienization was mostly an in-place transition which must then be explained in order to be understood.

The essential differences between *erectus* and *sapiens* skulls center on the size and shape of the braincase, and on the size and projection of the face. In most particulars Neandertals conform to the *erectus* pattern with only the large size of their brains being like *sapiens.* All hominids prior to 45,000 years ago are of one design, and since that time they all conform to the modern type. Some major transformation occurred throughout the world within a span of 10,000 years or less.

Theories of a new type of man (ourselves) evolving and replacing the preceding types do not allow for the continuation of racial traits in many areas right through this transition. Theories of gene flow and selection to spread the modern design do not allow nearly enough time. Neither view explains what it is about *sapiens* that is superior to *erectus.* The cultural trait of language fills all the requirements of advantageous behavior, rapid transmission, and preservation of line traits in the anatomy.

The last step in the development of language was apparently the phonemic principle of using meaningless sounds in meaningful combinations. This permits a large vocabulary which was otherwise impossible with the limited number of sounds that could be produced and distinguished. This in turn made spoken language an important communication system with high survival value. Complex and changeable social organizations then became possible for the first time.

Improved development of the vocal apparatus in man centered on elongating the pharyngeal space just above the vocal cords. Given the importance of speech, evolution of a superior speaking apparatus would procede independently in all areas with selection from available local variations. The development of the pharynx causes a lowering of the base of the braincase and a pulling in of its sides, lengthening of the mastoid process, reducing and pulling back of the face, and all the other differences that make *sapiens* skulls different from *erectus.*

The transition probably began somewhere in the northern hemisphere among Neandertals or another undiscovered type with an equally large brain. The spread of language would be rapid and was followed everywhere by the anatomical transition over the next few thousand years. Only in southern Africa, and to some extent in Australia, is there evidence of actual population replacements at this time.

THE PROBLEM.

There is general agreement that there is a species worth of difference between *Homo sapiens* and *Homo erectus.* The morphological gap between clear specimens of each is of about the same magnitude as that which would separate two closely related species living at the same time. This concept of morphological gap is our only measure of sequential species because the normal test of noninterfertility is not applicable. The skulls from Java and Peking, and others dating half a million or more years ago, are quite similar to one another and they differ sharply from all those of modern man. The problem is where to draw the line between these two species. Should this be a time line or a morphological transition, and whichever it is, what criteria are to be used?

One school of thought would have *sapiens* appear and then subdivide into the various subspecies or races of today. The other school sees what might be called racial differences among *erectus* which continue through this species-level transition. The antiquity of human races is thus at issue. As discoveries of fossil hominids have accumulated, it has become increasingly evident that no remains older than about 40,000 years ago are of the modern type. Claims of greater antiquity are regularly made, and just as regularly are dismissed after long and careful examination.

The monophyletic opinion would have one group of *erectus* evolve into *sapiens* about 40,000 to 50,000 years ago. These would then replace all other hominids as they developed into the various races. Only one phyletic line of *erectus* would then be our ancestors. It then becomes pointless to look for racial traits in most of the old skulls because they would have no direct bearing on the same or similar traits in man today. In contrast, the polyphyletic view is that the *sapiens* condition was a threshold that was crossed by all or most of the *erectus* phyletic lines. This would allow for racial differences (line traits) to develop among *erectus* which would continue in each geographical area through the common transition (grade traits) into *sapiens*. The various older fossils could then be assigned to the ancestry of particular races.

If races are no older than *sapiens,* then we are faced with two problems that demand answers, the timing of classical adaptations, and the persistence of line traits. The American Indians' ancestors passed through and adapted to the Arctic filter at least 12,000 years ago. The amount of time that has passed since then is almost one-third of the whole duration of our species. If the Amerindians have differentiated so little in response to climatic selection in 12,000 years, how could Old World climatic races have developed so much more in just 40,000 years? The amount of variation in terms of classical traits in the Old World is at least ten times as great as is found in the New World. This would certainly imply about ten times longer for such differences to evolve, and that goes well beyond the earliest *sapiens* remains. If one gives the native Americans even more than 12,000 years in these continents, as many would, then the problem is only compounded.

The counter to this has often been to assign ever greater antiquity to the modern anatomy in the Old World. Clearly *erectus* fossils are securely dated as recently as 50,000 years ago or less. If one postulates earlier *sapiens* then we would be dealing with two separate, culture-bearing species at the same time. This might not be impossible, but it certainly introduces some difficulties as to why one did not promptly replace the other. Fossil evidence of early *sapiens* has been diligently sought and is occasionally announced. The news coverage and financial support that immediately follow such claims should indicate one of the major motives for such efforts. Thus far the early *sapiens* discoveries have come and gone with predictable regularity, while non-modern remains beyond 40,000 years steadily accumulate.

Another way around this difficulty has been to backdate as much as possible of the *erectus* record. If reinterpretations of their dates can suggest older ones this not only gives more time for *sapiens* evolution, but it also gets good press—always the older the better. An added advantage of this is to push these not-quite-human ancestors farther away in time. It is interesting how emotionally uncomfortable some people feel about having such creatures so close in the family tree.

A final solution has been taxonomically to upgrade many of the more recent fossil *erectus* specimens into *sapiens*, thus allowing some of them to be ancestors of particular races. This also removes the stigma of recent unhuman ancestors by simply redefining them as human. Since the year 1960 it has become the fad to admit Neandertal man into our species as *Homo sapiens neanderthalensis*, and the Broken Hill man as *H. sapiens rhodesiensis*. Aside from a smooth vault and a large brain, Neandertal man has all the characteristics of *erectus*. Broken Hill is an *erectus* in all traits.

In addition to the American Indian timing contrast there is an equally impressive objection to recent development of races. This follows from the clear evidence of certain line traits that can be seen in many of the *erectus* fossils and which occur today among *sapiens* in the same regions. These include both classical traits like nose form and body build, as well as some genetic traits, in the sense used here, such as malar (cheek bone) position and Inca bones. If *sapiens* developed out of only one line of *erectus* they should all show the line traits of that particular group, particularly the nonadaptive traits. It is demonstrable that this is not the case. Peking *erectus* show perhaps half a dozen good line traits of the genetic type that continue to be found in the modern eastern Asiatic populations. European *erectus* show a few Caucasoid traits, and Javan specimens show some Australoid traits. So far there is little to connect African *erectus* with modern populations. This may not be impressive but it seems to be enough to rule out a monophyletic origin for *sapiens*.

A polyphyletic origin for *sapiens* is clearly indicated, but this raises many more questions. On one of these we can be emphatic; the races by any definition are not separately evolving lineages, because if they were they would be separate species. The genus *Homo* has always consisted of a single species at any one time, fully interbreeding, but with racial distinctions being well developed. It must be remembered that these racial distinctions were, as they are now, of two types, classical traits of the climatic races and genetic traits of the descent groups. And these two categories corresponded rather less in the past than they do now.

CRANIAL CONTRASTS.

To understand the *sapiens* revolution it is first necessary to pin down just exactly what we are talking about. There are many aspects that may or may not be involved, but the logical starting point would be the cranial characteristics by which the two species were contrasted in the first place. The original and subsequent skull finds from Java are the basis for the *erectus* type. To these may be added the Peking skulls, a few skulls and other parts from Africa and Europe from a similar date, and the somewhat more recent Solo man of Java.

Compared with all modern crania, these *erectus* show the following distinctions: The braincase is platycephalic or low-vaulted in relation to its length and breadth. The brow ridges are prominent, vertically thick, not divided over the center of each orbit, and are especially massive at their outer corners. The forehead is low and receding. The occipital ridge for neck muscle attachment is very prominent and includes the most posterior point on the skull. Most of the braincase consists of a series of nearly flat planes between a system of longitudinal and transverse ridges. The skull walls are about twice as thick as modern ones. The skull is broadest at about the level of the ears. The mastoid processes turn sharply inward as they descend, and are rather small for the size of the skull. The region of the foramen magnum (spinal cord opening) is high up under the base of the skull. The bone immediately anterior to the foramen magnum (basioccipital) is nearly flat instead of sloping upward and forward. The brain is about two-thirds the modern size, but ranges from 800 cc to 1300 cc according to absolute body size. The face, jaws, and teeth are larger, on the average, than in modern skulls; in each geographical area the local *erectus* is regularly larger of face than the modern *sapiens*. The entire face is anteriorly projecting because of its size. The chin region of the mandible is retreating. (See Fig. 50.)

This rather impressive listing contrasts the grade traits of *erectus* with those of *sapiens*. More traits can be found in other sources, but they are mostly line-trait contrasts resulting from comparing *erectus* in one area with *sapiens* in another. Clearly a considerable transformation of the skull took place. Interestingly, there is little or no postcranial distinction between the two species. Neandertals and possibly Peking man had very specialized bodies, but again these are line traits, not of grade, and also only temporary.

The Broken Hill skull from southern Africa (formerly called the Rhodesian man) shows all the traits of *erectus* and must be so classified. This was rather neatly demonstrated when I sawed off the face from a cast of this skull and asked students to identify it. Those who

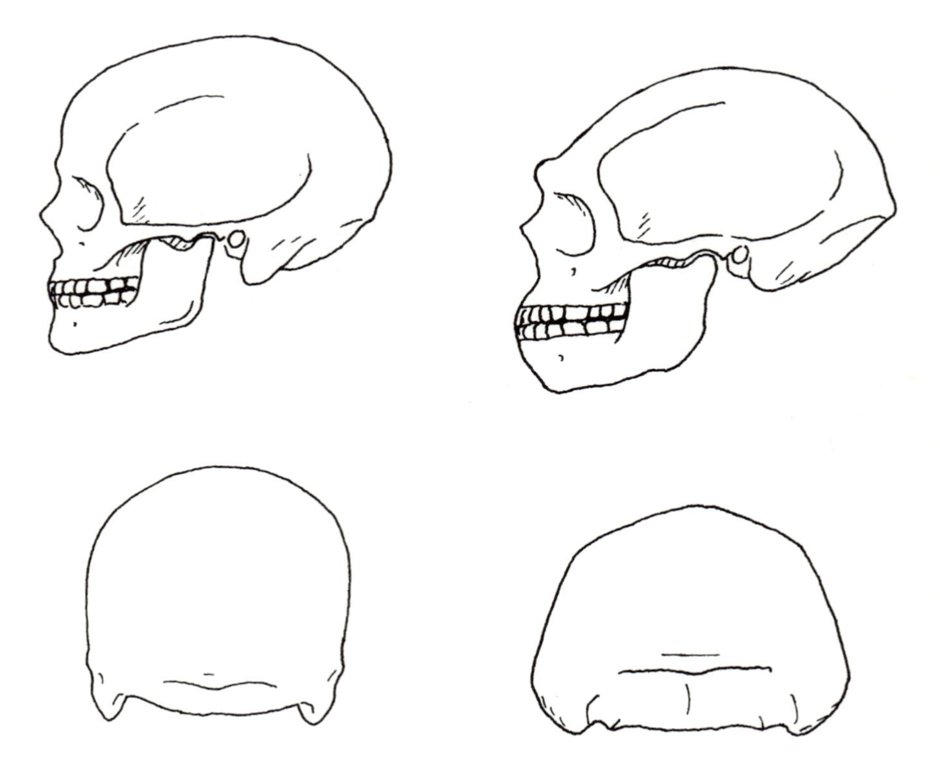

FIGURE 50. Skulls of *erectus* and *sapiens*. These general outlines show the long-noted differences from the side (above) and the rear (below). The *erectus* skull (right) has a smaller brain, flatter braincase, projecting brow ridges, larger face, lack of chin projection, muscle crest high on the back of the head, gabled shape of braincase with widest part at the base, and inturned mastoid processes.

did not recognize the specimen immediately called it *erectus* and could point out all the traits when questioned. The reason Broken Hill is often classed in our species is because of its apparent age of just 45,000 years, and for no better reason.

Neandertal man from Europe and the near east may now be compared with the listing of *erectus* traits given above. Neandertals have modern-sized brains contained in cases that are smooth and which bulge out over the ear region and over the occipital ridge. In all other respects they fit the *erectus* design. From earliest to latest of *erectus* times there is almost no change in the basic type. Average brain sizes increase, but except for the Neandertals, this is only a normal consequence of increasing body sizes. Another consequence of increasing body size in the later specimens is a relative increase in development of brows and other ridges. There is not a progressive modernizing or gradual evolution going on during *erectus* times; it is an evolutionary plateau. Neandertals are the one exception to this in their modern size of braincase. Some earlier European fossils which may or may not be classed as Neandertals also had brain sizes somewhat above the *erectus* average of elsewhere in the world.

If one considers brain size to be the prime trait of *sapiens*, and that all else followed from that, then Neandertals must be admitted into our species. The trouble with this idea is that Neandertal anatomy was around for at least 50,000 years with no further change, then abruptly was succeeded by fully modern man. If Neandertal was just a racial variant of ourselves, then why has his physical type been replaced?

Except for the brain size and some direct consequences of it, Neandertal is an *erectus* who persisted up to about 40,000 years ago in Europe. There the replacing type, known from about 30,000 years ago, is a fully modern form, commonly called Cro-Magnon. In Palestine a good Neandertal skull from the Tabun cave (a small female) dates from 45,000 years ago, and some rugged *sapiens* skulls from the neighboring Skhul cave date from 35,000 years ago. In each region the time of changeover is bracketed to within 10,000 years. If the two areas are treated together it must be within 5,000 years. It may be even less because the last Neandertals show no particular trend toward becoming more modern looking.

Elsewhere in the world there is not such clear timing, but what there is suggests a similarity short gap. In southern Africa the Broken Hill skull has been dated by tool association to 45,000 years ago, but this is on a time scale that is currently being questioned. Still, I find nothing particularly wrong with this date from a morphological point of view. Broken Hill was a particularly large individual with the largest eye sockets (a good measure of body size) of any fossil hominid yet known.

His 1300 cc endocranial capacity is acceptable for a non-Neandertal *erectus*, but the skull is not quite as ridged, crested, thick, or rugged as might be expected for such a large man. It may be just individual variation, but I sense a touch of something beginning to change here. Another specimen from southern Africa, the Florisbad skull, is also dated at 45,000 years and is a rugged but perfectly good *sapiens.* Neither of these dates is quite firm and a 5,000 or even a 10,000 year gap could be introduced between them. Other African *erectus* and *sapiens* crania also bracket this transition time but with a wider gap or more uncertain dates.

In China the last representative of *erectus* is the Mapa skull of early Upper Pleistocene date, which probably means more than 50,000 years ago and possibly twice that figure. Somewhat later in the Upper Pleistocene are a number of skeletal remains, notably the Tze-Yang and Liu-Kiang skulls which are good *sapiens* and show some of the genetic line traits from Peking times. There is no clear measure of the time gap here, but there must be at least 10,000 years between the two types as far as these specimens go. More crania could only narrow the gap.

The only remaining area that contains discoveries of late *erectus* and early *sapiens* is Java. The late *erectus* is Solo man and might again be dated anywhere in the Upper Pleistocene, though probably more than 50,000 years ago. These are followed after an unknown interval by the two fossil *sapiens* skulls from Wadjak. Like all early skulls of our type they are somewhat large and heavily built by modern standards.

There is generally a major change in the stone-tool industry traditions at or near the time gap that includes the anatomical transition of sapienization. In general, the newer kinds of stone tools from all areas are made in greater variety, are made to conform more easily with the fracturing qualities of the local stone material, and the tool types have more restricted geographical distributions. One cannot help getting the impression that some major improvement in the way of life occurred with this change in technology. Often a major increase in population is also indicated. It would be tempting somehow to equate the technological and life-style changes with those in the cranial anatomy.

The foregoing is only a short sketch of the timing and lithic data available. This and much more all seem to indicate some major change throughout the inhabited world, in about a 10,000 year period or less, which was followed by ever increasing diversity and advancements at a pace unknown before. At about this same time human brains were expanding to 1500 cc (if they were not already at that level). Faces were reducing in size and pulling back leaving chins projecting, while brow ridges were being incorporated into vertical foreheads. Foramen magnums were lowering and basioccipitals were becoming steeply sloped. Mastoid processes were enlarging and becoming vertical. Muscle attachments at the sides and backs of the braincase were moving towards the center of the skull, making it shorter, narrower, and taller. Braincases were becoming thinner and less angulated. In short, they were being remodeled into the *sapiens* design.

REPLACEMENT MODEL.

Most older theories postulated the appearance of *sapiens* in some limited region and the subsequent spread of this type as a new species over the world replacing the archaic *erectus* with no interbreeding. The evidently short period of time available for this transition would be compatible with this replacement theory, but there are some problems.

It is commonly taken as self-evident that *sapiens* cranial anatomy is superior to that of our brutish predecessors. On closer examination this fails to hold up, and indeed the *erectus* skull is actually the better design for virtually all purposes. The brain is far better protected from injurious blows, the face is likewise stronger against breakage, larger teeth will last longer with a gritty diet, and even the cranial hair will hang to the sides of the brow ridges instead of in the face (assuming the forehead is bare). A closer look at the reconstructable throat anatomy indicates *erectus* could swallow with less chance of getting fluids into his trachea. It is not enough to simply say that we are *sapiens* and prevail today. In some manner *erectus* was quite inferior, and until we can point out exactly what that difference is between us, we will not be able to say how and why the change occurred.

The replacement theory also fails because it cannot account for the persistence of certain line traits which are seen before and after the transition. The case for Peking *erectus* to Mongoloid *sapiens* includes Inca bones, shoveled incisors, enamel pearls, mandibular tori, and anterior cheek bones, just to name the most obvious. Admittedly this is the best case we have of continuing line traits, but it is enough to make the point. If *sapiens* originated elsewhere, his arrival in eastern Asia would have terminated those line traits with the replacement of the local *erectus* form. If *sapiens* originated from a descendant of Peking man, then these same line traits should equally characterize the rest of humanity today, which they do not.

It was long thought that the clearest case of population replacement was in Europe where not only the Neandertal anatomy but also his Mousterian tool tradition was abruptly superceded by very different forms. We now know that the tool change was at least partly in-place and gradual, but still very rapid by most Pleistocene standards. There is even evidence now of an overlap—the new technology with the old anatomy, at least it looks that way from some scraps of bone. This is as it should be, because an evolutionary change begins with new behavior and this is only gradually followed by selection for the best anatomy to express this new behavior. The stones should, and do, show the change first.

SELECTION MODEL.

The alternative theory is that it was just the genes, not actual people, that flowed out of the *sapiens* source area to overwhelm the world. This would involve some selective pressure favoring the new anatomy wherever gene flow causes its appearance. The same problem arises here just as with the replacement model—there is no obvious anatomical superiority in the various changes to justify their differential perpetuation.

The selection model also suffers from another fatal flaw in that there is simply not enough time for it to operate. Favorable variations will pass from one breeding population to another by occasional out-group matings. In the new population these will become more common in the next few generations because of their presumed superior adaptation. Then random matings will pass the superior genes on to the next breeding population, and so on.

It is difficult to determine rates of propagation for this process, but some rough limits can be set. If we assume a baboon-like social organization in troops of 30 to 50 individuals and with modern hunters' population density we get breeding pools of something like 30 km diameter each. If their life-spans were only a little shorter than ours, say a reproductive generation averaging 20 years, it would take 100 years for five generations of selection within such a troop. From a most favorable, centralized location in Iran, it would take about 27,000 years for the new traits to spread over the inhabited world. The baboon troop model may not be correct, but in view of the following considerations it seems the most likely. The five generations of selection is probably the rashest assumption here, and ten or more would be far more likely. All things considered, a figure of about 30,000 years seems to be the very minimum for this kind of transition by selection, and two or three times as long is more likely. The archeological record does not permit that much time.

Combination theories can also be advanced where a certain number of individuals move out to occupy new areas at the expense of the resident *erectus*, but who also interbreed with some of that local population. This can preserve some of the speed of change which is possible only with the replacement model. It also allows for the incorporation of some local genes to maintain the line traits that have already been described. Since the line traits noted here are mainly nonselective, the incoming *sapiens* population cannot be in overwhelming numbers or these traits would tend to disappear. Small increments of new *sapiens* would still require a long time for selection within each breeding population or their traits would rapidly become diluted over space.

These various theories all fail because of persistent line traits or from not enough time available. Combinations of both replacement and selection fail from a little of each and from dilution of traits. There would seem to be no normal biological process that could effect such a consistent anatomical change over such a large area in such a short period of time.

CULTURAL EXPLANATION.

The obvious remaining possibility to account for sapienization is that the spread of a behavioral trait triggered a world-wide selection for the same general anatomical changes to better perform the behavior in question. Some kind of learned activity could spread from one population to another more rapidly than any genes if it were sufficiently advantageous. The several generations of selection in each group are not necessary.

The learned behavior in question must be something that any *erectus* was capable of performing when given the opportunity. It would be something that could have taken as much as a few years to master, but not a lifetime, and certainly not five or ten generations. It must be a behavior that can be transmitted from one individual to another, or collectively from one social group to another, with or without physical interbreeding. The behavior must be one that is equally advantageous in all kinds of environments. Above all, it must be a kind of behavior that gave the possessors an enormous advantage over those who did not have it. And finally, the *sapiens* cranial anatomy must be a design that facilitates superior performance of this same behavior. With this last requirement it would follow that all *erectus* populations, after acquiring the new behavior, would select within themselves for the same anatomical variations that characterize *sapiens* today.

Given the above description, identifying the new behavior as language was quite obvious. This does not mean language in its totality was invented at one time and place, but rather there was some final step in its development that changed it from a good call system into a medium for communicating ideas. This is not the proper place for a full analysis of the change involved, but some thoughts on the subject may be in order.

There are two major aspects of human language which are distinct from all or most other animals' communication systems. These are symbolism and phonemics. Symbolic language means simply that a given signal stands for something that is agreed upon. To analyze such a signal will not tell us its meaning because this is arbitrarily assigned to each of them. Just because two signals look alike (sign language) or sound alike (words) does not indicate that their meanings are at all similar. Symbols mean what their users want them to mean.

Symbols can represent things that are not being directly perceived by the senses. This may have a bearing on their development because it enabled our ancestors to communicate about things that were elsewhere or elsewhen. A great mental time span that encompasses images of past and future events will as easily build images of present things that are out of range of the senses. If such a mind exists, for whatever reason, it is a secondary problem just how the symbols came to be developed to communicate these images.

Individual symbols, by word or gesture, communicate images of things and/or actions. These can be strung together in sequences which tell more than the total of the symbols by themselves. Here, of course, I am referring to what the linguists call morphemes, the minimal signaling unit that carries meaning. In some languages each morpheme stands alone as a word, while in others they are grouped together in clusters of as many as ten or more for each word. When these morphemes are given in sequences they can affect each other's meaning by proximity, or the order in which they occur, and thereby add more information.

By analogy to the morphemes' ordering adding meaning, the sequence of sounds in a single utterance adds meaning. In fact this is almost the entire source of their meaning. Probably the most unique aspect of human language is what may be called the phonemic principle. The individual sounds, or phonemes, in our speech do not by themselves carry meaning—but their combinations do. This appears to be unlike the communication system of any other animal where the minimal signaling unit always carries meaning. The wag of a dog's tail or the twitch of his ears will always carry meaning to another dog if it can be perceived at all. These signals are not made up from a combination of units that are meaningless by themselves. Dolphin "language" may have defied analysis because it too is made up only of meaningful signals. Human language corresponds roughly to the idea of alphabetic writing; our phonemes which carry no meaning are represented by letters, and our morphemes which do carry meaning are represented by words or syllables. (This is not always exactly true but it gets the idea across.) Dolphins can produce a great variety of distinct sounds, enough so that with a meaning assigned to each of them they can convey any thoughts they wish. These meanings may be modified in various ways by what might be called sound order, as opposed to word order, but they have enough sounds that they may not be forced into using them only in combinations as we are.

The anatomical basis of symbolic communication is easy to pin down, at least in gross terms. It is in the size of the brain and the number of its contained nerve cells and connections among them. Neuropsychologists have long known that mental time span correlates closely with brain size, regardless of phylogenetic contrasts of the animals in question. A big fish will have a better mental time span than a mouse if its brain is larger. Apes have greater abilities at memory and anticipation than do monkeys simply because they have more brain. We exceed the apes for the same reason.

Experiments on language learning by chimpanzees in recent years have at long last given us some clear measure of their symbolic capacity. Compared to ours it isn't much, but it does exceed all other animals with which we have established communication. In spite of the enthusiasm about chimp language it comes nowhere near human standards. If one had a four-year old child whose vocabulary and mistake rate were like these chimps, it would be considered defective. Given the chimp brain size of less than one-third of ours, this correlates nicely. With the dolphin equaling us in brain size, their reputed symbolic language is not surprising. I am waiting for someone to train an elephant to move his trunk in meaningless twitches which have meaningful combinations.

With this and a good deal more to go by, it is evident that we can make some rough estimations of the mental time spans of our fossil ancestors. Most of the australopithecine fossil material shows little more space for the brain, nor for the blood vessels to feed it, than there is in the living apes. We need not presume, as some have, much greater intelligence for them. Some revisions of australopithecine phylogenies may indicate some had brains of larger, but not *erectus*, size and corresponding mental abilities. With *Homo erectus* we are dealing with brain sizes about midway between those of the larger apes and man. Their mental time spans and symbolic capacities should also have been somewhere in between, but not necessarily exactly midway. In Neandertal man we find a brain size the equal of our own, even though they qualify as *erectus* in almost all other respects. It would follow that Neandertals could match us in their awareness of the passage of time, and preumably also in their ability to think in terms of symbols. How well they could communicate their symbolic thoughts is another matter.

The anatomical basis for the phonemic principle doesn't exist as such, but we might be able to infer its presence. If regular and frequent use of spoken language occurred only after the development of phonemics made it effective, then indications of evolution of the speech apparatus in general may also be a sign of phonemics in particular. Lieberman and Crelin (1971) have recently updated some attempts to show that Neandertals were greatly limited in their speaking abilities. They have reconstructed the Neandertal throat anatomy to indicate a very high position of the larynx and a virtual absense of the pharyngeal cavity above it. This is very much like the condition found in apes and in human infants who, while noisy, cannot produce nearly the sounds that adult humans can. There has been much criticism of Lieberman's work as is to be expected for any important ideas, whether true or not. On the whole there is something very different about the anatomy of the throat in Neandertals and in all other *erectus* remains, which would include all crania older than about 40,000 or 45,000 years. Directly or indirectly it would appear that all the differences between *erectus* and *sapiens* skulls follow from the contrast between their vocal apparatuses.

It has not been established that the phonemic principle was in fact the invention that constituted the final step in language development. It is clear that of all the basic elements that make up language ability, phonemics would have to be the last one added. If anything else were missing, phonemic distinctions would not be of functional use. Likewise, it is not directly shown that phonemics began with the transition to *sapiens,* but if this were not the case we would be hard pressed to explain this transition.

ANATOMICAL TRANSITION.

Variations in sound production come from a number of places ranging from the vocal cords themselves to the lips. Immediately above the vocal cords is the pharyngeal cavity which can alter in shape to become one of the most important sources of variations, particularly of vowel sounds. This space and its consequent contribution to speech production is unique to *sapiens* and it is not well developed in the apes or even in our newborn children. From the normal mammalian condition, our pharynx is formed mainly by the lowering of the larynx, or voice box, a substantial distance down the neck. Neither the larynx, nor direct evidence of its position is fossilized, but there are, nonetheless, clear signs that indicate its probable position in various fossil hominids.

The digastric muscles insert in the back of the chin and run first to the hyoid bone which is at the top of the larynx. From the styloid processes near the mastoids, the stylohyoid ligaments also go to the hyoid bone. Some researchers claim to be able to see the direction in which these muscles and ligaments pointed in Neandertals, and thus can determine the exact position their hyoids occupied in life. I cannot agree about the digastric muscles, but the direction the styoid processes point would have to be in about the direction of the hyoid. Neandertal styloids appear to point somewhat higher or forward than in ourselves. This indicates their larynx was either placed quite high, or else it was very far forward and this wouldn't make anatomical sense. (See Fig. 51.)

The basioccipital bone forms a buttress behind the rear of the nasal cavity where it starts to turn down and become the pharynx. In the formation of the human pharyngeal cavity, this region becomes elongated downward and its back wall assumes a more vertical position than in the apes. The nasopharyngeal air tract in the apes and in newborn humans is a long, gentle curve into the neck. In the adult human condition this tract makes a more abrupt turn of almost a right angle.

To a large degree the angle of the basioccipital parallels this change in slope and length of the soft parts that rest against it. The basioccipital in effect hinges at its forward end while the rear part swings down and forward as well. This rotation of the basioccipital brings with it the foramen magnum and the general area of the central base of the braincase. As this area moves down and forward the neck vertebrae are necessarily shifting in the same direction. These vertebrae then continue to form the back wall for the softer structures in their new positions. (See Fig. 52.)

The changes which are described above will effectively increase the height of the braincase simply by drawing the center of its base downward. As the base of the brain is drawn down relative to other structures, something else must move in laterally to compensate for this move. The sides and back of the cranial base will move inward slightly in order to make up for this difference. This slightly narrows and shortens the braincase, thereby completing the process of eliminating the platycephaly, or flat-headed effect.

Closing up the cranial base also moves inward the line of muscle attachments that runs around the back of the skull from one ear region to the other. This means that the head cannot be moved with such force as before. Increasing the braincase height by lowering its base

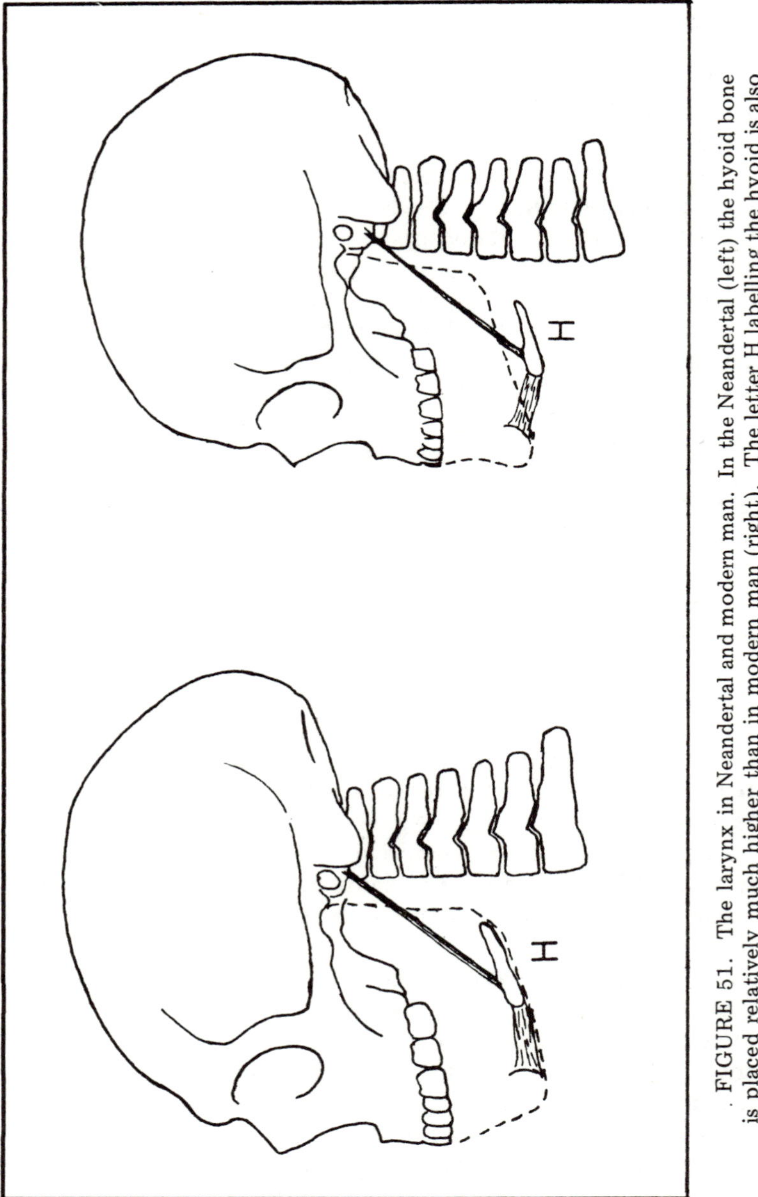

FIGURE 51. The larynx in Neandertal and modern man. In the Neandertal (left) the hyoid bone is placed relatively much higher than in modern man (right). The letter H labelling the hyoid is also placed directly over the larynx which is just below that bone. The hyoid and the larynx probably occupied the same positions in relation to the neck vertebrae in both cases. As the larynx moved downward the vertebrae moved with it and the skull bottom protruded down as well.

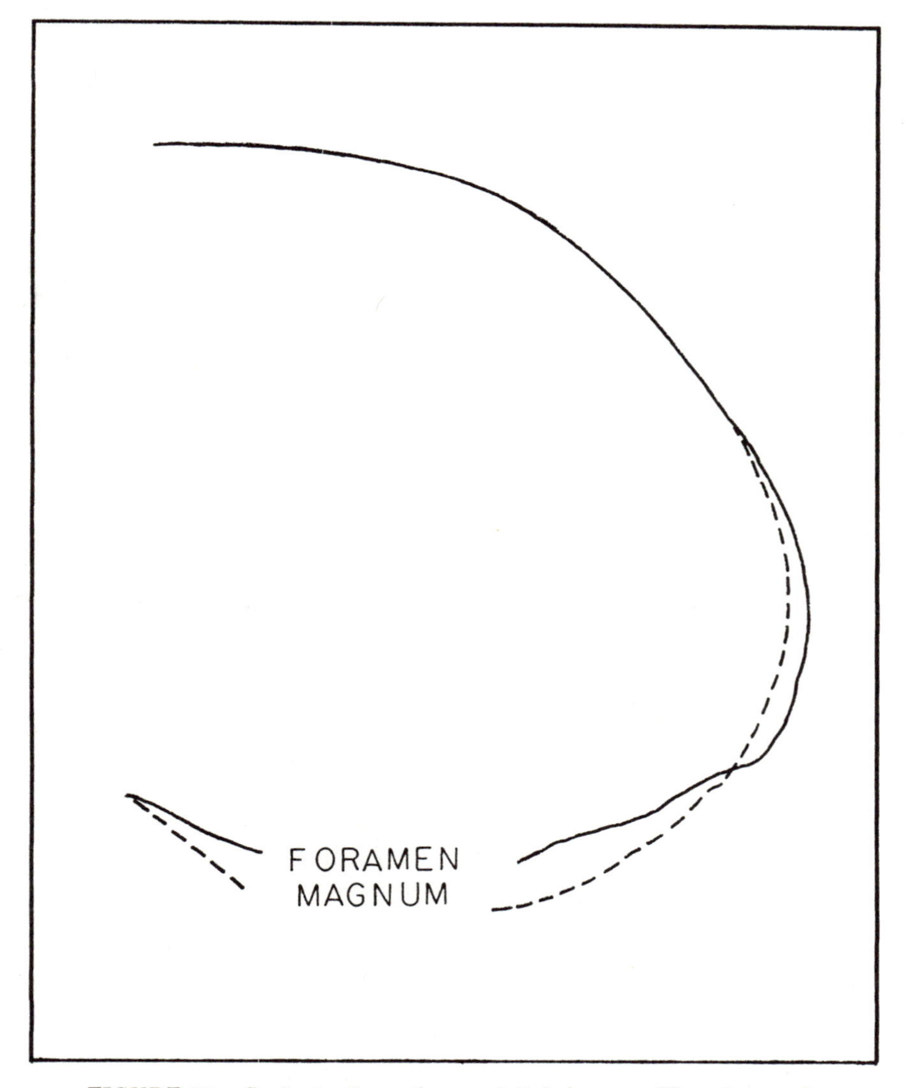

FIGURE 52. Sapienization, the occipital bone. The change from Neandertal (solid line) to *sapiens* (dashed line) is shown here in the occipital bone as seen in longitudinal section with the skull facing to the left. The pharynx is elongated, the larynx is moved down, the neck vertebrae move down with it, so the area around the foramen magnum (spinal cord opening) must move down as well. This tips the basioccipital, just ahead of the foramen magnum, as though it hinges at its forward end. The added space created at the bottom of the braincase is compensated for by an inward movement of the skull base immediately above.

only adds to this effect. It is not clear whether some advantage was gained by this change of muscle leverage. The new design permits the head to be moved with greater speed but with less power than before. In any case there was no great selective pressure to maintain the forceful head-moving design.

As the foramen magnum moves down and forward it carries with it the condyles which attach it to the first vertebra of the neck. The skull slides forward and back on this first cervical joint, actually rotating on a transverse axis located just above the occipital condyles. As these condyles are moved this axis of front-to-back rotation moves with them. As this axis moves down and forward the mastoid processes must lengthen in order to move the muscle attachments at their tips to a lower position. This is significant only when the head is tipped far backward and the mastoids are then pointing forward. They must project far enough forward beyond the axis of rotation so that the muscles originating from the sternum can pull down on them and tip the head upright again. (See Fig. 53.)

The same sternocleidomastoid muscles that pull the head forward also help to rotate it from side to side when used separately. Apparently good leverage is required for this action and the mastoid tips must maintain a reasonably lateral position. As the sides of the skull come together slightly and the mastoids elongate a bit, the entire process must take on a vertical orientation to keep the tip from moving in too. Thus the mastoid ceases to be inflected as in *erectus* skulls. (See Fig. 54.)

Changes in the facial region all begin with the tongue which moves back and turns down into the throat. The back of the tongue constitutes much of the anterior wall of the all-important pharynx. This is not accomplished by an elongation of the tongue (compared with apes), but simply by a change in position of about a constant-sized structure. This movement back and bending down behind can be seen by following such topographic features as the foramen cecum. This indentation is near the center of the ape's tongue and at the back of the human tongue because the rear half of the originally nearly horizontal tongue has now turned to a vertical position. (See Fig. 55.)

As the back half moves down into the throat, the front half of the tongue is drawn back a corresponding distance. In order for the tongue tip to move food around the incisors and to lick the lips, the entire front of the mouth must be drawn back too. The chin maintains its position for tongue and digastric muscles to have full action space. Teeth get smaller in order to fit in the withdrawn jaw space available to them. The rest of the upper face also tends to pull back with the jaws, but not quite so much, thereby reducing prognathism or jaw projection. (See Fig. 55.)

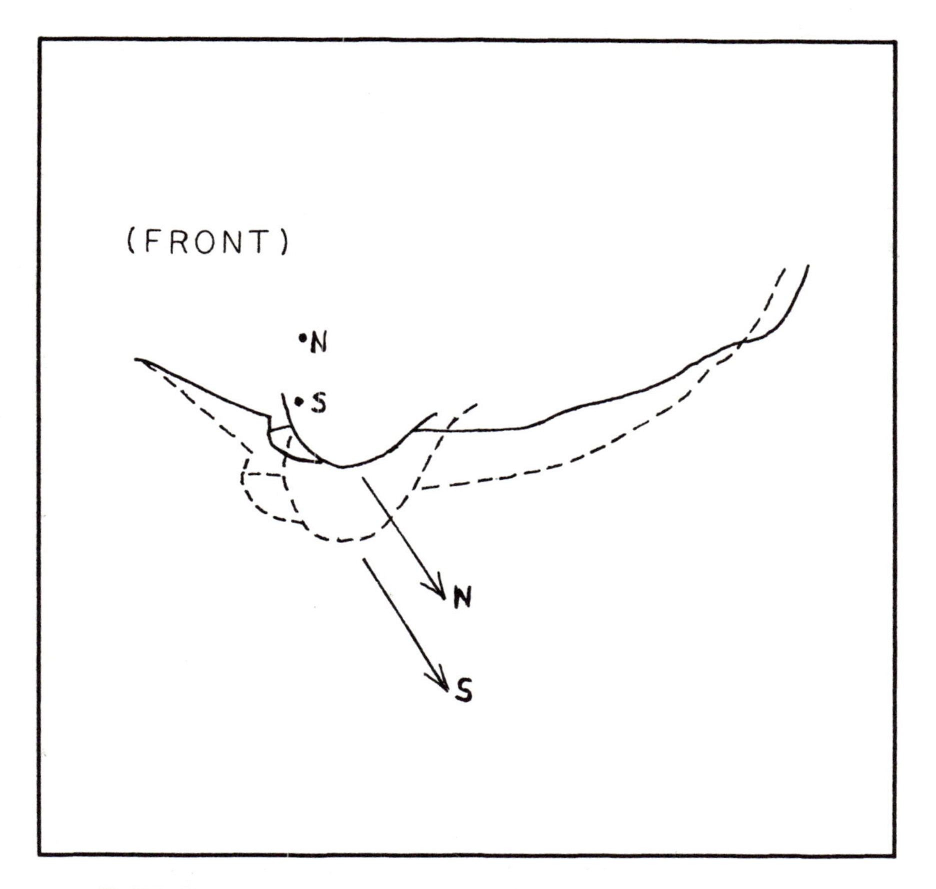

FIGURE 53. Sapienization, the mastoid process. The Neandertal occipital condyles (solid line) to which the first vertebra attaches are located much higher up in the skull base than in the *sapiens* (dashed line). These condyles determine the location of the axis of rotation just above them. When the head is tipped far back the sternocleidomastoid muscles pull in the direction indicated by the arrows. If the head is to be rotated forward, the line of pull must pass in front of the axis of rotation. Thus, as the axis moves down with the condyles, the mastoid process must similarly be extended downward.

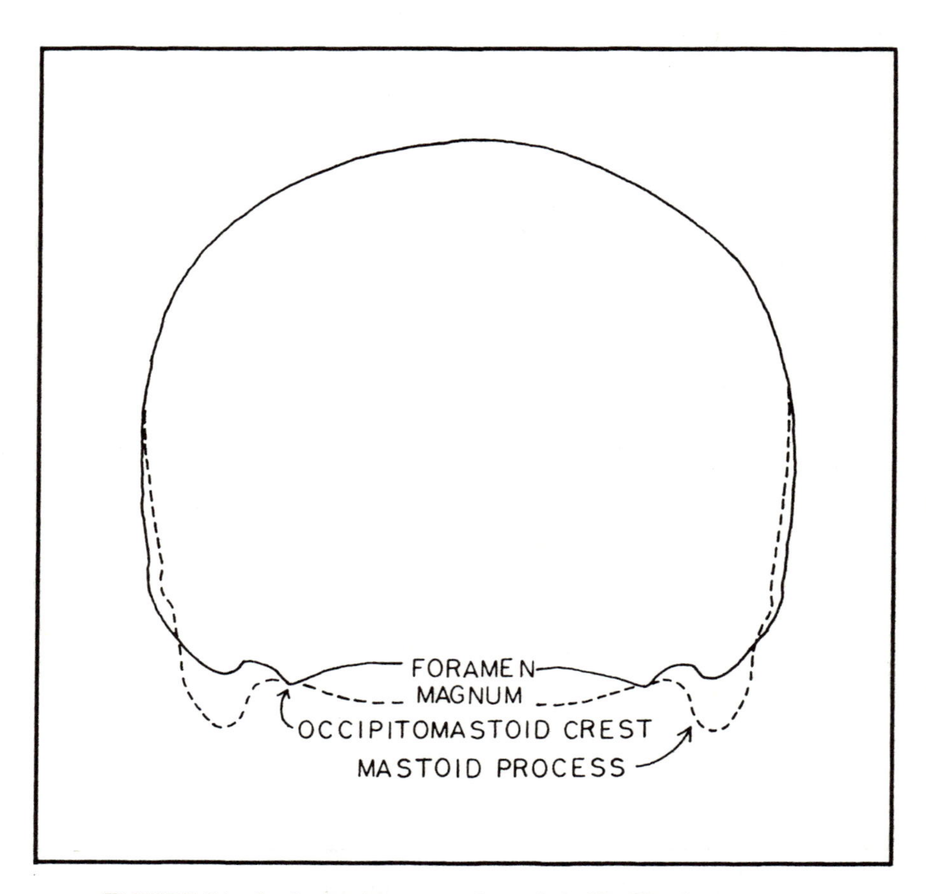

FIGURE 54. Sapienization, rear view of skull. The foramen magnum moves down from the Neandertal position (solid line) to the *sapiens* position (dashed line). The added space is compensated for by pulling in the sides of the base as well as the rear (Fig. 52), thus eliminating the platycephaly or flattened shape. As the mastoid processes extend downward (see Fig. 53) their tips must stay well to the sides to accomplish rotary movements of the head. Because the upper part of the mastoid moves inward and the lengthened tip does not, this gives a vertical orientation for the entire process. The projecting occipitomastoid crest of the *erectus* skull is actually the only part of the skull base that does not move.

The optical orbits and nasal cavity move farther underneath the frontal lobes of the brain as they pull back. Because of limited vertical space available, these structures, especially the orbits, reduce in size in order to fit. The upper rims of the orbits, otherwise known as brow ridges, become incorporated into the forehead and thus cease to project. There will usually be some added nasal projection as well because this nasal chamber will tend to hold its original length while the structures around it pull back. (See Fig. 55.)

With this the transformation of the *erectus* skull into that of *sapiens* is complete. There are some weak points in this causal chain of alterations that all began with the formation of the pharyngeal cavity. On the whole, however, it holds together logically and accounts for why our skulls have acquired such a seemingly poor design. The test of whether a skull was designed to maximize speech production is not just the basioccipital slope or the relative length of the palate, but rather in the entire *sapiens* vs. *erectus* cranial contrast. It must also be remembered that small skulls of either species will be more sapient in their design in some features, and large skulls will be the reverse. Thus a small *erectus* will resemble a large *sapiens* to some degree in many of the features described here. But when similarly sized skulls are compared there are strong contrasts in all these characteristics.

HISTORY OF THE TRANSITION.

One of the most obvious questions is where did this transition to *sapiens* begin. On anatomical evidence we can point a strong finger at the Neandertals because they show at least two items that may have been prerequisites. One of these is their brain size which equals our own. An increase to this brain size regularly appears as part of the sapienization process in all other areas, thus making it one of the basic traits. The symbolic capacity implied by this size of brain may also be a prerequisite, but this is not as directly evident. If it wasn't the Neandertals, then another population with similarly large brains must be the source.

The other trait is the absence of what I call the tongue shelf. In all other *erectus* mandibles there is a shelf of bone projecting back behind the lower incisors as if to provide a surface on which to rest the tip of the tongue. In some Neandertal jaws, as in *sapiens*, this shelf is missing and the inside of the symphasis drops nearly vertically. I don't know how to interpret this feature in the Neandertals as it seems to imply a beginning of the vocal adaptation, but it is not accompanied by any of the other pertinent traits.

Late *erectus* specimens are known from enough of the inhabited

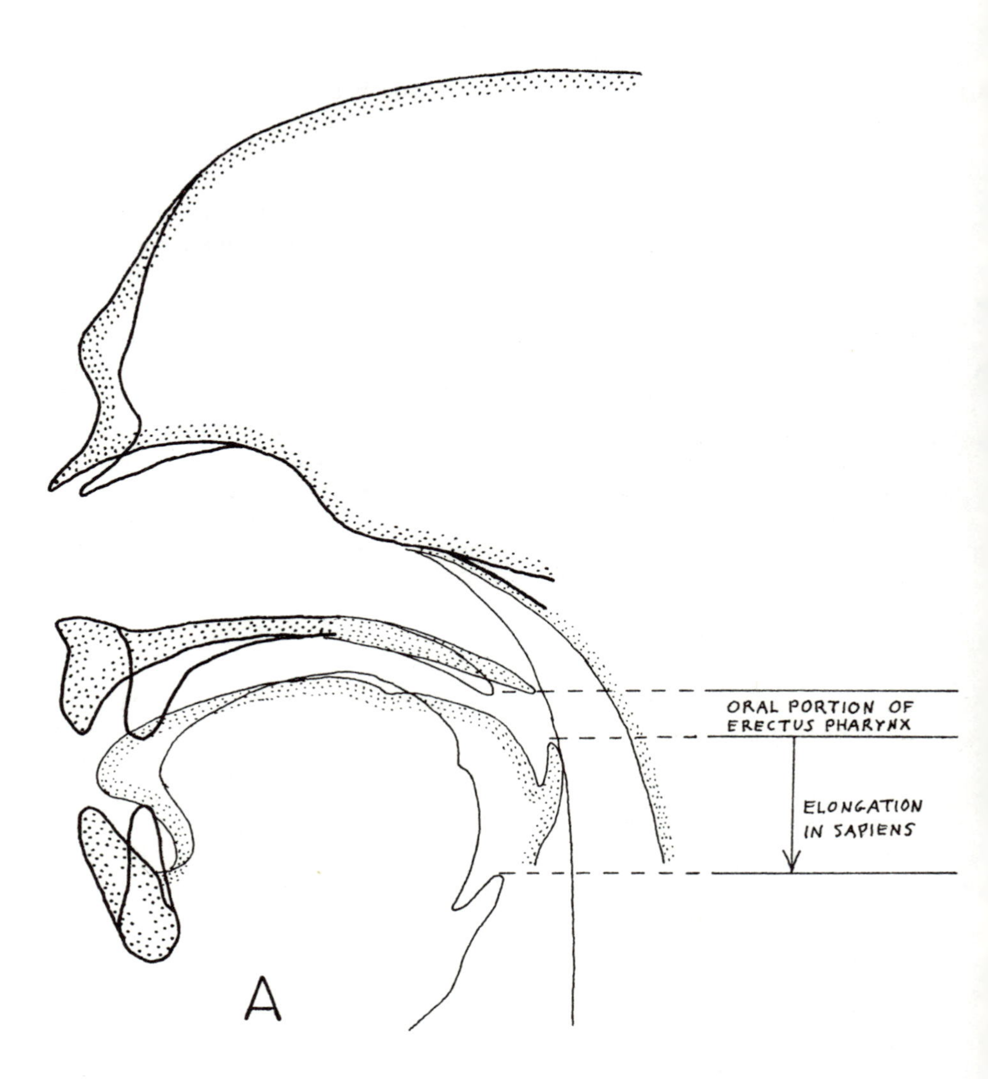

FIGURE 55. Sapienization, the face and throat. Neandertal and *sapiens* structures are superimposed in both pictures, bone being shown with heavy lines and soft parts in fine lines. On the left (A) the Neandertal outlines are stippled, on the right (B) the *sapiens* outlines are stippled. Movements of various parts are indicated by arrows, tongue tip (T), foramen cecum (FC), epiglotis (E), vocal cords (VC), and basion (Ba)

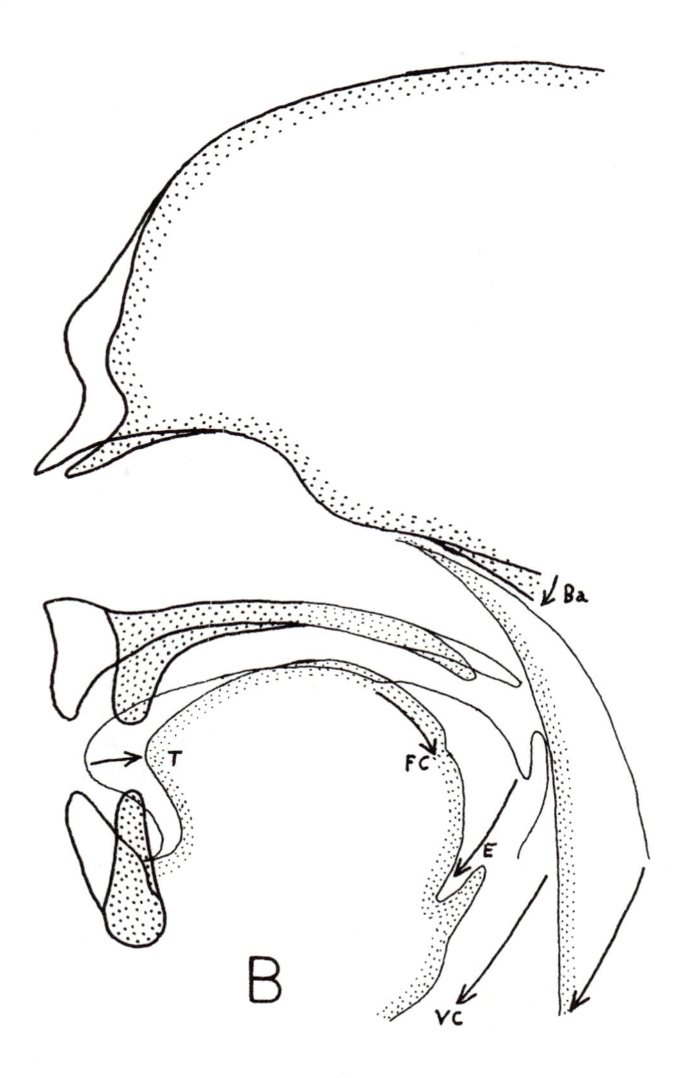

or front edge of foramen magnum. The pharynx is elongated by pulling the epiglotis down and forward, and by pulling the tongue back and partly down the throat. As the tongue tip withdraws, the teeth and most of the face also pulls back. The face gets smaller in order to fit under the frontal lobes of the brain. The chin remains unmoved to keep space for the tongue and throat muscle.

world of that time to rule out most areas for the origin of *sapiens*. India still remains a blank, as does much of eastern Asia. If a large-brained, late *erectus* lived in either of these areas it would also be a candidate for *sapiens* origins. On present evidence of dating we can probably rule out Europe for the beginning. This leaves only the eastern Mediterranean area and the plateaus of Turkey and Iran as the most probable, but hardly the proven source. It may be no coincidence that the Neandertal skull with the largest endocranial capacity, Amud man, was found in Palestine.

On other grounds a more northern region might be argued for. If phonemic language were preceded by communication with each sound carrying a fixed meaning, then the vocabulary would have been severely limited in terms of short utterences. A large inventory of symbolic concepts would then have to be expressed by hand, face, and body gestures if they were to be communicated at all. One needs light in order to see such gestures as well as an unobstructed line of sight. In northern climates, toward the edge of human habitation, summer darkness of eight hours per night may set the normal sleeping duration. Midwinter nights of twice that length would preclude most communication for eight of those hours unless they spent all that time around fires. A *sapiens* origin along the northern fringe does not accord with the dating unless the transition was very rapid and occurred between the dates of 40,000 and 35,000 years ago. The other possibility is a *sapiens* origin in the northern China area where present archeological evidence says little, one way or the other. The somewhat Neandertal-looking Mapa skull from southern China would fit such a picture, but does not prove it. Aside from a generally northern source, the exact location cannot presently be pinned down.

The spread of sapienization would be a diffusion of the ideas involved in fully developed language, followed by an in-place selection for those anatomical traits that would improve this language facility. If the last step of human language were the phonemic principle to increase the spoken vocabulary, then this habit should have spread rather rapidly. A complex call system would have been common to all *erectus*, probably one much more varied than that found in any of the living apes. To modify this into a phonemic vocabulary should prove to be no great difficulty for large-brained hominids. To teach it to smaller-brained hominids is also not too difficult because we do this every generation today.

The advantages to be gained by more rapid communication of symbolic thoughts are numerous. Quick changes of plans in hunting expeditions, perhaps much of cooperative hunting in itself, would be facilitated. Probably the most important aspect to acrue from improved language facility would be in the realm of what we use language for the most today—social organization. Building, shifting, and dismantling social groupings are the hallmarks of man. Not only do we have complicated social structures, but unlike other animals, we can change these quickly and sometimes fairly easily. People in organized social groups can accomplish things that no individual, or collection of individuals, can do.

Conflicts between adjacent populations would not be equal contests if only one side had an effective and flexible organization. Here would be one of the major exceptions to the rule of hunters not being able to overrun the territories of other hunters with similar numbers and adaptations. For the most part, this language facility would probably come in such modest increments that no great difference would normally exist between any two adjacent populations. The initial idea and any improvements on it would spread rapidly, while adaptation of the superior speech apparatus would occur more slowly. A ripple of minor conflicts may well have spread with the beginning of sapienization, but little more is indicated for most of the world.

In southern Africa and to some degree in Australia, much more than a ripple of conflict is indicated. A long pause in the spread of sapienization at some natural barrier would permit a build-up of a differential in its development. Then a spill-over of more fully developed *sapiens* into the *erectus* lands should have had disastrous consequences to the resident population. It has been discussed earlier how this may have led to a total population replacement in southern Africa and a massive incursion into Australia.

9.
CONCLUSIONS

SUMMARY.

The method of mapping trait distributions and comparing them with each other and with all other possible phenomena is the major basis of this work. From this it can be seen that studies relating race with intelligence are of no pertinence to anything. These studies have always begun by assuming the very thing they are trying to test—that mental differences have distributions that coincide with certain physical differences. Any intelligence test that begins with a sample of whites and a sample of blacks has failed right there. The pooling of such data into these two categories is a rash assumption and can obscure any real differences, if such exist.

Mapping of separate trait distributions led inevitably to the dual system of racial classification. This system challenges the unified concept of race that we all grew up with. If the idea of common descent can be separated from the observation of shared physical traits, then this work will have met with some success.

The antiquity of race is another touchy subject and I have concluded that racial differences do indeed go back in time to long before our species level of organization. It does not exactly follow that we can trace specific races back a million years. The dual nature of race was even truer then than it is now.

The readers of this book, from anthropologists to laymen, should find nothing to support any concepts of racial superiority or inferiority.

RACE AND INTELLIGENCE.

In the preceding chapters many readers will have noticed that no mention was made of the possible relationship between racial categories and intellectual abilities. The more astute readers will have realized that no such relationship has ever been demonstrated. In fact, by the procedures that are normally used this would be essentially impossible. This follows from the manner in which data has always been gathered on this rather sensitive subject. Researchers have been very careful to use properly selected samples of sufficient size for averaging and other statistical manipulations. In so doing they have invalidated any racial aspect of their work because they have assumed what they set out to prove in the first place. This is that intelligence differences, if any exist, will have the same geographical distribution as skin colors or whatever trait is being used to select the sample.

There is a general problem here which relates to the gathering of data on many other racial characteristics as well. The only valid procedure is to map the distribution of the trait, preferably in the ethnographic present, and then to compare it with other trait distributions, with climates, with genetic barriers, or whatever. Correlations will emerge from this mapping of the data and cannot be assumed before one even begins.

The error that is so frequently made is that of pooling data into preconceived categories. Fortunately this has not been done with most genetic traits, but one might consider what would have happened if such pooling had occurred. The dry earwax genes peak in northern China at 98% and decline in frequency from there in all directions in proportion to distance, and regardless of other trait distributions. If we had initially decided it was a "Mongoloid" trait and pooled our data accordingly, we would have a gene frequency of about 80% for Mongoloids and 17% for Caucasoids. This would have been called a good trait for distinguishing the two "races" and its real distribution would have been obscured.

The same reasoning can be applied to the frequency of the gene for B blood in Europe. Classical traits tend to divide this continent into a northern half of larger and less pigmented peoples, and a southern half of smaller and darker ones. Clearly the "natural" division of Europe is north vs. south and this could be tested against blood group data. Sure enough, with a horizontal line drawn through Vienna, the north averages 12% B genes and the south averages 10%. If another line is drawn vertically through Vienna the continent is now divided into quadrants. Pooling of blood types within each of these gives the following figures:

NW 8%	NE16%
SW 6%	SE 14%

Our slight north vs. south distinction was indeed correct, but it is greatly overshadowed by an east to west distinction of over two to one. Pooling blood data into categories determined by classical traits would have effectively obscured this very impressive east-west clinal distribution. The implications become all the clearer if we multiplied all these B gene frequencies by ten and called them I.Q. scores.

Other very "scientifically" controlled experiments have been made to study the physiological effects of alcohol consumption, of artistic abilities, of sense perceptions, of disease resistance, and the like. Most of these are of no value in comparing races because they all assume the distribution of trait rather than demonstrating it. All such studies run the same risk of obscuring the very differences they are looking for, simply by the assumptions on which they pool their data. The only valid procedure is to plot the variations of a trait geographically in order to see how they distribute themselves. Then the data may be pooled, but only in the categories suggested by the data, not by the investigator.

A few errors of this sort may have crept into this book though I have tried to watch out for them. The forward set of the "Mongoloid" cheeks does not appear to have been mapped by itself, and then this map examined to see if it corresponds with the distribution of coarse, straight, black hair. Through direct encounters and examination of photographs one can get at least a rough picture of these distributions and they do seem to be coincident. The epicanthic fold follows the distribution of the above traits also, but much less closely and seems to fade out in some areas where the others persist. How many other "Mongoloid" traits are similarly coincident, and how many are just assumed to be, is hard to determine. The traits used here are those with known distributions or are those which can easily be judged. Some traits may seem conspicuous by their absense here or by their curt treatment, but this is generally because the kind of distributional data that is needed simply is not available.

Measurements of intelligence are about the worst I have ever seen in terms of lack of availability of proper distributional data. This is rather surprising for such a potentially important subject. The current furor in some scientific circles about racial intelligence is all a waste of time on both sides because no properly racial data has been produced.

Intelligence is certainly in large part a functional expression of the central nervous system. Gross malfunctions of this system are known to impair intellectual performance, and some of these malfunctions are inherited. It would be a reasonable assumption that there are lesser variations in this system, also inherited, that have small effects on intelligence. It is even possible, though this has hardly been shown, that such minor variations might also have some differences in their geographical distributions.

Suppose for the moment that we can measure mental differences independently of cultural conditioning. Suppose we knew which variations were superior. (If we were all Einsteins, who would collect the garbage?) Suppose we knew which were inherited and how. If we knew all this our information would still be meaningless in terms of race unless we plotted the distributions geographically.

Pooling intelligence data by skin color categories is all very interesting but why pick that measure as the basis for pooling? We might compare I.Q. scores of blue-eyed vs. brown-eyed Europeans, tall people vs. short people, lineal vs. lateral, A vs. B vs. O bloods, sticky vs. dry earwax, loops vs. whorls, round heads vs. long heads, or any other trait contrasts. Why single out skin color? Even if a correlation is found, it still would remain to be shown if it were important (see European B blood) or if the boundaries coincided (see dry earwax). The differences some people claim to detect among modern Americans may be correlated with nose form instead of skin color—that seems about as likely to me.

Suppose we found that Koreans had different I.Q. scores than Chinese, on the average, and now we want to give a figure for the combined nationalities. Do we weigh the two equally? Do we weigh the figure for China twenty times more because of its greater population? Do we reconstruct some past population figures—which past and whose estimates? How do we expand this to include all the so-called Mongoloid peoples, including the Amerindians? We must find some way to reach such a figure if we are to compare Mongoloids with Negroids. Then how do we weigh the Africans vs. overseas Negroids, and so on.

All these problems are encountered even without touching on the difference between climatic races and descent groups. By now the reader should see how pointless all previous work has been on this subject.

DUAL RACE SYSTEM.

The distinction between climatic races and descent groups is the most original and important contribution of this work. Race theory up to now has always made the assumption that the two aspects automatically go together. Hopefully it has been shown that they do not, and that they logically should not.

In the past many researchers have noticed the discrepancies in distributions between classical and genetic traits. There have been four major attempts recently to cope with this. Kroeber, like those before him, simply ignored the genetic traits and categorized people according to the similarities in their classical traits. This was still long enough ago that he could get by with it. Boyd went to the other extreme and grouped people according to their genetic traits alone. He was working on the assumption that common descent was biologically the most meaningful measure of affinity. Garn tried to separate these into two levels, geographical races distinguished by genetic traits, and their subdivisions distinguished by classical traits. He did not make this distinction explicit, but it can be read from his racial criteria. Coon made the last heroic effort to keep classical and genetic traits together in his subspecies. His system strains a great deal, and it works as well as it does largely because recent human movements have brought some of the boundaries into better agreement than they were before.

The dual system simply side-steps the whole issue by not trying to make the two distributions agree. Racial traits can be lined up on a scale from those most environmentally selective (skin color) to those most drift affected (MN bloods). Technically a racial classification can be made for every one of these traits. They are all distributed around the world by selection and/or drift with little connection to each other. It just happens that these traits mostly cluster at the two ends of the selection-drift scale. With only some over-simplification we can construct a set of selection races and a set of drift races. Those based on selection are here called climatic races, while those based on drift are called descent groups.

About 10,000 years ago the natural distributions of these two systems showed no particular tendency to coincide. Their mapped areas are given in Figs. 30 and 49, and they can also be compared in chart form. It will be seen that the order here flows from west to east in an arc around the Indian Ocean.

Descent Groups	*Climatic Races*
South African	Bushman
	Pygmy
North African	Saharan
European	Caucasoid
Asian	Mongoloid
	Ainu
Indonesian	Veddoid
Papuan	Negrito
Australian	Australoid

Sapienization evidently caused a disruption in the two extreme areas of southern Africa and Australia. Human movements of this sort could bring the boundaries of classical and genetic trait distributions together. In Australia this was so long ago that classical traits are mostly rearranged according to climate, while genetic traits have not fully evened themselves out. In Africa it makes no difference because the human movement ran to the end of the world anyway.

The agricultural revolution was a much more overwhelming human movement which spread both classical and genetic traits from the originating sources. The near-eastern source was the most impressive of these with a spreading of populations into Europe, northern Africa, and much of Asia. Secondary sources, evidently triggered from there, spread from western Africa throughout the sub-Saharan region and from central Asia throughout the far east. Each of these movements advanced a somewhat unified racial frontier which tended to run together the classical and genetic traits and to give a more unified picture. These events are much too recent for selection and drift to have settled the traits back into more natural distributions.

Since 1500 A.D. further human movements are mainly a continuation of the trends of the preceding few thousand years. Much of this has been with the added push of industrialism and overseas transportation as well. These have facilitated the long-distance spread of Europeans and Africans into climatic regions, especially in the Americas, to which they were sometimes environmentally preadapted. Other expansions continued overland out of China, across Siberia from Europe, and into southern Africa. Even these have not yet obliterated the old dual system of human categorization, and probably never will entirely.

If and when civilization comes to an end, the forces of natural selection and drift will re-establish climatic races and descent groups on a somewhat new basis. Caucasoids will hold in some of their new environments, Negroids will prevail in the American tropics, Southern Mongoloids will fade out, the Saharans should return, and even the Ainus may rise again. Genetic groups will be repooled in new proportions between the usual kinds of barriers, minorities will drop out, new drifts will occur, new mutations, etc. How long this will all take depends in part on how far and how fast civilization falls, but in any case 100,000 years should lead to a new stability in natural man.

One might ask which racial system is the "real" one. To this I can only answer, both of them. Race classifications in the past have generally given about equal weight to similarity of visible traits and to common descent. Since these can now be separated, it would follow that both concepts are applicable to race. If one must choose, as I have, to use the word "race" for only one system, this becomes pretty much a matter of personal choice. My own interests lie more in physical adaptations than in genealogies, so climatic races gets priority and the term descent group had to be invented for the other system. Someone else might have named them differently.

If this is still confusing, a similar situation with a nonhuman animal may clarify one's own thinking by moving the problem a little farther away from the ego. The Irish Wolfhound is a breed of dogs that was considered more or less extinct by the year 1862 when a concerted effort was begun by George A. Graham to revive them. His procedure was to locate dogs which were supposedly at least part Irish Wolfhound in their ancestry, and also other dogs which showed the appropriate characteristics, regardless of their origin. After many decades of judicious breeding, a type of dog emerged that looked and acted much like the old descriptions. In terms of genetic continuity, however, the recreated breed had little in common with the original one. Is the old Irish Wolfhound extinct or are they still with us today? It depends on where you choose to place your emphasis, on the phenotypic traits that can be seen, or on the actual ancestry. (When one of these beasts steps on your foot you are more impressed by anatomy than by genealogy, in spite of what you may say about his ancestry at that moment.)

ANTIQUITY OF RACE.

In broad principle I must cast my lot with Weidenreich and Coon on the great antiquity of human racial diversity. This is not so unusual, as most researchers are now moving strongly in that direction. Still there are some major differences that the reader will already have appreciated. The most obvious of these is that the dual system of racial classification makes it impossible to trace racial history in the form of clear units that correspond with today's categories. Well-bounded subspecies don't exist in the scheme presented here. Every trait has its own separate history. Lumping these into climatic races and descent groups simplified things a great deal, but even this step conceals much of what has really been going on. To lump all these traits into a single set of races is even simpler yet, but this would go too far, and so much becomes concealed as to make the concept of race almost meaningless.

Racial history is now rather difficult to write. One cannot easily follow the dual system through time and space without some confusion. Each human population, past and present, fits into two systems at the same time and performs according to two kinds of rules. There are two different plays being acted out in the history of mankind, but with only one set of actors.

The concept of the ethnographic present is our best base line for beginning the investigation of human diversity. It soon proves inadequate when it becomes evident to what extent people had moved during the several millenia before then. The next base line of 10,000 years ago, chosen to antedate agriculture, is not an original concept here. It was used by Coon who called it early post-Pleistocene and mapped his subspecies as of that time also. In this work I have mapped both the climatic races and the descent groups on this base line of natural man. This was the last time at which the two kinds of classification were completely independent of one another. No equivalent maps for more recent times are given with this dual system, but they can easily be deduced, at least approximately, from the text. From the long-term view of human history this pre-agricultural time line is the natural one, and we are today living in a partially artificial situation which may not last long.

Farther back in time one crosses the *sapiens-erectus* threshold which is also critical in terms of racial history. The geographical adjustments that occurred with this transition are perhaps not so important as the fact that in most places there was racial continuity directly through the event. In the maps and discussion of *erectus* at 100,000 years ago, one can see very much the same pattern of climatic races and descent groups as is picked up more clearly at much more recent dates. Again, race and group boundaries do not correspond, and there is no reason why they necessarily should. The various adaptations to climatic differences were well underway with the first *erectus* a million years ago. The various barriers to gene flow were about the same then as now, and genetic areas of common descent began their process of differentiation at the same time.

When we try to trace our origins over the last million years or so it gets very confusing. Who is the "our" whose origins are being traced? My own northern European anatomy is mostly easy to account for, but how much influence there was from the near-eastern agriculturalists is difficult to say. Where did my brother ultimately get his brown eyes—from those same agriculturalists or from the Lapps? Why are we Rh positive instead of negative? To what degree am I a direct descendant of Cro-Magnon man, of Neandertal, and of Heidelberg man? These questions may not be too difficult, but for most of the rest of the world a literal tracing of racial origins is even more difficult.

UTILITY.

As a final wrap-up I should address the question of what the purpose of this book is and why should anyone read it. This has all been written with three types of readership in mind: professional anthropologists, university students, and interested laymen. For the anthropologist it is not well enough documented and footnoted to be a useful research tool. For the layman it is probably far too technical for easy reading. Students will object to it on both grounds. By steering a middle course I will have failed to satisfy either extreme, but this may yet be the most effective way to advance a new idea.

The concept of racial duality may prove too complicated to be of interest to most readers. Simpler ideas are much neater because they are easy to remember and to repeat without risk of distortion. Much of what is presented here has been simplified in order to work toward that goal, but one can go only so far. Possibly some interest will be generated in classifying individuals within each system, though populations are the more proper subject material for this. Classification in terms of classical traits is rather straight forward, and only the names of some of the climatic races are new. Classification by genetic traits is more difficult as few of us know our major blood types and even fewer know if we have Inca bones. Checking earwax and fingerprints can be fun but this won't tell us much. It was lots of fun thirty years ago trying to estimate the three numbers of our somatotypes, however pointless. Now maybe we can do something of the same order in assessing our proper descent groups.

The time level given for natural man of 10,000 years ago seems to remove this whole scheme from present-day relevancy, but it cannot be helped. The human expansions that resulted from agriculture have partially unified the two systems of racial classification, but not completely. The utility here lies both in understanding past developments and in making sense of the many discrepancies that still exist today. The unified concept of race that has been generally assumed is the basis of much misunderstanding and is the source of many prejudiced views. This dual system clarifies the problem without getting oneself into the ridiculous position of denying the existence of race. Too many anthropologists in recent years have tried to work against racial prejudice, and only ended up making fools of themselves by denying something that anybody can see with his own eyes.

The sapienization process has been a large and technical part of this work. Much of it is still somewhat speculative and untested. Some of my colleagues advised me not to include this subject, or at least to tone it down. It was included because this was the only way to account for certain trait distributions, and to leave them unexplained would be even worse. Sapienization is an essential concept in order to clarify the antiquity of races, and how this could work through a species-level change. And finally, its inclusion here serves as a trial balloon for some parts of the concept. Criticism is expected.

Perhaps the major utility, from a practical point of view, is exposing the futility of all present research on the subject of race and intelligence. The dual system of classification was not essential to make that point, but it helped. All such studies, racist or otherwise, must be done again against a geographical background if they are to have any meaning. There are many other studies of racial differences which also must be re-examined because they too are based on pooled samples selected from categories that were assumed to be realistic.

There is a great deal of new information presented here, and even more that has been known for a long time. What is most original is the arrangement of all the data, new and old. In general, I have avoided moralizing or drawing ethical conclusions from all this, thinking instead that the reader can do this for himself. It doesn't seem likely that this work will have any repercussions on race relations in the world today, and if it does I hope it will be for more peace. I would not want to be in the position of the German rocket scientists during World War II. Their job was to put the rockets up, but what they did when they came down was not their responsibility.

SELECTED BIBLIOGRAPHY

Biasutti, R. 1957. *Razze E Popoli Della Terra.* Turin: Unione Tipografico.

Boyd, W. C. 1950. *Genetics and the Races of Man.* Boston: D.C. Heath.

Brues, A.M. 1977. *People and Races.* New York: MacMillan.

Coon, C.S. 1939. *The Races of Europe.* New York: MacMillan.

________ 1962. *The Origin of Races.* New York: Knopf.

________ 1969. *The Living Races of Man.* New York: Knopf.

Coon, C.S., S.M. Garn, and J.B. Birdsell, 1950. *Races*, Springfield, Ill.: Charles C. Thomas.

Garn, S.M. 1961. *Human Races.* (First Edition) Springfield: Charles C. Thomas

Keith, Sir Arthur 1949. *A New Theory of Human Evolution.* New York: Philosophical Library.

Krantz, G.S. 1968. Brain Size and Hunting Ability in Earliest Man. *Current Anthropology,* Vol. 9, No. 5, pp. 450–51.

________ 1976. On the Nonmigration of Hunting Peoples. *Northwest Anthropoligical Research Notes,* Vol. 10, No. 2, pp. 209–216.

Kroeber, A.L. 1948. *Anthropology.* New York: Harcourt, Brace.

Lieberman, P. and E.S. Crelin. 1971. On the Speech of Neanderthal Man. *Linguistic Inquiry,* Vol. 2, pp. 203–222.

Montagu, A. (Ed.) 1964. The Concept of Race. London: Collier-MacMillan.

Mourant, A.E., A.C. Kopec, and K. Domaniewska-Sobsczak. 1979. *The Distribution of the Human Blood Groups and Other Polymorphisms.* London: Oxford Univ. Press.

Sheldon, W.H., S.S. Stevens, and W.B. Tucker. 1940. *The Varieties of Human Physique.* New York: Harper and Brothers.

Weidenreich, F. 1945. The Brachycephalization of Recent Mankind. *Southwestern Journal of Anthropology,* Vol. 1, No. 1, pp. 1–54.

________ 1947. Facts and Speculations Concerning the Origin of Homo Sapiens. *American Anthropologist,* Vol. 49, pp. 187–203.

INDEX

Composition: Set in 10 pt. Century Schoolbook
by American Typesetting, Inc.

Mechanicals: Format and graphics by
Driftwind Farm Enterprises

Presswork: Printed on 55 lb. Gladfelter
Spring Forge Vellum by Alpine Press, Inc.

Binding: Bound in Holliston Roxite A49245
by Alpine Press, Inc.

Jacket: Printed in two colors on Mead Offset
Enamel by Hampshire Press, Inc.